The International Companion to Edwin Morgan

INTERNATIONAL COMPANIONS TO SCOTTISH LITERATURE

Series Editors: Ian Brown and Thomas Owen Clancy

Titles in the series include:

International Companion to Lewis Grassic Gibbon
Edited by Scott Lyall
ISBN 978-1-908980-13-7

International Companion to Edwin Morgan
Edited by Alan Riach
ISBN 978-1-908980-14-4

International Companion to Scottish Poetry
Edited by Carla Sassi
ISBN 978-1-908980-15-1

The International Companion to Edwin Morgan

Edited by Alan Riach

Scottish Literature International

Published by
Scottish Literature International
Scottish Literature
7 University Gardens
University of Glasgow
Glasgow G12 8QH

Scottish Literature International is an imprint of
the Association for Scottish Literary Studies

www.asls.org.uk

ASLS is a registered charity no. SC006535

First published 2015

A CIP catalogue for this title
is available from the British Library

ISBN 978-1-908980-14-4

**Kingston
University**
London

ASLS acknowledges the support of Kingston University
towards the publication of this book.

Contents

For Marshall Walker

in partial repayment of a debt we'll never want to close. – A.R.

Series Editors' Preface

When in 2009 the first of the series of *Companions to Scottish Literature* under our editorship appeared under the aegis of the Edinburgh University Press, we had a vision of the scope and range of the series which extended to nineteen potential volumes, some based on literary periods, some on overarching themes and some on specific authors. As the years passed, other topics were recognised and added. By 2013, fifteen volumes in the series had appeared, but Edinburgh University Press had also decided that it no longer wanted to continue publishing new titles in the series. We remain grateful to them for their support for those first volumes and the community of Scottish literature scholars and lovers worldwide must be grateful to the Association for Scottish Literary Studies, which after reviewing the position, decided to take on completing the original vision for the series under the aegis of its academic imprint, Scottish Literature International. After the gap of a year to manage transitional matters, the 2015 tranche, therefore, represents under the series title, *International Companions to Scottish Literature*, the continuing fulfilment of the series editors' original vision, with the welcome addition of further topics. These will take the number of volumes produced well beyond twenty.

The 2015 tranche includes two volumes originally envisaged: the thematic volume on Scottish Poetry edited by Carla Sassi, which complements the 2011 volume edited by Ian Brown on Scottish Drama, and the volume on Edwin Morgan, edited by Alan Riach. The third volume, on Lewis Grassic Gibbon, edited by Scott Lyall, is an addition to the original vision, and one highly appropriate. Gibbon studies have developed strongly in recent years and this Companion is much needed.

As readers will see, these volumes continue to attract contributors of international standing and the highest quality. From the start, we have argued the complexity and profundity of the issues that Scottish literature embodies and addresses. The editors and authors of the 2015 volumes play a full part in helping fulfil the vision with which the series in its initial form began, to problematise in the most positive and creative way any easy notion of what Scottish literature is. The generic and linguistic complexity of the poets, poet-playwright and novelist these volumes address illustrates that vision.

Ian Brown
Thomas Owen Clancy

Acknowledgements

The volume editor would like to thank Alasdair Gray for permission to reproduce his portrait of Edwin Morgan on the cover of this book. Thanks also to the Andrew Tannahill Fund for the Furtherance of Scottish Literature at Glasgow University, which helped make this possible. The painting was commissioned by the Saltire Society in association with the Scottish Arts Council in recognition of a lifetime's achievement, and awarded to Edwin Morgan in 2003. It is now held by the Hunterian Art Gallery at Glasgow University. The Department of Scottish Literature at Glasgow University covered the cost of the index, made by Stewart Sanderson: my thanks to both. Most of all, I would like to record my thanks to the maestro, Morgan himself, for his deft encouragements, unfailing generosities and lasting friendship. *Mektub.*

A Brief Biography of Edwin Morgan

Edwin George Morgan was born on 27 April 1920 in Hyndland, in the West End of Glasgow. His father, chief accountant of an iron and steel merchants firm, was, like his mother, reserved and politically conservative. Morgan grew up gifted, lonely, intrinsically curious and publicly self-restrained. Moving with his parents to Pollokshields, then Rutherglen, he went to school at Rutherglen Academy, then Glasgow High School. He began publishing as 'Kaa' (the name of the unobtrusive, comprehensively observant rock-python in Kipling's *Jungle Books*) in both the High School *Magazine* in 1936 and later the *Glasgow University Magazine*, having entered Glasgow University in 1937 to study English. His study was interrupted in 1940 when he was called up for war service. After considering registering as a conscientious objector, discussions with parents and friends led to his joining the Royal Army Medical Corps, serving in Egypt, Lebanon and Palestine.

After demobilisation in 1946, Morgan completed a first-class Honours degree and, despite an option of research at Oxford, he stayed in Glasgow when the English Department offered him a lectureship. His full-time employment there continued from 1948, through a professorship in 1975, until retirement in 1980.

After the war, he published under his own name, reviews and translations appearing in a range of periodicals. His first two books appeared in 1952: *The Vision of Cathkin Braes* and a translation of *Beowulf*. Translations continued throughout his life alongside original poetry: his *Collected Translations* is almost as large as the *Collected Poems*; his version of Racine's *Phaedra* won the Oxford–Weidenfeld Translation Prize in 2001.

The 1950s were difficult, as he struggled to confirm his self-confidence in social, sexual, poetic and professional worlds. A decisive change began in 1962, when he met and fell in love with John Scott, a factory storeman from Lanarkshire. Their relationship continued until an argument, about which Morgan felt considerable regret and sorrow, shortly before Scott's early death in 1978. Though they never lived together, there were regular international holidays and home visits. After the 1950s' oppressions, there was a buoyancy in Morgan in the 1960s. Even prohibitive laws – homosexuality was illegal in Scotland until 1980, so that throughout his university career, Morgan could not openly admit his sexuality and expect to keep his job – could be managed.

1968 saw the poetic breakthrough, a carefully designed hardback collection, *The Second Life*. This established Morgan as a major poet of the era – and an innovator. Having studied American poets – North American Beat and Black Mountain poets, South American concrete poets – Morgan's technical adaptation and dealing with popular cultural material opened new possibilities in Scottish poetry. This liberation extended throughout the 1970s: films, news items, the ephemera of modern living, entered poems with as much facility as references to a wide range of literature, science and technological developments. Never owning a computer, he wrote poems as if computer-designed, probing serious political questions about technology's effects, never shy of worst scenarios, always seeing virtues in possibility. Asked by the National Museum of Scotland for an essential modern item, he selected a recording of Yuri Gagarin's voice speaking from outer space – bringing together domestic and galactic technology, love of languages and political curiosity. Deploring political oppressions, he always applauded revolutionary hope, translating into Scots the Communist Mayakovsky's poetry.

He continued playfully inventing forms and perspectives while addressing issues of utmost seriousness in Europe's highest classical verse form, in the 'Glasgow Sonnets' and in 1984, in the book-length sequence *Sonnets from Scotland*. These reaffirmed Morgan as dedicated to Scotland, reimagining the nation as a potentially independent state. In the 1980s, this politically decisive statement was crucial to Morgan. Equally so was, in 1990, the public declaration of his homosexuality. His work was widely taught in schools, well liked and loved by many. Nonetheless, reactionary condemnation followed. Sections of the Church received his dramatic trilogy about Christ, *A.D.* (2000), with hostility. Morgan accepted the risks: dramatising Western literature's most ancient text, *Gilgamesh*, and writing more poetry, his commitment was undiminished by age or ailment. Diagnosed with prostate cancer in 1999, he responded with a dialogue poem between two human cells, one healthy, one cancerous. His last major sequence of poems, *Love and a Life* (2003), collected in *A Book of*

Lives (2007), was openly autobiographical, recounting varied experiences of love. Best known in the 1970s as a poet of personae, brilliantly giving voices to unspoken things and creatures all around us – inimical like the hyena, sexy like the apple, simply incomparable (the Loch Ness Monster) – here he talked as himself, solitary, resourceful, vulnerable, enduring.

Poems of Thirty Years won the 1983 Saltire Society Book of the Year Award. In 2002 the society awarded him the Andrew Fletcher of Saltoun Award for notable service to Scotland. In 2008, *A Book of Lives* was Scottish Arts Council Book of the Year. He was commissioned to write a poem for the opening of the Scottish Parliament building on 9 October 2004, read on the occasion by Liz Lochhead. Awarded an OBE in 1982 and the Queen's Gold Medal in 2000, he became first Poet Laureate of Glasgow in 1999 and Scots Makar in 2004, holding this post till his death in 2010.

Abbreviations of work by Edwin Morgan

AD	*A.D.: A Trilogy of Plays on the Life of Jesus* (Manchester: Carcanet Press, 2000).
B	*Beowulf: A Verse Translation into Modern English* (Manchester: Carcanet Press, 2002 [first publ. 1952]).
BL	*A Book of Lives* (Manchester: Carcanet Press, 2007).
BS	*Beyond the Sun: Scotland's Favourite Paintings* (Edinburgh: Luath Press Ltd, 2007).
C	*Cathures: New Poems 1997–2001* (Manchester: Carcanet Press, in association with Mariscat Press, 2002).
CB	*Crossing the Border: Essays on Scottish Literature* (Manchester: Carcanet Press, 1990).
CP	*Collected Poems* (Manchester: Carcanet Press, 1990).
CT	*Collected Translations* (Manchester: Carcanet Press, 1996).
D	*Demon* (Glasgow: Mariscat Press, 1999).
DON	*Dreams and Other Nightmares: New and Uncollected Poems 1954–2009* (Edinburgh: Mariscat Press, 2010).
E	*Essays* (Cheadle: Carcanet Press, 1974).
FGS	*From Glasgow to Saturn* (Cheadle: Carcanet Press, 1973).
FVB	*From the Video Box* (Glasgow: Mariscat Press, 1986).
G	*The Play of Gilgamesh* (Manchester: Carcanet Press, 2005).
HHAA	*Hold Hands Among the Atoms: 70 Poems* (Glasgow: Mariscat Press, 1991).
IP	*Instamatic Poems* (London: Ian McKelvie, 1972).
LL	*Love and a Life: 50 Poems by Edwin Morgan* (Glasgow: Mariscat Press, 2003).
NNGM	*Nothing Not Giving Messages* (ed. Hamish Whyte) (Edinburgh: Polygon, 1990).
NSP	*New Selected Poems* (Manchester: Carcanet Press, 2000).
PTY	*Poems of Thirty Years* (Manchester: Carcanet Press, 1982).

SOD	*Sweeping Out the Dark* (Manchester: Carcanet Press, 1994).
SS	*Sonnets from Scotland* (Glasgow: Mariscat Press, 1984).
TND	*The New Divan* (Manchester: Carcanet Press, 1977).
TSL	*The Second Life* (Edinburgh: Edinburgh University Press, 1968).
VOR	*Virtual and Other Realities* (Manchester: Carcanet Press, 1997).
WHV	*Wi the Haill Voice: 25 poems by Vladimir Mayakovsky* (translator) (Cheadle: Carcanet Press, 1972).

INTRODUCTION

Presence, Process, Prize

Alan Riach

The Presence

On 27 April 2010, Edwin Morgan was ninety years old. A gathering of people approached him as he arrived in his wheelchair in the Mitchell Library in Glasgow, passing from one conversation to another in small groups, sharing warm words, in an appropriately quiet, festive fashion. The occasion was amicable, without friction or animosity, a collective of goodwill. In his company, we were all friendly, but every one of us paid attention sharply when the necessary moment arrived and he was invited to cut his handsome birthday cake. He extended his hand with purpose, the slight tremble steadied, and Alasdair Gray's voice rang out, 'Use the knife, man!'

This book is a companion to a life's achievement in work that could never have been predicted fifty, or even ten, years before his death a little later the same year, on 17 August 2010. Morgan continued to write, publish and take new directions to the end, and point forward towards different possibilities, but with one deep driving force, active long after his death. This introductory chapter considers two questions that take us to the heart of Morgan's work, and to that driving force.

The two questions are: Why is it that, for Morgan, the most essential motivation is exploration? His essential affirmation is 'the intrinsic optimisim of curiosity' or, as he says himself, 'Unknown is best'.[1] And what is it that makes Morgan's work such an enabling, encouraging oeuvre in modern poetry?

The driving force we will come to later.

Turn the clock back ten years from the ninetieth birthday to the celebration for Morgan's eightieth birthday and the little book of tributes produced for the occasion, *Unknown Is Best.* The title was taken from a line in the poem Morgan himself contributed to the book, entitled 'At Eighty'. It begins:

> Push the boat out, compañeros,
> Push the boat out, whatever the sea.

This is bad advice, of course: *whatever* the sea? The wise man does not push out the boat into oceans murderous with elemental hostility, and no one in a long career of negotiated public identity and private disposition demonstrated that truth more clearly than Edwin Morgan. But of course, this is a poem, not literal advice. It works by metaphor. It continues:

> Who says we cannot guide ourselves
> through the boiling reefs, black as they are,
> the enemy of us all makes sure of it![2]

The turbulent seas and raging rocks are there, and whatever it is that opposes us all ensures that the world is difficult. But the poem enacts a defiance: 'who says we cannot guide ourselves?' The metaphor is one of self-determination, but it is not a glib assurance. What keeps it tense is the reality of opposition, whoever would foreclose the extension of human life to which we are healthily disposed. The words of the pioneer of socialism in Glasgow during the First World War, John MacLean, as quoted by Morgan in his commemorative poem from 1973, come to mind: 'We are out / for life and all that life can give us'.[3] And thus the conclusion:

> Out,
> push it all out into the unknown!
> Unknown is best, it beckons best,
> like distant ships in mist, or bells
> clanging ruthless from stormy buoys.

This suggests that the co-ordinate points by which we must navigate our voyages are not always reliable, and are subject, themselves, to the tides and torrents of time. In turn, that might remind us also that there is something deeply serious in the seeming frivolity of the aural pun in that last word, 'buoys'.

The precedent here is Walt Whitman's 'Song of Myself' with 'Old age superbly rising!' and the exclamatory praise, that

> Every condition promulges not only itself, it promulges what grows
> after and out of itself,
> And the dark hush promulges as much as any.
>
> I open my scuttle at night and see the far-sprinkled systems
> And all I see multiplied as high as I can cipher edge but the rim of
> the farther systems.
>
> Wider and wider they spread, expanding, always expanding,
> Outward and outward and forever outward.
>
> My sun has his sun and round him obediently wheels,
> He joins with his partners a group of superior circuit,
> And greater sets follow, making specks of the greatest inside them.
>
> There is no stoppage and never can be stoppage,
> If I, you, and the worlds, and all beneath or upon their surfaces, were
> this moment reduced back to a pallid float, it would not avail in
> the long run,
> We should surely bring up again where we now stand,
> And surely go as much farther, and then farther and farther.
>
> A few quadrillions of eras, a few octillions of cubic leagues, do not
> hazard the span or make it impatient,
> There are but parts, any thing is but a part.[4]

So Whitman sails on into the cosmos and inhabits it with his song. Whitman's originality is breathtaking, but there is ambivalence here. Is this truly a poetry and ethos embracing 'others' or is it in fact endlessly self-extending vanity?

The urge that drives us towards other things and other lives than our own is what gives Morgan's poem a tension, both individually, as a poem, a made thing, but also, in Whitman's phrase, as 'but a part'. To collect these parts is to engage in a process, and the process for Morgan is encompassed not only in his *Collected Poems* but also in his plays, criticism, translations, letters – a life's work – and then in what this enables and encourages beyond that.

In his little book on Herman Melville, *Call me Ishmael*, the American poet Charles Olson proposes that the story of a great historical era can be read to its final end in the nineteenth century, in three great odysseys: 'The evolution in the use of Ulysses as hero parallels what has happened in economic history.'[5] Homer's Ulysses pushes against the limits of the known world, the Mediterranean, and in this way he projects the archetype of the West to follow, the search, to reach beyond the self. By 1400, Dante finds Ulysses in Hell, among the evil counsellors. He has become an Atlantic man. In the *Inferno*, he speaks to his crew like Columbus, urging them further forward: 'O brothers! [...] who through a hundred thousand dangers have reached the West, deny not, to this brief vigil of your senses that remains, experience of the unpeopled world behind the sun.'[6]

He bends the crew to his purpose, and drives them west. After five months on the Atlantic, they see the New Land there on the horizon, but a terrible storm blows up and they are drowned and destroyed before they reach land.

I once asked Edwin Morgan about his poem 'At Eighty' and reminded him that Dante placed Ulysses in Hell for giving his crew the same advice. He smiled mildly and replied, 'Perhaps Dante was wrong.'

It's significant that Odysseus's final voyage is referred to by various significant twentieth-century poets, including T. S. Eliot in *The Waste Land*, Ezra Pound in *The Cantos*, Hugh MacDiarmid in *To Circumjack Cencrastus* and Derek Walcott, in both 'The Schooner *Flight*' and *Omeros*.[7] But the point here is really that for Homer and Dante, Odysseus is pushing against the limits of the known world. Back to Olson:

> The third and final odyssey was Ahab's. The Atlantic crossed, the new land America known, the dream's death lay around the Horn, where West returned to East. The Pacific is the end of the UNKNOWN which Homer's and Dante's Ulysses opened men's eyes to [...] Ahab is full stop.[8]

'Ahab is full stop' – but is he? 'The end of the UNKNOWN' – but is it? Is the world ever really conquered, either in economic history or in human exploration?

Morgan, in his Odyssey, takes us from the darkness and constraint of mid-twentieth-century Scotland into the twenty-first century. Olson's map of history shows us the globe and we can recognise the truth in what he is saying. We cannot repeat those journeys, but every setting out is a new beginning, and the open complexity of all journeys is the domain of the arts. Understanding this is to resist the vanity of all efforts to bind and contain imaginative life, to resist the mechanical excess of systematic meaning, and to teach that intelligence and sensitivity reside with an irreducible openness, never with the closed.

The work of Edwin Morgan is to affirm this irreducible openness, a home to sensitivity and intelligence, a lasting assurance. In 'The World', from *The New Divan*, (1977) he writes:

> I don't think it's not going onward,
> though no one said it was a greyhound.
> I don't accept we're wearing late. [...]
> I don't believe that what's been made
> clutters the spirit.[9]

In an ethos of pervasive angst and contagious ennui, that is an astonishing thing to say. And in his translation from Eugenio Montale's poem 'Mediterranean', from 1959, Morgan writes:

> You first made me know
> That the puny agitations
> Of my heart were only momentary motions
> In yours; that there lay at the base
> Of my life your terrifying law: to be as various
> As vast, yet fixed in place.[10]

This is why 'unknown' is best: it generates exploration, and exploration generates discovery, and enablement and encouragement become the most essential elements in Morgan's work.

In the little book of tributes *Eddie@90* there are eighty items, essays, poems, salutations, records of delight, each one of them announcing Morgan as an encouragement, an enabler, a friendly catalyst: his characteristics are in words like 'welcome', 'invitation', 'kindness', 'dedication' – that positive view, energised, generous, poetically and culturally promiscuous – or to quote Alan Spence, 'For [...] forty years [...] Edwin Morgan has been an inspiration, a benign presence.'[11]

What makes him such an encouragement? Where does this come from?

The Process: Five Lives

It may be helpful to read Edwin Morgan through five periods of his writing life, each a further part of the process. The first (1952–68) is that of *Beowulf* and *The Vision of Cathkin Braes* to *Starryveldt* and *Emergent Poems*, the poet coming out of and through the aftermath of the Second World War.

The early Morgan is not the playful shape-shifter or the marvellous ventriloquist, computer programme-subverter and science fiction singer, translator, teacher, transmission-master. The other side of wonder is terror, horror, loneliness, equally the product of a human response to the sublime. The sea is 'as various / As vast' but it also drowns all puny human agitations, momentary motions are constantly lost in time, yet fixed in place. The early Morgan is lonely, voicing a difficult soliloquy in the Day of God's Wrath, 'Dies Irae', the first poem in the *Collected*: uttered in 'the blaze and maelstrom' by a 'Mortal voyager in the far flood of the north' whose 'ship long since had struck its rock, and sunk', who wakes from the nightmare 'hurricane of the wrath' and feels 'the hoar chill of dawning on the sea / And shrieking of the wind and savage gulls'.[12] And he is the poet of the late 1940s who records the clashing armies and monsters of the night in *Beowulf*:

> The man old in worth sat unrejoicing
> Bearing, enduring grief, strong
> Sorrow for his soldiers, when they saw the footprint
> Of the hated, of the accursed spirit; that strife
> Was too strong, too long and too malignant![13]

Morgan's *Beowulf*, first published in 1952, is a hard, grinding poem of clenched knuckles, thwart and frustration, tones palpable in both language and narrative. It is an accurate translation but also displays and deploys the character Morgan himself was at that time. In the 'Preface' to the 2002 edition, he tells us that it was begun 'shortly after I came out of the army at the end of the Second World War' and 'was in a sense my unwritten war poem'. He concludes: 'I would not want to alter the expression I gave to its themes of conflict and danger, voyaging and displacement, loyalty and loss. *Inter arma musae tacent* ["In time of war the muses are silent"], but they are not sleeping.'[14]

For Morgan's poetry, this is the first transitional moment, from the 1940s and 1950s through to the 1960s, and the development into that endlessly playful, open encourager, that benign inspiration he was to become, from *Beowulf* (1952) to *The Second Life* (1968).

So the second life is the period of the book of that title and its successors, *From Glasgow to Saturn, The New Divan* and *Poems of Thirty Years*, flourishing, in serious play, redressing his own history and affirming potential (1968–84). Throughout the 1970s, we could chart the poetry of the Morgan most people know and love, the instamatic Morgan, the humane and sympathetic observer and recorder, unafraid of Glasgow Green at night and how to speak of it in a Scotland still so sexually repressed, or of the desperate blind man in the snack-bar, the woman urinating openly in Central Station, but equally, joyously, unafraid of celebrating the giggling girls with their 'linoleum chocolate' or the trio of festive young people walking up Buchanan Street on a cold Christmas evening, or the energy that pulses and 'promulges' visibly, in the children in Joan Eardley's painting, as they run under the broken sign of a sweetie shop in Rottenrow, before the bulldozers do their necessary, rightful job.[15]

Each one of these poems is a short narrative, a kind of epiphany, a momentary vignette, not a fragment, because each has a coherence, but an episode isolated and connected to the process. Each one is only part of the story. Each one reminds us of Whitman's phrase again, 'anything is but a part'. From them we can infer the poet, not as romantic ego, active intervention, moral judge, but rather as citizen, someone in the play who is also watching the play. The poem is the made thing but there is the world beyond it, full of its own celebrations that are cognate with but not the same as poetry. Morgan is in dialogue, engaging with odd things, like typographical mistakes, or articulating unpredicted speech, writing the songs and monologues of creatures without voices of their own.

Morgan's playfulness was not universally popular. In 1980, Norman MacCaig published a book of poems called *The Equal Skies*, where the contents list promises a poem called 'Little Boy Blue' on page 21. Turn to page 21 and you find the title, 'Little Blue Blue': simply a mistake, in MacCaig's eyes, but, for Morgan, an inspiration. Morgan's poem 'Little Blue Blue' appears in his first 'Collected' volume, *Poems of Thirty Years* (1982), in the final section of hitherto uncollected poems, and gives us this unforgettable hybrid character, the last of the children of the 1960s, son of sea and sky, with his electric-blue guitar, denim jeans and jacket and dove-blue boots, sailing the seas and whizzing up to Scrabster in a cobalt Talbot Sunbeam. 'Everybody loves a blue angel', the poem tells

us. Not so. I once asked Norman MacCaig what he thought of the poem. The snarl was more prominent than the appreciation of inventiveness: 'Typical clever Eddie,' he said.[16]

That cleverness was how he was thought of then, not always as benign or enabling but rather as evasive, eluding directness; even, perhaps, dishonest. See him alongside his contemporaries, MacCaig, Sorley MacLean, George Mackay Brown, and the quality of vatic authority in their poetry is a strong contrast to Morgan's tentative, provisional identities, his deliberately exploratory forms.

We can identify this historically of course. Morgan's commitment to what he calls Futurism has its connections back to the first Futurists, poets and painters, artists of the collage, and as such at some distance from – indeed opposed to – the authority of the individual lyric poet. Such an authority rises emphatically in the Romantic tradition that runs at least from Shelley to Yeats and Sorley MacLean. For the Futurists, however, collage is a visual experience of multiple perspectives and colliding points of view. The priority of visualisation, evident in Morgan's scrapbooks, is present also in verbal and intellectual presentation, an articulation comprising different voices, sounds, ideas, musical forms, as collage was a method applied to literary works as various as Marinetti's *Zang Tumb Tuuum*, Apollinaire's *Calligrammes*, Eliot's *The Waste Land* and poetry by any number of writers from William Carlos Williams's *Paterson* on.

For W. B. Yeats, poetic form had to be cohesive, grammatically justified, comprehensive and coherent, whereas for Ezra Pound, in *The Cantos*, it is structured by compilation, making an epic of fragments. The opposition is between a singular voice giving full expression from a central position, and a multitude of voices in continual play, a representation of differences, personae.

Consider Morgan in this context, engaged very much in representing and playing with differences, and therefore standing at some distance from his contemporaries, MacLean, MacCaig, Mackay Brown, each one writing poems that would articulate full expression, in bardic directness or sly irony, from a single position. Almost all Morgan's work keeps regular syntax and observes grammatical rules, using conventional and accessible sentence-structures and verse paragraphs (with the exceptions of sound- and language-game poems), and yet he seems prophetic of a general twenty-first-century condition much closer to collage. The internet and social media make writers of everyone, and differences are constantly in play.

But this comes at a cost. MacLean, MacCaig and Mackay Brown are increasingly historical figures, which is not to diminish them or their work. Indeed, they are both enabled and bound by their priorities and geographies, but in a way that Morgan is not. This is more than simply the fact that they died in the 1990s, while Morgan lived on till 2010. It is more too than the fact that Morgan is a poet of the city in a way that none of these contemporaries were. And it is more than acknowledging Morgan's proleptic engagement with computer technology and virtual realities. He never owned a computer, rejecting the offer of a gift of one when in his eighties. He stuck to his portable typewriter until it finally broke down. He never worked with online resources. Yet the point is rather that Morgan's capacity for change allowed him to develop through two further transitional moments, and these are emphatic. They move him well beyond the position of the clever, playful, academic poet of the 1970s to the writer who would become Scotland's Makar, her National Poet, officially made laureate in 2004.

This is the third life, the era of *Sonnets from Scotland*, liberating the vision of the nation, and of *From the Video Box*, *Hold Hands Among the Atoms* and *Virtual and Other Realities*, when Morgan was engaging imaginatively with new technology and new history (1984–97).

The first of these transitional works is *Sonnets from Scotland* (1984). I visited Morgan once with a student who was writing a thesis on his work. She asked him which one, of all the poems he had written, was his favourite. Impossible to answer that one, he said. I asked him then, could he say if he had a favourite book of all of them? And he thought seriously for a moment and said, '*Sonnets from Scotland*.' He felt an affection for this one.

This is significant because this book sets out the proposition of a multifaceted, outward-voyaging, yet also introspective and multi-dimensional national identity, 'as various / As vast, yet fixed in place' – both aspects balanced, beginning with the proposition of an invitation: we are visitors ourselves, on earth, as Sigourney Weaver almost says as Lieutenant Ripley in the last line of the last of the *Alien* films: 'I'm a stranger here myself.'[17] Interstellar travellers arrive to explore Scotland, past, present, future, actual, imaginary, ruined, razed, dystopian or illuminated, festive, self-determined, awakened from sleep by the call of a far horn over a land that lies still, there, present, waiting. At the end of the sequence they depart, but there is no ending any more than there was a beginning. It is all in process. Both ending and beginning are provisional, in actuality and imagination, which is where the sequence itself began, with the first poem – not in order of arrangement but the first to be written – 'The Solway Canal'. Here, anonymous travellers sail in a hydrofoil through the Cheviot Hills in a foggy April dawn, past the high steel bridge at Carter Bar and wet rock walls on either side, to see waterfalls marking 'that northern island of the Scots' as the sun comes up on the Eildon Hills, shining down to 'the Canal's drowned borderers' graves'.[18] The scene is magical, which is to say, inexplicable, but the images: a man-made canal marking the border, the mysterious Eildons, drowned graves, and visitors observing all these things, make new imagining more possible. The poem implies that the world can be changed, and will change anyway, so we'd better be part of it, and take part in it.

Morgan's stature arises not only from the poetic oeuvre and the critical and scholarly accomplishment but also from his personal example, a man who helped enable so many of the generations immediately following him, in various ways, politically and publicly, as well as personally. It is familiar to locate *Sonnets from Scotland* in the history of resistance in post-1979 Scotland, when the aftermath of the referendum and the general election of that year had so conspicuously disenfranchised Scottish voters. The book signals Morgan's stepping into the national tradition in a new way, placing himself in a direct line with Hugh MacDiarmid. If *A Drunk Man Looks at the Thistle* is our *King Lear*, then *Sonnets from Scotland* is our *A Midsummer Night's Dream*, troubling, transformative, ultimately hopeful, rising – to quote Sorley MacLean in this context – on the other side of sorrow. And that line follows through to Morgan's poem for the opening of the Scottish Parliament, the most directly engaged civic political poem of our time, a different kind of encouragement. This is the poem in which Morgan advises Scottish parliamentarians to work responsibly for the people of Scotland, knowing that full independence has not yet been given to them. This is the Morgan who, in his will, left one million pounds to the Scottish National Party in the belief that it would help in the long process of delivering an independent Scotland once again.

The fourth life is at the turn of the millennium.

At the end of the twentieth and the beginning of the twenty-first centuries, Morgan produced two works which are essential and complementary in his story: a slim volume called *Demon* (1999), later collected in *Cathures* (2002), and *A.D.: A Trilogy of Plays on the Life of Jesus* (2000). Here, he describes the range and purpose of the gods of human kind. In the third of the *A.D.* plays, *The Execution* (Act 1, Scene 4),

Jesus is telling a story to a crowd, inviting people to 'Reach out; think; listen; argue with me'. Then he almost quotes a poem Morgan himself had published in the 1973 collection *From Glasgow to Saturn*, 'The Fifth Gospel'. The poem begins: 'I have come to overthrow the law and the prophets: I have not come to fulfil, but to overthrow.' Later, we read: 'It is not those that are sick who need a doctor, but those that are healthy. I have not come to call sinners, but the virtuous and law-abiding, to repentance.' We are advised: 'Give nothing to Caesar, for nothing is Caesar's.'[19]

Now, in the play of thirty years later, Jesus is given these words:

> Take a crossbow to the bloated belly of convention.
> I have not come to fulfil the prophets,
> Though some will say I have. I am myself
> A prophet never dreamed of; my remit
> (If I fulfil my life) is to free worlds,
> Not this one only, from guilt, hate, death itself.
> You have all heard of the kingdom of heaven,
> But it is not what you think it is.

The people suggest what it might be: a republic, a commonwealth, an empire, just as we might say, an independent Scotland, a free state. Jesus's answer is this: 'We'll see, we'll see.' And then he tells the parable of the mustard seed.

> Take a mustard seed. Very small, is it not?
> You wonder what could possibly come of it.
> Goodness, it could sit in a sparrow's eye!
> But plant it, water it, watch and wait for it.
> It spreads, it lengthens up like a bush, it's a tree,
>   with branches.
> Branches with birds, birds bursting with song.

The inevitable voice from the crowd interrupts him: 'What about the mustard?' And he replies:

> You get the mustard,
> You get the mustard all right, for your meat,
> But that is not the point of the parable.
> What is the point of the parable?

The voice from the crowd, pragmatic, offers: 'Dinny despise the wee things.' And Christ agrees, but goes further than piety:

> That's right.
> Never despise children. Never despise the poor.
> Never despise the outcast. But there's more.
> The seed, the bush, the tree: it's a process.
> The kingdom of heaven is not a thing,
> Nor is it a place, it is alive, it grows.

And he continues:

> [...] it lives.
> It is not even something you can search for,
> Though the paradox is that you must do so
> With your heart and soul.

And concludes:

> The kingdom of heaven is among you.
> It is this very moment waving like leaves
> And sending the most delicate roots in the world
> Out through your doubts and the fears of the time.[20]

Morgan is not only the benign and encouraging Eddie, then, but also the man who insists 'unknown is best'. It is too easy to undervalue the seriousness of his 'supreme graffito', the punning 'CHANGE RULES'.[21] Its message, the danger it warns of, the excess of familiar comfort, works both ways: 'rules change'. They change through time and they can change some things immediately. The Demon poems clearly speak of this: when serenity turns to complacency, the Demon is there to 'rattle the bars', not trying to get in, nor out, but driving the gatekeeper dogs berserk, and in that context, the playfulness of benign inspiration keeps its edges keen. He is the lovable poet of many voices: but where did those voices come from? Out of what dark? The wonderful playful song of the Loch Ness Monster, up from the deep, profoundly unimpressed with the world around him – or her, who knows? – the sexy, coquettish apple, its words winking and its skin shining at the susceptible reader, are voices we hear alongside that of the hyena, laughing with its tongue lolling out, waiting for the foot to slide, the heart to seize, for the fight to the death to be fought to the death.[22] These voices came from long gestation in isolated dark, the mustard seed, in a world of bias and thwart, frustration and dismay, and, indeed, despair. Both Morgan's living Christ and his resourceful, irrepressible Demon triumphantly rise from such spirit and ground.

There is one final period of transition that follows from this, the fifth life, the period of *Cathures*, *Love and a Life*, *The Play of Gilgamesh*, *A Book of Lives* and *Dreams and Other Nightmares*, being himself (2002–10).

Critical appraisals of Morgan often make the point that the most salient characteristic of his work is its variousness, the diversity of forms, voices, styles he used, over six decades of writing. His friend and publisher Michael Schmidt puts the matter critically: 'The case against him is that he is *too* versatile. The real Edwin Morgan never stands up.' Yet, Schmidt says, he believes there is 'an "I", autobiographical, candid, strong and vulnerable, who articulates those poems which seem most durable'.[23] This single self occupies the last of his works most fully.

Turn the clock back again to 1990. Glasgow is designated the European City of Culture. Morgan is acknowledged unofficial city laureate – the official position is confirmed a few years later – and in this year, in the *Glasgow Herald* newspaper and other publications, he openly talks about his sexuality, and 'comes out'. Now, there are many things that might be said about this moment but here what is being emphasised is that it signals a civic and, indeed, national fact, a recognition that must be insisted upon: that sexual repression enforced by law, religious diktat and social convention with its bloated belly requires the crossbow challenge of public discourse. And there is courage required to step up to that challenge. Further, the degree of liberation brought about by this openness, this declaration of 1990, had its poetic consequences in the autobiographical sequence of 2003, *Love and a Life*. Here the great ventriloquist has given way to the single mortal man, speaking of his own life and loves explicitly and tenderly, as if to remind us that any human experience is always different.

This is at the heart of *The Play of Gilgamesh*, based on the oldest written story in the world, where the hero-king and the earth-creature Enkidu have to reconcile themselves to the 'fixed' law of mortality, and understand the value it confers, in all its 'various and vast' manifestations, upon the living. If Morgan's example is a benign inspiration, which it is, and if, as he says, 'unknown is best', it is because he has taught us never to despise the outcast, always to remember the process.

The Prize

In 'Poetry' from the sequence *Grafts / Takes* (1983), we are given three moments illustrating poets at work. In the first, Virgil tells prospective visitors he is installing a new hypocaust (an ancient Roman central heating system), and is not to be disturbed while writing *The Aeneid*, approaching a crucial moment in 'tragic Carthage'. In the second, Byron excuses himself after six hours of drink and dancing, yawns, goes home, and writes six brilliant pages of *Don Juan*. In the third, Wordsworth sends his dog ahead to warn him if anyone is coming who might overhear him murmuring his poetry as he composes it in his solitary wandering in the Lake District. Morgan tells us Wordsworth might seem 'crazed' but then he corrects himself:

> Not crazed. Bith in eorle indryhten theaw
> thaet he his ferthlocan faeste binde,
> healde his hordcofan, hycge swa he wille.[24]

This is a passage from the old English poem 'The Wanderer' (lines 11–14), from *The Exeter Book*, *c.* AD 600–1000, and in Morgan's own translation reads:

> It is true I know
> that the custom shows most excellent in a man
> to lock and bind up all his mind,
> his thought his treasure, let him think what he will.[25]

In other words, play your cards close to your chest, until you know you have a winning hand or, as Morgan puts it in the final stanza:

> Who admits he's fought until he's won
> and drawn the victory into anecdote
> or hung it by the fire upon a string?[26]

The fight requires presence, continues through process, and the victory is not merely anecdote but a life's work encompassed, the prize. But the prize is now part of the process, requiring the presence of others.

An old English riddle is the last poem in his last book, *Dreams and Other Nightmares*, first published on his ninetieth birthday and launched at the event described at the beginning of this chapter. The solution is 'Creation' and this is also the answer to the notion that the limits of human understanding of the world have been reached. The three Odysseys are over. Yet the world is not ended, nor even, as Morgan says, cluttered. There is still immense space and time to explore. The placement of 'Creation' at the end of his last book, fixed in place, might suggest its significance as a deliberated point, a final judgement. For the word 'Creation' is more than a noun. It is an enactment, a reminder of the verbal movement it represents. It is an indication of the unknown, 'promulging what grows after'. This is Morgan's Futurist manifesto, a promise of how things are yet to be. It might be considered alongside Morgan's judgement, delivered in the voice of his alter ego Pelagius, in the 2002 collection *Cathures*, that what must come will arrive without taint of original sin, and with 'only human grace'.[27]

This is the 'deep driving force' noted at the beginning of this chapter.

This collection of essays is intended to explore the world of Edwin Morgan and act as a companion to his multifaceted trajectory through space and time. 'Who admits he's fought until he's won' is a question that dogs the whole trajectory, until, admission assured and victory confirmed, the whole story can be entered into and enacted through the expositions of his readers. The process continues. The beat goes on.

CHAPTER ONE

The Once and Future Pilot

James McGonigal

The sense of energy that readers respond to in Edwin Morgan's poetry comes partly from its recurrent imagery of movement across space and time. This was there from the start – in 'the blaze and maelstrom of God's wrath' that opens his first collection, *Dies Irae* (1952), and in the same volume's muscular translations from Anglo-Saxon, with 'The Seafarer' exploring 'sorrow's abodes, / The welter and terror of the waves' (*CP*, 24, 32).[1] And movement continues to the end. 'Epilogue: Seven Decades' closes *Collected Poems* in 1990 while at the same time revealing the glint of an opening out into the astonishingly productive eighth and ninth decades that would follow: 'When I go I want it bright, / I want to catch whatever is there / in full sight' (*CP*, 595).

When they first appeared in *The Second Life* (1968), Morgan's science fiction poems seemed to epitomise this questing energy. What is worth noting now is not just their novelty within 1960s Scottish poetry but the range of approach taken to a new kind of poem. In 'Spacepoem 1: from Laika to Gagarin' (*CP*, 194), bilingual wordplay links the Russian space programme of the late 1950s and early 1960s to avant-garde sound poetry of the tumultuous decade that followed (while also harking back to the 'trans-sense' language of *zaum* developed by Russian Futurists such as Khlebnikov and Kruchenykh whose work Morgan knew well). The dramatic monologue of 'In Sobieski's Shield' (*CP*, 196–98) is infused with science fiction's tense trope of worlds lost and found, as the poet explores anew the human capacity for determined hopefulness amidst horror in a grim planetary landscape beset by mineral storms. 'From the Domain of Arnheim' follows a more lyrical path, where the emotional impact of human encounters across the boundaries of historical epochs shakes both the observers and observed, so that each remains haunted by what has been glimpsed (*CP*, 198–99).

Time, not space, was, for Morgan, the final frontier. Writing to the young poet Richard Price in 1992 he declared:

> The sea, which is most of the earth, is very frightening, but that is probably a good thing, since if we all came from it originally it would be wrong to want to return to it, like returning to the womb: we have to shake the drips off and go out, onto land, into the air, into space, eventually into time.[2]

This was a view he had held since the late 1930s, when he read two books on precognition by J. W. Dunne: *An Experiment with Time* (1927, extended 1934) and *The New Immortality* (1938). We know the approximate date of his encounter with Dunne's ideas on parapsychology and the post-Einsteinian physics of spacetime because those volumes are listed towards the end of 'Books I Have Read (1927–1940)'[3] alongside other works studied for his undergraduate courses before he had to abandon university for National Service in 1940.

Dunne's work created considerable interest in the 1920s and 1930s, engaging public intellectuals such as H. G. Wells and J. B. Priestley in debate as well as academics with an interest in parapsychology. Part of the impact of his writing derives from the contrast between the bluff no-nonsense style of this Anglo-Irish ex-military engineer, sportsman and aeronautical pioneer and the surprising way he engages with the new physics of relativity to postulate a four-dimensional series of parallel time-worlds, and uses this to explain the otherwise puzzling precognition of future events in certain dreams (he provides a number of credible examples obtained under experimental conditions).

A key feature of Dunne's system is the role of an observing consciousness in the second time-dimension which thereby possesses a wider angle of vision than the sleeping dreamer in the narrower dimension of our present historical world of instants and memories, passing and past. This wider angle allows the observer (who also inhabits the dreamer's consciousness and is indeed in parallel or serial identity with him or her) to see future events that hence can become embedded in the dream material. Whether or not this is true, it is noteworthy that an observer figure, or band of observers, became central to Morgan's science fiction poems. One thinks of the development of the observer role from 'From the Domain of Arnheim' to 'Memories of Earth' (*CP*, 330–40) and 'The New Divan', with its all-seeing sages above the vagaries of human strife in love and war (see poem 81, *CP*, 322–23). Other watching figures also haunt the 'Divan' series: 'lords of the night' (poem 48) or the 'writing angel / with its vast perhaps' (poem 71). The travelling visitants of *Sonnets from Scotland* are the fullest manifestation of this idea across the multiply imagined times and spaces of Scotland (*CP*, 437–57), with the traditional sonnet form here appearing to act as a reassuringly familiar field to catch or record such forces, alien though not unfriendly.

The impact of Dunne's ideas on a young poet may also help to explain the curious role in Morgan's creative life of his Scrapbooks, which he reworked from a childhood collection of curious facts and illustrations at exactly the same period as he encountered this new explanation of time and serial identity, and which he continued to fill on his return to university from war service in early 1946, extending the Scrapbooks into many large volumes until the early 1960s.[4] These are bound folios or ledgers of kaleidoscopically juxtaposed photographs, cut-outs from newsprint, literary, biological and other scientific texts, art work (some of it his own) and autobiographical detail including accounts of dreams – all presented as an intellectual collage with care for balance or contrast.

These 'artist's books' appear to combine surrealism and science. Morgan saw them as a significant part of his 'complete works', an extended commentary on twentieth-century life as filtered through one sensibility. But each page also presents poised intersections between past, present and future, the latter mainly represented by space travel and other scientific developments in astronomy and anthropology. Archaeology figures too, as the time-science of vanished cultures, and it is interesting to see its role continued in 'The New Divan' (see poems 32–35, for example, on desert excavations: 'Under the sun, dig up a king. / His whole retinue had been burnt like coal / to warm his afterlife'). Phantasmagoric scenes in this long poem frequently reflect Morgan's experience as a young soldier of encountering in reality the Middle Eastern landscapes, ruins, artefacts and native cultures that he had cut out and stuck down in his boyhood scrapbooks. Transposing images and ideas beyond historical chronology, then, was an early focus of intellectual and aesthetic interest that would come to shape his later poetry.

Translation offered further opportunities to encounter distant cultures in a way that was intimate and yet disciplined. We might also speculate on the role of translation in Morgan's artistic life as helping him to make a creative breakthrough into the sense of an eternal present, or universal arena of poetic forms. He concludes *Hugh MacDiarmid* (1976), his lucid study of a great poetic father-figure, with a Shelleyan perspective. Warning readers of MacDiarmid's autobiography *Lucky Poet* (1943, 1972) 'not to look for any straight chronological unfolding of the events of his life' he praises instead this

> chaotic repetitive [book], bursting with suggestive ideas, curious facts, instant flytings, brilliant analogies and pages of vers libre looming like extracts from that huge Shelleyan poem 'which all poets, like the co-operating thoughts of one great mind, have built up since the beginning of the world'.[5]

In Morgan's poetic development in the 1940s and 1950s, translation and original poetry ran in parallel, the former frequently outpacing the latter. Editors often seemed to prefer the translations to his early poems, which can seem strident or 'willed'. In this context, he developed out of his exprience of translation a quasi-mystical and doubtless comforting understanding of the translator and the translated poet as equal partners before the 'original' poem, which pre-existed both. After the necessary and thorough preparatory work, he would begin a search for equivalence across two languages, but not of the words of the foreign language so much as

> the words of *the poem itself*, which has attained some sort of non-verbal interlinguistic existence in the mind. [...] Without wishing to be mystical, I believe there seems to be some sense [...] in which the poem exists independently of the language of its composition.[6]

He then goes on to refer to Walter Benjamin's 'difficult but percipient' essay, 'The Task of the Translator' (1923): 'It is the task of the translator to release in his own language that pure language which is under the spell of another, to liberate the language imprisoned in a work in his re-creation of that work.' Such a view of the ideal original poetic form clearly held attractions for a youngish poet struggling to find his own voice, and discovering some self-affirmation as a 'co-author' (at least) in the act of translating a poem.

Morgan's translations roam in space – from Russia to Italy, Spain, Hungary, Brazil. But they also work through time: from Anglo-Saxon to late-Hibernian Latin; from a Renaissance French and Italian Petrarchan love poetry of estrangement to the 'revolutionary' use of demotic Scots language to express the avant-garde socialist vision of Mayakovsky, 'wi the haill voice'. The process was helped in Morgan's case whenever he felt a particular engagement with the personality of the poet he was translating. Such involvement and identification – not only with Mayakovsky, but with Attila József and Sándor Weöres, Maurice Scève and Eugenio Montale – derived partly from a sense of co-habitation with their minds in a poetic home beyond individual and narrow lifespans.

The free-ranging activity of translation across voices, languages and cultures was a kind of travelling by proxy. It is to be contrasted with the solidity and deliberately narrow compass of the place where those translations were made: for Morgan was born, lived for most of his creative life and died within the same square mile of Glasgow's West End. He did, however, travel widely on holiday and also professionally to give lectures and readings, and found himself constantly drawn to the pulse of street life, with Cairo and Naples being particular favourites – partly because they reminded him of Glasgow. Writing to his publisher Michael Schmidt in April 1972 he admitted

> I am really a very native Glasgow-loving root-clutching person, and the mechanics of travel fill me with angst, yet I seem to be meant or doomed or prodded to go to place after place, city after city (but cities I love in any case, all cities) – Paris, Amsterdam, Cologne, Innsbruck, Stockholm, Bergen, Helsinki, Leningrad, Moscow, Kiev, Tripoli, Tel Aviv, Durban, Washington, New York [...].[7]

The travelling continued well into his seventies, from Lapland to Albania, from Iceland to New Zealand. Thus there is a constant theme in Morgan's life and poetry of voyage from and return to a centre where modern life reshapes itself into the future. Growing up in a dark metropolis that also sparked with energy and technological inventiveness, he never learned to distrust the modern city, but was forever engaged by its practical sciences and potential for change. To him, Glasgow was like the America it faced across the Atlantic – restless, experimental, willing to tear things down and start over, with an oddly energising unpredictability that derived from a major conurbation's social and linguistic tensions.

Living as a gay poet and academic in this mainly proletarian city, Morgan's daily experience was that of a person who travels simultaneously in multiple spheres – of sexual habits, social class codes, technological and also aesthetic experimentation. Past and present experiences intersected with future potential, this last being a political as well as a poetic conviction. In life as in art he chose optimism – not an option but a duty – determined to 'go with the planetman / in duty and in hope from moon to moon' (*CP*, 394).

In those closing lines from 'The Moons of Jupiter' in *Star Gate: Science Fiction Poems* (1979), the planetman is Morgan himself. The whole sequence is an elegy for his friend John Scott (1918–1978), to whom he would dedicate his collected *Poems of Thirty Years* (1980). Scott had died of cancer and, worse, estranged from Morgan, who now bitterly blamed himself for failing to resolve their quarrel of a year earlier, despite a close relationship since the early 1960s. His closeness to Scott seems now emblematic of a quietly determined rebelliousness in Morgan's nature, as one of 'that band of tranquil defiers' who break free from base and set off on a different trajectory in 'A Home in Space' (*CP*, 387–88). Their relationship had combined love and sexual transgression, cross-class engagement and anti-sectarian defiance. Scott was a storeman from a large working-class Catholic family in Lanarkshire, whose religious background would have barred him from employment in the Morgan family firm of Arnott, Young and Company on Clydeside, because of discriminatory employment practices then pertaining.

This significant ship-breaking and metal recycling firm had been founded by Morgan's maternal grandfather, and his father was chief accountant there. The irony of the contrast between their daily business, which provided for his comfortable family home and private education, and his own love of the sea and ships would not have been lost on Morgan. It may have fuelled his socialist and republican sympathies. 'Red' Clydeside was in his early life a bustling scene of shipbuilding and lading, castings-off and moorings. The decline of its marine industries in the 1970s and 1980s dismayed him:

> The North Sea oil-strike tilts east Scotland up,
> and the great sick Clyde shivers in its bed.
> ('Glasgow Sonnets' vi: *CP*, 290)

So the symbolism of seas, voyages and ships that extends through his verse may be a form of psychological redress. His early long poems both feature sea voyages: *Beowulf: A Verse Translation into Modern English* (1952) and *The Cape of Good Hope* (1955). He came to see the translation as in a sense his 'unwritten war poem' with 'its themes of conflict and danger, voyaging and displacement, loyalty and loss'.[8] Both poems are therefore connected with Morgan's journey as a young recruit round the Cape of Good Hope towards war service in Egypt.[9] The impact of this experience would emerge most clearly in hindsight: in the image of the soldiers 'all crowded onto the wet deck, leaning on the rail, our arms / on each other's shoulders, gazing at the savage outcrop / of great Africa' in 'The Unspoken' (*CP*, 182).[10] Even this moment of joy, the poem states, could not match the discovery of the new emotion of falling in love with John Scott. Nor could love find its match even in the memory of the poet's excited contemplation of a more recent scientific voyage – of the sputnik launched with a dog aboard, and 'the faint heartbeat sending back its message / steady and delicate'.

Most of our journeys lack such intensity, of course. It is worth remembering the mundane forms of transport in Morgan's poetry, notably the Scottish buses that as a non-driver he used constantly, and which, thus, became the setting for many poems of human encounter. These journeys might offer inebriated reflection, as in 'Good Friday', or sexual opportunity and threat, as in 'Christmas Eve' (*CP*, 164, 283), or the sense of watching street theatre on the move – the young man boarding a bus carrying in one hand his other hand, chopped off by 'a cleaver in Royston' ('Tale of a Hand', *C*, 34).

Cars figure rarely and often strangely. Most memorable perhaps is the Mercedes Benz 'driven' by a dead man straight at a brick wall in an early testing procedure for safety air bags, using a cadaver to simulate a human driver (*CP*, 218–19). This appears in his *Instamatic Poems* (1972), a series which, elsewhere in the *Complete Poems* selection from it, features a Land Rover, three funereal gondolas, Paolozzi's 'crashed car exhibition', the interior of the Pioneer-10 space probe, as well as, in 'Glasgow 5 March 1971', two passing drivers who 'keep their eyes on the road', deliberately avoiding engagement with a violent assault and robbery taking place on Glasgow's main Sauchiehall Street. (Each poem is dated, referring to actual events reported in newspapers or on television.) In contrast with the interaction and chatter of the city's public transport, then, Morgan tends to link cars with alienation.

He loved aircraft, particularly the Concorde jet in which he once flew to Lapland and back in a day, reconstructing the trip in a supersonic revisioning of Milton's sonnet 'On Time'. Time speeded up appears to slow down: 'Afterwards that day seemed a week, / a fortnight, a world, Puck's world'. He was allowed into Concorde's cockpit which he compares to the space shuttle (on which he had already booked his passenger place for a future public flight) and describes himself as

> never tired of stars, always longing to sit
> in the brilliant cone, even with chance, even for a time.
> (*CP*, 529–30)

That love of speed and energy was imaginatively reborn in old age with his *Tales from Baron Munchausen* (Edinburgh: Mariscat Press, 2005), based on the fantastic journeys of its eponymous teller of tall tales – journeys by wolf-drawn carriage, or on self-made wings across the Channel (dragging an English ship home by grappling irons), or high above the battlefield astride a cannonball.

All of this creates in Morgan's poetry an atmosphere of exhilaration, forward movement and the fascination of things glimpsed in passing, like the pheasant seen from the Aberdeen train, captivated by a piece of winking glass and creating 'a Chinese moment in the Mearns' (*CP*, 152–53). Or glimpsed from a different dimension, as in Jack London's longing look back down from Heaven towards San Francisco Bay and his days under sail: 'Tell them / they cannot make me a heaven / like the tide-race and the tiller / and a broken-nailed hand / and the shrouds of Frisco' (*CP*, 430–31). Places recently visited may be transformed by insertion into an ongoing sequence, as when the eponymous hero of *Demon* considers the frozen marshlands of Auschwitz in Poland or a white beach near Durrës, Albania (*C*, 91ff.). What gives a depth of perspective to such fleeting poems is the intersection of realities (China/Scotland; Paradise above/below; history/eternity), and this is also a feature of Morgan's poetic exploration of outer space: 'space that needs time and time that needs life', as he concludes in 'A Home in Space' (*CP*, 387–88).

Within Morgan's lifetime, advancements in information technology significantly altered our perception of time, speeding up communication flow while increasing the scale of consequences from its breakdown. His 1960s computer poems, written at an early stage of this development, are prescient but good-humoured instances of miscommunication: the Computer's First Birthday Card, First and Second Christmas Cards, Dialect and Code Poems (*CP*, 522, 177, 142, 276–77). The darker 1980s brought 'Computer Error: Neutron Strike' to his vision of potential futures in *Sonnets from Scotland* (*CP*, 453). Hauntingly within its scene of desolation, 'the videos ran on, sham death, sham love'. The destabilising nature of televisual and virtual imagery is explored in *From the Video Box* (1986) (*CP*, 479–500): 'melting the boundaries between art and reality [through] hilarious or sinister juxtapositions', to quote from poem 21's advertisement for a 'portable chameleon television'.

It is not all advanced technology. In poem 25 Morgan focuses on the winner of 'that strange world jigsaw final', supposedly televised. He is 'a stateless person [...] small, dark, nimble, self-contained', who is able, after days and nights of almost superhuman concentration, to complete a jigsaw of an aerial image of one featureless stretch of mid-Atlantic: 'to press that inhuman insolent remnant together'. That summary of the poem probably makes it seem the most boring TV programme imaginable, but Morgan's control of the pacing, tension and physical detail of the contest turns it into a vivid parable of the creative mind, as it slowly, patiently, with determination, stamina and huge force of intelligence pieces together a work of art from tiny details until it emerges, meaningful and complete. This poem has appealed to many poets because its very theme seems to be imagination – the ability to create pictures from fragments of experience, real or fictitious. But it also harks back to Morgan's early mosaic-making construction of the Scrapbook pages and his patient creation of a differently patterned reality, fitted together from pieces of other particular times and spaces in a new medium.[11]

From the Video Box plays with multiple perspectives. As readers we are involved in reconstructing mental images of Morgan's statements from imaginary viewers of never- (or not-yet-) produced television programmes, statements which are supposed, however, to have been recorded in an actual device. This was one of the video boxes set up in the early 1980s by the new and innovative Channel 4 in several British cities. These allowed viewers to record their television critiques which were then edited for broadcasting on a real programme called *Right to Reply*. So we might argue that Morgan's interests in spacetime and the possibility of serial versions of reality, as suggested by J. W. Dunne, appear to have continued long into his creative life.

He had, of course, continued to read and reflect upon science journalism. The influence of indeterminacy, sub-atomic theory and astrophysics can be seen in the genial 'Particle Poems 1–6' and fearsome 'The Mouth' in *Star Gate* (*CP*, 384–86, 388–89). The wave–particle duality that provides the experimental basis for quantum mechanics also adds a dimension to the late and chronologically based sequence 'Planet Wave', which Morgan developed in two parts around the turn of the millennium with Scottish jazz saxophonist and composer Tommy Smith, and performed on several occasions with his band (*A Book of Lives*, 2007: 23–43). The sequence stretches from 'In the Beginning (20 Billion BC)' and moves through pre-historic and historic events and characters to conclude 'On the Way to Barnard's Star (2300 AD)'. Within that range, however, each poem includes a 'wave', and is counterpointed by the unpredictability of jazz improvisation.

Another counterpoint to Morgan's virtual travelling is to consider the impact on his poetry of journeys undertaken in different decades of his long life. The most significant are his month-long study tour of Russia and the Ukraine in April–May 1955; his British Council trip to Hungary in October 1966 to attend an international poetry conference in Budapest; a reading tour of American high schools and colleges in May 1971; and another British Council lecture and reading tour, funded by the Istanbul Turco-British Association, to Istanbul and Ankara in April 1979. He kept notebooks on these journeys and so we have access to his first impressions, but can also consider their re-emergence in his poetry and translations.[12]

Russia's energetic post-war rebuilding and the optimism of its people confirmed the poet in his socialism, and in his enthusiasm for Glasgow's massive 1960s projects of slum clearance and road building. His optimism is epitomised in 'The Second Life' (*CP*, 180–81), where renewal of self and city coincide. The journey also enabled him to identify closely with Vladimir Mayakovsky, having seen, for example, the same shop signs hung outside fishmongers in Moscow: 'A tin fish, ilka scale a mou / I've read the cries o a new warld through't' (*CT*, 37). The confident use of a bold Scots in these translations, a proletarian speech, was an aesthetic and revolutionary decision in its own way, possibly validated by Morgan's sense of having walked the same streets. These translations would eventually lead to publication by Michael Schmidt of Carcanet Press of *Wi the Haill Voice: 25 Poems by Vladimir Mayakovsky* (1972), the first of many collections.

Although he translated from more than a dozen languages, Morgan was particularly drawn to Hungarian poetry. His translations of Attila József and Sándor Weöres are remarkable. Morgan met the latter on his 1966 conference trip to Budapest and shared a reading, his translations of Weöres being already admired in Hungary. They had a meal in an old and atmospheric literary café, with 'instant poems and drawings exchanged multilingually and often "concretely" between Weöres and myself'. (Weöres spoke no English, though his wife did, but knew some French and Russian.) Morgan describes him in his travel notebook as 'an extraordinary man – small, puckered face, young-looking though about 50, great sense of fun (hence concrete and phonic poems). [...] Contrast between utterly dead official public conference and lively warm personal contact so extreme.'[13] This meeting between two similarly myriad-minded poets confirmed in Morgan his sense of Weöres's significance. He went on to publish a *Selected Poems* (1970) in the Penguin Modern European Poets series (*CT*, 59–101) as well as many further translations (*CT*, 469–82).

Morgan was also an enthusiast for American Beat poetry, with Allen Ginsberg and Anselm Hollo being particular favourites. Through their engagement with contemporary lives and youthful voices, often rootless and 'on the road', Beat writers helped liberate him from the psychological tensions constricting his early poetry. He deplored the lack of such engagement in much established Scottish poetry and throughout the 1960s sought to support new writers through reviewing, editing and publishing initiatives.[14] Thus the American figures of Ernest Hemingway and Marilyn Monroe open *The Second Life* (1968) in poems that combine elegy and social critique with an openness of form that owes something to his admiration of Whitman and Ginsberg. When he had the opportunity of a three-week reading tour on the East Coast in May 1971, his observations of American society were carefully recorded, complete with many samples of journalism and newsletters, car stickers and street signs: 'God is Alive', 'Pedestrians Subject to Arrest'.

This last notice was alarming, because a pedestrian's-eye view of street life was as essential to this poet as interstellar speed. In Turkey, walking along the shore towards the new suspension bridge over the Bosporus he passed through a maze of villages, noting:

> Garages, boatbuilders' yards, tatty little dark cafés with men playing backgammon & sipping tea, coal depots, fish-shops, a filthy old toilet with FERFI in Hungarian – why? Strong sense of street life, many men working and many not, leaning against trucks, dozing on barrels or coils of rope, arguing, bantering, or as often as not just mooching along, a few women but much outnumbered by men, a fair number of dogs, cats, all looking a bit scraggy & unkempt, many cats scavenging among the refuse & rubbish. What price 'quality of life'? Yet can an outsider judge? Because the externals are dirty & uncared-for, what follows? The Nazis had trim gardens.[15]

Later he describes a visit to the labyrinthine museum of the Topkapi Palace and then the contrast of the ascent outside through trees and columns towards a high kiosk – with the sudden appearance at the summit of the sweep of Istanbul and its surrounding seas that reduced him to tears.[16] The sources of his emotion were complex. He described the incident later in 'Istanbul', one of the glancing poems composed in the 1990s called 'Pieces of Me', a selection of which appeared in *Dreams and Other Nightmares: New and Uncollected Poems 1954–2009* (Mariscat Press, 2010: 38), published to mark his ninetieth birthday. Set alongside recent poems made from the dream imagery that had haunted some of his nights in the nursing home where he died, these late works return us perhaps to the earlier piecing together of Scrapbook fragments and his youthful contemplation of Dunne's serial work on dream time.

Another piece, 'Sidon', recalls his experience as a young soldier of watching a fishing boat being built on the shore, but in such a desultory way that month after month 'its see-through planks / framed their ravishing / patches of sea blue'. When the soldiers left a year later, it still stood 'in perfect unfinishedness, / a ruin in reverse' (p. 36). That startling image in old age suggests a reversal of time, and a voyage still potentially to come. From beginning to end, Morgan's poetry had dealt with time and its see-through spaces, the gaps and indeterminacies that can reveal the unexpected. Even if that boat, completed at last, should set sail and for want of a pilot be lost, the poet might still hope to find washed up on shore 'a shred of sailcloth' and to reuse that piece, as he does at the close of 'The New Divan' (*CP*, 330), to bind together his far-travelled works.

CHAPTER TWO

Edwin Morgan's Scrapbooks

Dorothy McMillan

One afternoon not very long ago I was looking at Edwin Morgan's Scrapbook number nine.[1] At page 1708 my eye caught writing that was familiar to me: it turned out to be on a postcard sent by Charles Salter to his colleague, in the English Literature Department, Edwin Morgan. Here it is:

> Dear Eddie ('enchanted eddy')
>
> It is a thankless task writing to you as the script will only have permanence if you reject the illustration, otherwise you will strip off the one to stick the other into your scrap book: in any case the emblematic effect of the genre of picture p.c – the turning over – is lost. I am being very unintellectual but it is such a relief one's remarks being listened to with respect, this is largely because they are made in a language foreign to the other members of the party. I am writing this in the hut shown.
>
> Charles Salter

Both men are, of course, illuminated by this card but a closer look reveals even more about Edwin Morgan's characteristic methods in his Scrapbooks, methods which I suggest reveal and half conceal much about the essays and poems that he produced in the period up to *The New Divan* in 1977. Morgan ensured that his friend Charles Salter got it both ways. He contrived to split the postcard in two and pasted the picture on the page opposite with two lines drawn to link the corners of the asymmetrically placed half-cards across the volume opening, so that the house referred to in the postcard is clearly identifiable and one imagines Charles Salter in it writing the card. I find this delightful – funny, friendly, resourceful – but also indicative of a kind of need for control, an intention to defeat constraints by a refusal to be limited by what seem to be obvious limits. Of course you cannot have both sides of a postcard at once – unless ... This is, as Morgan writes below, 'Sharp Scrapbook Practice'. In this way he circumvents the rules while refusing to ignore them.

The postcard also raises questions about the intent of the Scrapbooks: Charles Salter must have seen them; indeed, the postcard suggests they were common knowledge among Morgan's colleagues, or at least those who knew him more intimately. Elsewhere there both is and is not a kind of audience implied. Sometimes an audience is directly addressed but elsewhere the books are introverted, turned in on themselves, like their pages, hugging their secrets. Nevertheless, one has throughout a sense that one is being invited in perhaps to rediscover one's own history as well as the history of the whole universe. I certainly encountered my own past in disconcerting ways. Page 3276 of Scrapbook Fifteen carries a story from the *Sunday Mail* about forty-nine students, a number 'foreign' or 'coloured', charged with breach of the peace after a party in Buccleuch Street, Glasgow, in 1961. I had a lucky escape, then, for it was the following year that I went to a boozy party in that flat. The same volume contains news of Yuri Gagarin, Kingsley Amis, a visit of visiting Russians to Tunnocks Bakery – 'They make sputniks we are told but they cannot make caramel wafers' – and the hanging of eighteen-year-old Francis 'Flossie' Forsyth, which I am ashamed to admit I had forgotten.

In an interview with Donny O'Rourke in 1989 Edwin Morgan explains that the Scrapbooks contain 'things that had caught my eye and had struck me in some kind of way'.[2] At O'Rourke's suggestion he agrees that the Scrapbooks might have been a 'surrogate activity' for writing poetry, since they stopped just before his poetry started to achieve success and wider readership with *The Second Life* in 1968. Morgan's biographer, James McGonigal, provides indispensable information about the Scrapbooks as part of the digitisation project ongoing at Glasgow University Library.[3] He stresses that Morgan regarded the Scrapbooks as part of his oeuvre and sought some kind of publication. Edwin Morgan was surely right to regard his Scrapbooks as works of art or a work of art, but the problems of reproduction may well prove insuperable. Only some kind of exhibition which enables the attenders to experience the physicality of the Scrapbooks can convey their special quality.

For a start McGonigal's commentaries on fourteen digitised page images (some of double openings) take about five thousand words and there are, as McGonigal is careful to point out, over 3,600 such pages, some more crammed than others but only a few in the last declaredly unfinished volume leave any uncovered pieces of page: the scraps go to the extreme edges of the page and sometimes fold over to go beyond the page without going out of bounds. And the pages are even more crammed than this suggests, for images are superimposed on images and captions are stuck on top of pictures so that the effect is often almost three-dimensional. Sometimes the surreal effects of superimposition are deceptive so that the reader must tentatively touch the page to distinguish what has been found by Morgan from what has been created by him. McGonigal's commentaries are always illuminating but they are not, nor do they pretend to be, definitive: it is almost always possible to make up several stories about the relationships of the images to each other. Sometimes, the intent, the story, is unmistakable as in the war and anti-war pages of Scrapbooks Three to Six. Even then there may be surprises: the last page, the inside back cover, of Scrapbook Four has a three-quarter-page colour image of Altdorfer's *Die Alexanderschlache*, which is a fitting, if ambiguous, comment on the most recent 'war to end all wars', but below is an unattributed quotation:

> It stood the record of many sensations of pain, once severe, but now softened; and of some instances of relenting feeling, some breathings of friendship and reconciliation, which could never be looked for again, and which could never cease to be dear. She left it all behind her, all but the recollection that such things had been.

This seems just right, setting the quiet, private and personal against the world-shattering. But where is it from? Well, these are the thoughts of Anne Elliot in *Persuasion* as she leaves Uppercross and her youthful love, as she thinks, for ever. Jane Austen is the last writer I would have expected Morgan to invoke at this point, indeed at most points: if one were looking for gaps in the Morgan encyclopaedia Austen might well come to mind – she doesn't even get into the index of any books by or about him. Yet here she is, as astonishing as she is appropriate.

In one sense, then, the sixteen Scrapbooks are indescribably plenitudinous. The first volume has cuttings, ranging in size from full page to a single phrase or word from *Country Life*, *The Bulletin*, *The Times*, *Reader's Digest*, *Beaux-Arts*, *The Observer*, *La Belle France*, *Italia*, *Woman's Journal*, *Evening News*, *Prediction*, *Chambers's Journal*, *National Geographic*, *Outline of Literature and Art*, *Picture Post*, *Wonders of All Life*, *Revue Française de Prague*, *Lilliput*, *Weekly Illustrated*, *Parade*, the *New Yorker*,

World Digest, *News Review*, *Studio*, the *Sunday Express*, the *Sunday Post*, various, unidentified art books and magazines (Western and Eastern, ancient and modern, high and low), and there is also lots of cut-out or handwritten poetry in various modern languages as well as Anglo-Saxon and Latin, normally untitled and unattributed, Tifinagh script from the Musée de l'Homme carefully copied, cigarette cards, a few family photographs, and some of his own drawings and designs. It seems utterly chaotic, without discrimination or discipline – a playful bear, lying on his back and touching his toes, rubs shoulders with a Piero della Francesca nativity from the National Gallery – and for the reader presents endless *TLS* Christmas quizzes and *Independent* Christmas details puzzles.

In another sense, however, the Scrapbooks are rigidly controlled. The cut-outs are carefully trimmed: they never overlap without design and they go exactly to the edge of the page. The variations in size of the cut-outs and cuttings give an appearance of care. Morgan's own writing where it provides captions, or, as is sometimes the case, whole poems, or prose pieces, is meticulous to the point of obsession. The pagination is painstaking even to the point of labelling inside-cover pages a and b. The mirror writing of 2127b, the inside front cover of Scrapbook Eleven, is irreproachable. The inside front cover of Scrapbook One has a couplet from Ronsard, four lines from *Paradise Lost*, Book Five. The cuttings and cut-outs are taken from *Zoo* magazine, and so on and on. Perhaps, one thinks, any geeky boy with access to these resources could have done all that, but this is not so. It requires an extraordinary capacity for taking pains as well as sheer cleverness to get it all together.

Of course, the later adult Scrapbooks contain images and sentiments that would have been unthinkable from the boy who began them. Increasingly tiny cut-outs of male figures in posing pouches appear in odd places.[4] Mostly these seem obsessive space-fillers, like the little pen doodles that also separate and connect larger pictorial or textual cuttings, but some are more artfully placed. After all, these beautiful male bodies were often in the first place posed to mimic classical statues or paintings: take away the posing pouch and the figure becomes Apollo. Place the poser differently again and beefcake takes on a sacred quality: as the side panels of a triptych; as the diminutive *putti* at the foot of an altar-piece; as the half-reclining figures on the Medici tombs.

Elsewhere larger male bodies are juxtaposed, bluntly stuck on top of more sinister landscapes. On page 1909 a very carefully cut out young man, naked to the waist and looking down provocatively perhaps at his lower invisible self, is placed slightly to the left on a colour photograph of an atomic blast in an ocean. The young man seems to rise, as it were, above the sands, and a tiny red flag to the right on the sand surely announces that all love, all desire, is extremely dangerous. Is this collage about bombs or boys? What's the difference? And below, to complicate the questions, is a portrait photograph of Hart Crane and, lest that might load the dice, to his left is Sibelius in profile. In the bottom left corner is a gold Omega automatic watch (watches and clocks are ubiquitous) and on Crane's left the head of a young man, perhaps only a schoolboy, looks over his left shoulder, turning away from it all. I cannot even begin to invent a connecting story for the facing page 1910, which includes prominently an engraving of a dog in huntsman costume, engraved by Grandville for *Scenes de la vie privée et publique des animaux* and captioned 'Un des chasseurs novices pour lesquels rien n'est sacre', a colour plate of Breughel the Elder's *Haymaking*, a photograph of a native boy dreamily paddling a canoe, a thumbnail of a young man naked to below the navel holding a magazine, an even smaller pic of a young man, clothed, putting the shot ... The print cuttings include the story from 1790 of a young girl in Aberdeen who donned male clothes to enlist for the bounty and who, when caught, was merely required to return the money; an account by Angus Wilson given in a 1953 BBC talk of ludicrous questions asked of him as author; and, most extensively, an account of Lincoln's dark predictive dreams before he was assassinated. And there is more.

James McGonigal and Sarah Hepworth in a scholarly and ingenious article in *Scottish Studies Review* use 'two openings' and a further page to suggest various ways of understanding the design of the whole Scrapbook project.[5] As befits Morgan's biographer, McGonigal reads in and out of his subject's known loves and obsessions – visual art, space exploration, things Scottish, things international, things local, things sexual, things philosophical. Particular attention is paid to emblems, Glasgow being a centre for emblem studies, and to the kilt which pervasively clothes the figures of the Scrapbooks from Morgan himself to Andy Stewart.[6] In a recent email exchange James McGonigal, patient and helpful as ever, suggests that 'Russian Constructivism possibly provides a better guide to EM's praxis with the Scrapbooks than the surrealists/dadaists do – allowing in the political dimension, not just the psychological'.

The problem is where to stop, since it seems as if every art movement, every philosophical, psychological, political, scientific and religious exploration of the last century gets in somewhere and even as one thinks, 'Well, not much woman stuff here', a Paris fashion or a funny hairstyle pops up.

I cannot but imagine the serious and rather lonely eleven-year-old boy with his scissors and his paste and his pen and his ambition, putting the print and picture world around him into his jotter: 'infinite riches in a small room'. And when I look at Scrapbook Fifteen's naked pinup with his chain-decorated posing pouch and artificial horns carefully cut round, and the turban, filled with narcissi instead of a face, of Scrapbook Sixteen, the boy is still there with his scissors and paste and his intent purpose, but he is a boy who has lived through a hideous war, the atomic bombs of Hiroshima and Nagasaki, space travel, urban renewal, and some joyful and some more or less dark sexual encounters in desert camps, and Glasgow parks and bars. Scrap-collecting begins to seem a bit like an effort to ward off the monstrous, or contain it, or laugh it off, but the laughter is not always convincing, although it never quite dies away.

Small wonder then that Morgan's playfulness is always accompanied by rulefulness. Every joke, even a feeble or vulgar one, is in deadly earnest. The trivial and the deathly serious rub, indeed must rub, shoulders. And this seems to be a characteristic too of the early critical essays. Edwin Morgan never really bought into the business of academic criticism. Certainly some of his early essays conformed to the requirements of the conventional academic magazines in which they were placed and they are the worse for it. When Morgan was presenting himself as an academic literary critic, he tended to get the voice wrong. He was presumably rather ashamed of the patronising 'Women and Poetry' which James McGonigal mentions as probably the first academic essay he published; he certainly never republished it.[7] He published in the same journal a piece on Browne and Johnson that begins, 'It is hardly to be doubted that the idea of the function of prose as communication of the intelligible on a level which should make it hard or impossible to mistake the writer's meaning was accepted throughout the seventeenth as in the eighteenth century.'[8] The strangulated prose offers in itself a glimpse of how constrained and unhappy Morgan must often have been during the earlier part of his academic life when he was living in what he describes to Sydney Graham as his 'Academic Pseudo-vivarium', trying to write in a way that falsified his real responses.[9] He is much more alive in his more journalistic essays: 'A Hantle of Howlers', the most playful of the early essays, collects two hundred examples of student howlers 'from University Entrance papers in English Literature, marked in Scotland during the last eight years.'[10] It transforms mistakes by understanding error and incongruity as perception and insight. Like the Scrapbooks it takes on chaos and, getting it under control, makes poetry out of blunder and carelessness. 'A Glimpse of Petavius' (1963) is all over the place in an academic sense, linking and leaping without academic caution, and speaking from the heart: 'Our poetry needs greater humanity.'[11] And then there is the brilliant essay 'Three Views of Brooklyn Bridge', which charts the very different responses to the startling modernity of the bridge of Hart Crane, Vladimir Mayakovsky, whose poem Morgan translated into Scots, and Lorca, also translated by Morgan. Of Lorca's poem he writes:

> It is as if all eyelids had been removed, as if everyone was forced to stare, and run, and shudder, and stare again. To try to escape from the nocturne is futile: everything is false, vicious, or empty; the sham wineglass and the theatre skull are no nearer true humanity than the iguanas and crocodiles. In Lorca's Aspirin Age there are not even any aspirins, only the fever that wants them.[12]

How fortunate that Morgan deserted academic prose.

A love of exuberance, of excess, combined with a resistance to them, informs *The Second Life*, his first widely successful volume of poetry. *The Second Life* is a beautiful and a deliberate volume. Its production matters: it is a pleasure to hold but you know you are holding a book that cannot forget itself. Yet this self-consciousness about the appearance as well as the language of his poetry proved something of a hostage to fortune. Reviewing *The Second Life* in *Poetry* among other British collections, X. J. Kennedy sandwiched his remarks between a grudging assessment of Philip Hobsbaum's *In Retreat* and a generous endorsement of Ruth Fainlight's *Cages*, approved one rather feels because it refuses to make large claims. Kennedy praises the 'funny and ingenious' concrete poems, quoting 'Siesta of a Hungarian Snake' but endorsing Morgan's own signalling of their difference: 'I am not sure that the weary, stretched and overworked word *poetry* needs to apply to this sort of graphic art.' He likes the 'poetry' of the volume a good deal less, deprecating in particular the 'heavy-handed playfulness' of 'An Addition to the Family'. Still more savage is the comment on the conclusion of what has become one of Morgan's best-known poems, 'In the Snack-bar': 'this is the sort of thing Mrs. Hemans would have written had she been born in an age when mentions of cloaca are permitted.'[13]

Kennedy seems to have anticipated that 'In the Snack-bar' would attract comments like this one: 'In this poem, Morgan uses his acute skills of observation to describe the plight of a blind, infirm elderly man to make a social comment about how people treat those less fortunate than themselves'.[14] This puts me in mind of Veronica Forrest-Thomson, a poet that Morgan greatly admired, who is prompted by a similarly bluff reading of a poem by Sylvia Plath to ask 'why she should have bothered to write poems if this was what she wanted to say'.[15] Both Kennedy and the educators make the same error: they read a serious poem as if it were a sententious one. For dark though it is, 'In the Snack-bar' does not exclude the playful: it is outrageously dependent on pun, double entendre and mixed registers, and its conclusion works to show that the crowded ordinariness of the world is sustained by the blind, hump-backed monstrous old man whose 'trickle of water' fertilises life as much as the 'slidy puddles' of mixed sugar and rain in the snack-bar. X. J. Kennedy takes the sugar as the message and neglects the piss.

The Scrapbooks repeatedly mix the sugar and the piss. Scrapbook Six carries a photograph of the obscene upside-down hanging of Mussolini and his associates with the UPIM department store sign prominent behind them. The same page has a photograph of the fifteenth-century tomb of Sir Henry Pierrepont, who fought in the Wars of the Roses; viewers will be reminded of Albert Pierrepoint, the last English hangman. The page does not neglect to have its tiny posing pic. In this way, the Scrapbooks might help to counter the persistent gentlification of Edwin Morgan, a pulling of his teeth that has been going on, I think, since his cancer diagnosis in 1999. His response to that diagnosis was extremely courageous and he by no means went gentle into that good night. But, of course, knowledge of his suffering, of the treatments and the painkillers and so on inevitably changed public attitudes. For Carol Ann Duffy he was 'a great, generous, gentle genius', a proper enough sentiment but it makes him sound too nice. In the embarrassments and even tastelessnesses of the Scrapbooks perhaps we can recover some of the uncomfortable contradictions out of which he produced his best poems like 'Trio':

> The chihuahua has a tiny Royal Stewart tartan coat like a teapot-
> holder,
> the baby in its white shawl is all bright eyes and mouth like favours
> in a fresh sweet cake,
> the guitar swells out under its milky plastic cover, tied at the neck
> with silver tinsel tape and a brisk sprig of mistletoe.[16]

The generosity and hopefulness of this poem is not simply built on gentleness, it is in part the reward of being a dab hand with a pair of scissors and a glue-pot and of paying attention to more dubious young men in posing pouches.

Edwin Morgan may have become Scotland's best-loved poet but there is much in his Scrapbooks to suggest that he was an angry young man, even if he would never have allowed himself to be so described. He would certainly never have permitted the release that alcohol was for most of the angry young men. Most drinker-writers are not, of course, playful, although they may be funny: the playful and the skinful tend not to go together. Instead Morgan had to learn to release his anger so far and no further, he had to contain it within the edges as he contains the images of his Scrapbooks: so the black humour of the dramatic monologues of 'Stobhill' distances and controls the poet's anger about the almost-incinerated baby, still alive after an abortion.[17] He also had to contain his own misery, to learn to make fun of it. We should be in no doubt, however, that Morgan suffered some very black patches.

Scrapbook Ten shows Morgan very close to the edge, perhaps held back from it by gallows humour. It is one of the largest physically; it weighs one down to pick it up. It covers the period 1953 to 1955. 1953 was the year of the coronation of Elizabeth II, memorialised here by a poet who longed for a Scottish republic.[18] Unsurprising then that the volume also contains accounts of the executions of Charles I and Louis XVI and that Julia Margaret Cameron's 'The Passing of Arthur' sits alongside a satirical account of the art photograph's camped-up nostalgia. It was the year, too, of the death of Stalin and the conquest of Everest. The volume is still saturated with the awful effects of war: Trevor-Roper's account of the death of Hitler, Paolo Monelli's of the death of Mussolini, but most of all the persistence of the bomb. Page 1822 gives the *Glasgow Herald* report of the first atomic weapon tested by the United Kingdom on 3 October 1952 in the Monte Bello Islands. Churchill reported in the House that it cost over one hundred million pounds. Dr Penney, in charge of the test, was that year honoured by the Queen. A folded-up story from the *Herald* shows a photograph of a child masked in dressings and a dazed girl being literally carted off apparently by a Japanese home guardsman: Morgan has written 'Hiroshima' at bottom right and stuck a cutting at the top left, 'Oh, you'll get the idea when the Penney drops'. The black humour of the pun is not originally Morgan's but the lasting horror of the collage is.

Compare opening 2033–34. At the top of the verso are two cuttings: 'Morgan presents From Here to Eternity' and 'Open the window. Let the morning in—'. Most of the page is taken up by a typed letter, presumably typed out by Morgan, from Hart Crane to Waldo Hart.

110 Columbia Heights, Brooklyn, N. Y. 21 April 1924.

> Dear Waldo: For many days, now, I have gone about quite dumb with something for which 'happiness' must be too mild a term. [...] And I have been able to give freedom & life which was acknowledged in the ecstasy of walking hand in hand across the most beautiful bridge of the world, the cables enclosing us & pulling us upward in such a dance as I have never walked and never can walk with another [...]

I give here only part of Morgan's typescript which is itself only part of the whole letter. But the point is that this is Hart Crane at an ecstatic point in the composition of *The Bridge*. Down the right side of the letter are four roughly passport size photographs: a male head seems to be gazing longingly through bars. This may be Montgomery Clift, who starred in *From Here to Eternity*, but it could be James Dean; it does not look exactly like either man. Then, a tiny male figure on a beach; a newspaper photograph of two unidentified men possibly in uniform; a colour photograph of a TV with a stuck-on picture of a flashy sports car with two men in it. Further down, on the right of the page is a half-photograph in blue/green of something like underwater coral, the other half of which meets it from the facing recto. Across the bottom third of the page is a colour detail of the right (Hell) wing of Bosch's triptych *The Garden of Earthly Delights*, showing a blackened bridge over a fiery river with teeming hordes of the lost and damned. Over this Morgan has stuck a newsprint cutting: BRIDGE OF FIRE, and below in smaller letters 'River of Fire'. On the right side of the picture is a black and white cut-out of a naked, oiled male torso. At the top of the facing page a cut-out announces: LE SUPPLICE PAR L'ESPERANCE (the agony of hope) above a half-page night-time photograph of Brooklyn Bridge over which is applied a Cyrillic cut-out, мост жизни (Bridge of Life). Below, a tiny head of a posing male nestles beside a colour detail of the legs of Icarus visible above the water from Breughel's *The Fall of Icarus* (a favourite throughout the Scrapbooks). Beside are the lines of Hart Crane's *Voyages*, III:

> Infinite consanguinity it bears—
> This tendered theme of you that light

Retrieves from sea plains where the sky
Resigns a breast that every wave enthrones;
While ribboned water lanes I wind
Are laved and scattered with no stroke
Wide from your side, whereto this hour
The sea lifts, also, reliquary hands.

And so, admitted through black swollen gates
That must arrest all distance otherwise,—
Past whirling pillars and lithe pediments,
Light wrestling there incessantly with light,
Star kissing star through wave on wave unto
Your body rocking!
and where death, if shed,
Presumes no carnage, but this single change,—
Upon the steep floor flung from dawn to dawn
The silken skilled transmemberment of song;

Permit me voyage, love, into your hands ...

At the foot of the page tiny heads of young men are arranged round a photograph of three ships, one large and two small in the middle of an ocean.

Many stories inhere in these pages. I want to stress only that all of the young men of these pages – Hart Crane, Montgomery Clift or James Dean, Mayakovsky (invoked in the Cyrillic lettering) and Icarus – in one way or another celebrated what was for them modern technology and the pages remember some of them in joyful, even ecstatic moments, but none came to a happy end. Conversely we may chuckle at the cheekiness of the Giovanetti 'Max' cartoons scattered throughout, but much of the volume is close to despair.

The Scrapbooks, then, provide a kind of hinterland to Morgan's life and productions, at least to those before *The New Divan*. I think something really new did happen in *The New Divan*. Randomising his life experiences, as he does in the title poem, Morgan got them under control by setting them free, rather in the same way that he chose to complete his scrapbook project by leaving the final scrapbook unfinished. When *The New Divan* was first published a number of people that I knew said, 'Eddie has come out, at last.' They meant this to refer, I think, to his poetry and his sexuality simultaneously. His poetry had found a new kind of quality which he no longer needed so fiercely to control. It is a quality which is best defined not as 'light-hearted' but rather 'high-hearted'.[19] It is not that the anger that tempered the playfulness of his earlier work has gone, but rather that he has found a transcendent voice: 'A Girl' from *The New Divan* depends as much on outrageous puns as 'Stobhill' – 'One at least / of her doctors has said they will pull out / her life support systems over his dead body' – but the poet is unprotected by dramatic monologue and the parents of the Girl are given no quarter: 'Don't ever bury their dust / by their daughter's dust, that's all.' The right to make such judgements is supported throughout *The New Divan* by a loving attention to the 'blessed trivia that keep us from dying', a thought prompted by the early death of Morgan's admired young poet friend Veronica Forrest-Thomson.[20] Morgan had discovered the value of trivia over long years, ever since he was a boy, in part by using scissors and paste.

CHAPTER THREE

Full Flourish: Major Collections of the 1960s and 1970s

David Kinloch

A tree struck by lightning offers the image of an energised universe standing on its head. As Edwin Morgan writes in 'Three Trees', first published in his 1977 collection *The New Divan*:

> My roots burrow in rainclouds.
> I grow down to earth at midnight.
> I am the negative of a tree.
> [...]
> Roots up twigs down's the power.
> [...]
> I can't make it a world of chance
> but what I can, I do.[1]

This queerly inverted tree finds its unlikely neighbour in a 'water-skiers tree' and a new creature, an 'impacted windscreen tree':

> a tree of porphyry
> in hair-fine crystalline divisions showing
> the saved man at the wheel
> his shivering substance.

As John Ashbery had exclaimed some years earlier in his poem 'Some Trees',

> These are amazing: each
> Joining a neighbour, as though speech
> Were a still performance.[2]

All these trees are in relation and remind one – as Reginald Shepherd has noted with regard to Ashbery – of a Baudelairean universe where 'perfumes, sounds and colours correspond'.[3] But Nature in that late Romantic poem echoes in such a way that its individual constituents seem to merge in a 'unity', however dark and unfathomable. And there Morgan and Ashbery part company with the inspirational French poet, the emphasis placed firmly on images which transform the trees into networks or constellations that communicate unusual and fragmented ways of being in the world.

As Gilles Deleuze writes in his introduction to *A Thousand Plateaus*:

> We're tired of trees. We should stop believing in trees, roots, and radicles. They've made us suffer too much. All of arborescent culture is founded on them, from biology to linguistics. Nothing is beautiful or loving or political aside from underground stems and aerial roots, adventitious growths and rhizomes.[4]

Morgan's 'lightning tree', with its 'aerial roots', behaves with a voracity more akin to that of a weed, of 'couchgrass' (Deleuze, 9):

> skeletal quickeners
> briefest if bravest, a fuse of spirits
> of fear lit over fields. (*CP*, 349)

'Many people have a tree growing in their heads,' says Deleuze, 'but the brain itself is much more a grass than a tree' (Deleuze, 15). 'Three Trees', then, while it is also a version of Morgan's frequent use of the monologue to give inhuman entities a human voice, is a further clarification of the aesthetic that receives its most sophisticated and extended expression in the long poem 'The New Divan' (*CP*, 295–329). This makes the title of the collection in which both poems appear. This chapter's approach, therefore, will be to attempt to make sense of the 'full flourish' of Morgan's activity over the three major collections of the 1960s and 1970s by looking at the earlier books, *The Second Life* (*CP*, 145–202) and *From Glasgow to Saturn* (*CP*, 233–94), through the prism of *The New Divan*'s (*CP*, 295–382) achievements. In the process, it will also visit and map the 'constellations' of poetry that rhyme through these books, turning them into a deliberately loose confederation: concrete poetry, love poetry, epic poetry, Glasgow poetry and science fiction poetry.

*

Morgan was not a writer of manifestos per se – although his introductions to some of his collections of translations sometimes read in this way. But his manifesto does exist: disguised, modest in tone, almost an apologetic explanation for the ways in which his collections do not work. In response to a question about the links between the 'various aspects of his writing' in an interview with Robin Hamilton in 1971, Morgan commented:

> I don't think that I personally do see those links … I've always tended to do quite different things, and I don't try very hard to see whether they all come from the same thing or are all to some extent related.[5]

Four years later, in response to Marshall Walker's attempt to establish a relationship between Morgan's realist Glasgow poetry and the science fiction poems in *From Glasgow to Saturn* he remarked (*NNGM*, 54):

> Looking back I think the more imaginative side of it came first and getting down to the local part of the environment came later. There has been an attempt, perhaps, to bring the two together but it may be that I don't *try* to bring things together in that particular kind of way, that I rather like to keep things in fairly separate categories.

It was precisely this alternative vision of what a collection of poems could be that resulted in a refusal by Cape to publish *The Second Life* in 1965. It was turned down as being 'too various'. 'They seem to like homogenous poets', Morgan commented in a letter to Archie Turnbull (30 August 1965).[6] When Edinburgh University Press eventually did bring out the volume in 1968, the concrete poems were printed on different-coloured paper from what Morgan called the 'ordinary' poems and in an interview with Robin Hamilton he emphasised that this 'compromise' was a way of 'saying that it [concrete verse] was poetry and saying that it was something quite different' (*NNGM*, 26). The effect is intriguing: the obvious temptation has been to try to make connections between these different kinds of poetry, but it may be worthwhile contemplating *The Second Life* first and foremost as an extraordinary object rather than as a book, a cousin perhaps of Morgan's decades-long compilation of scrapbooks. The first computer-set book to be printed in Scotland, not only does it contain different colours of paper, but it is large and square in shape, designed to accommodate the long rangy line of many of the verse poems and the need of the concrete poems for space: 'The concrete poems are all in a sense "poems in space"', he wrote in a letter to Walter Cairns (13 July 1967).[7] This first edition sets great store by its visual effects: even the title itself is offered curiously to us in the form of a mirror image inverting the letters of *The Second Life.* This trope of reflection reminds one of the 'Mirror Stage' in Jacques Lacan's theories about the construction of human identities and, as John Vincent has commented, 'it puts one self in proximity with another not-quite-self and suggests a linkage between them', the 'second life' rippling out and away from the first, which stands on the bank to gaze uncertainly after its appearance.[8] These were, it should be noted in passing, bold and tenacious decisions taken by a forty-plus poet who had fought for years to understand his own nature and trajectory as well as to find a faithful publisher.

Fragments of a non-traditional poetic aesthetic begin, then, to come into view. The best place, however, to look to understand its typical characteristics and its full implications is the collection *The New Divan* with its desert landscapes, its demolition of 'arborescent' culture and the presence of the organising metaphor of the divan itself. Taking part of its title from the *Diwan* of the fourteenth-century Persian poet Hafiz of Shiraz, it is worth considering the various meanings this term has in the context of its source culture. Its poetic meaning is that of 'collection', but the orientation of this term receives its impetus from the other older senses of the word. Originally a 'divan' was a manuscript in which financial accounts were noted. Latterly this meaning was extended so that it came to mean 'government treasury' or chancery and was sometimes synonymous with the Caliph's court itself, a seat of government.[9] The idea of a chamber where debate or conversation was conducted, sometimes in a semi-supine position from benches or couches, is there in the mix as well. A 'Divan', therefore, potentially collects together many different voices, chattering, debating, contradicting, a place of variegated discourse, multiple lines of attack and defence. Nevertheless, the Divan also decides the law and keeps accounts. It is not difficult to see how these various meanings relate to the hundred short poems or stanzas of 'The New Divan', each between eleven and eighteen lines long. Often described as Morgan's belated 'war poem' because set in the Middle Eastern landscapes where the poet saw out the Second World War, it nevertheless offers an extremely oblique approach to the war, ranging over a wide span of time and space. In all his discussions of the poem Morgan was at pains to stress its non-linear structure. Indeed the term 'structure' itself gave him pause for thought (*NNGM*, 136):

> [...] it deliberately does use a kind of randomness in the sense that one is not following a story that really goes forward step by step. Characters appear and reappear. You're not certain whether the characters are autobiographical or not. That kind of randomness is something that did attract me. And, if you like, the idea of non-structure almost as a structural idea in itself – in a sense that a good deal of the poetry of the Middle East [...] deliberately is almost anti-structural and almost in fact thinks that we in the West are too obsessed by structure, and we drive our readers too hard. In Arabic or Persian poetry they're rather fond of the idea that a 'divan' as they call it, a collection of poems, is something that you enter; you move around; you can cast your eye here and there, you look, you pick, you perhaps retrace your steps.

Here then is the sense of a 'collection' as a dynamic space where the reader can 'enter' and move around. And while the autobiographical voice is undeniably there, particularly in the final short lyrics where the soldier Cosgrove makes his appearance, many other voices, those of lovers both straight and gay, travellers of one kind or another, despots and victims are presented in a deliberately disorienting kaleidoscope of semi-oriental images.

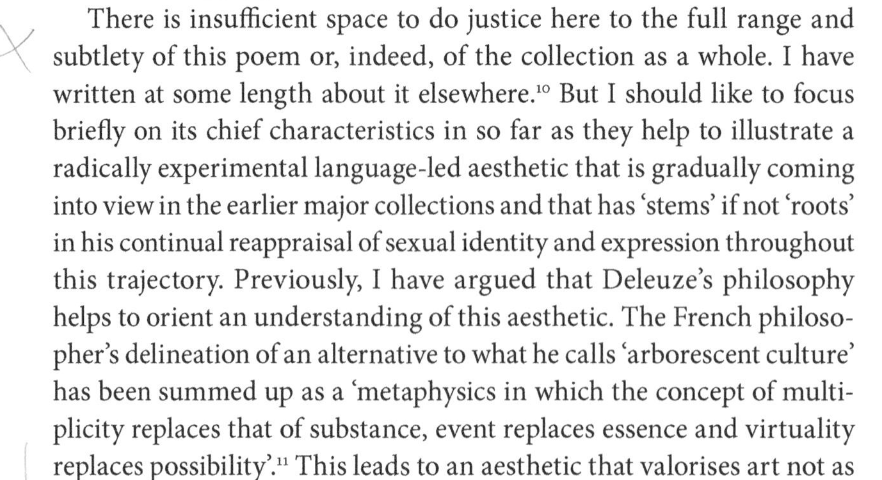

There is insufficient space to do justice here to the full range and subtlety of this poem or, indeed, of the collection as a whole. I have written at some length about it elsewhere.[10] But I should like to focus briefly on its chief characteristics in so far as they help to illustrate a radically experimental language-led aesthetic that is gradually coming into view in the earlier major collections and that has 'stems' if not 'roots' in his continual reappraisal of sexual identity and expression throughout this trajectory. Previously, I have argued that Deleuze's philosophy helps to orient an understanding of this aesthetic. The French philosopher's delineation of an alternative to what he calls 'arborescent culture' has been summed up as a 'metaphysics in which the concept of multiplicity replaces that of substance, event replaces essence and virtuality replaces possibility'.[11] This leads to an aesthetic that valorises art not as a re-presentation of reality, but as an experience, an event in its own right, 'that proceeds by way of sensibility, the body and sensation.'[12]

Thus, 'The New Divan' ignites a series of adventure-driven and erotic trajectories in which the 'substance' or singular 'meaning' of the poem is hard to pin down and in which personalities and places are various and ill-defined. As poem 27 has it: 'He was the master of ungathered things' (*CP*, 303). Purportedly a poem 'about' the Second World War or inspired by his experiences in the Middle East during the 1940s, the war itself is mostly an immanent presence. When it does flare intensely into view, as it does in the final poems of the sequence, it is to present war essentially as an absence of meaning via the image of the dead body of an officer from which life has departed (*CP*, 330):

> drained of blood, wasted away,
> leg amputated at the thigh,
> wrapped in a rough sheet, light as a child,
> rolling from side to side of the canvas
> with a faint terrible sound.

The lines are all the more effective in that the precision of this scene contrasts so strikingly with the many other stanzas in which we search in vain for stable contours (*CP*, 319):

> A pattern
> a swirling moment gave went quickly.

But if war is just that – an ultimate absence of meaning – it is basically unrepresentable. It is not available to 'sense', but is so possibly to 'sensation', to a poetry able to evoke and suggest by means of its sometimes opaque syntax and deliberately incoherent imagery. If this, indeed, is the aesthetic 'law' promulgated by Morgan's 'Divan', then it is wilfully and defiantly broken in the terribly clear image of the dead body in the poem's penultimate stanza. This is what matters, he says, this body, our body, our only reality which war entirely negates.

If, as I have argued elsewhere, Deleuze, sensation-focused sound poems like 'Shaker Shaken' and Morgan's work in 'Five Poems on Film Directors', printed later in the *The New Divan,* help us to read the long poem, we still have to try to identify the cultural co-ordinates from which this aesthetic emerges.[13] One of the main features of Morgan's work that marked it out as distinctly different and innovative over the course of the 1960s when his first important collection was published was his investment in concrete poetry. At first sight, nothing could be further removed from the problematics of a long poem like 'The New Divan', but that they were intimately connected in his mind is clear from the interview he gave to Marshall Walker in 1975 (*NNGM*, 56):

> [Concrete poetry] also affects things like the length of a poem, the feeling which is fairly general that it is extremely hard to write a long poem nowadays but nevertheless there's a hankering after doing it somehow, and it is a question of just seeing how you can bring together the idea of a lengthy work and the idea of quickness or simultaneity or modernity or something of that kind.

I will touch on the intrinsic merits of Morgan's concrete verse later, but here it is evident that his experiments in this area helped him to think about the form of a truly modern poetry, a form or forms that encompass and express the modern experience of a speeded-up universe, forms that acknowledge the importance of the concept of space and of the materiality of the poem, a dynamic object oriented in relation to the physical dimensions of the page. It also offered poems in which meaning is hard won, hedged around by ambiguity, infected by polysemy. Poem 18 in 'The New Divan' offers the following lines that seem sceptical of a traditional lyricism (*CP*, 300):

> You want the lyric line, you want the words
> to lay their length against you like – like what?

while poem 92 actually includes a rather dyspeptic glance back to the 'computer poems' of his previous collections. What he calls elsewhere in the poem 'disoriented angels hooked on sense' (*CP*, 319) give up their pretensions to be mouthpieces for a discredited monotheism and give way to the efforts of information technology (*CP*, 327):

> let computers mass the injuries
> let computers mess the injuries
> let computers miss the injuries
> let computers moss the injuries
> let computers muss the injuries
> of merely mortal times.

In the context of the Divan's exploration of a war-plagued, apparently senseless universe, what in the past delivered playful sound and visual poems turning on the substitution or addition of key syllables, consonants or vowels here delivers an implicit acknowledgement of both art and science's exhaustion. Nevertheless, concrete techniques and principles undoubtedly helped Morgan achieve the distinctively disruptive and fragmented movements of an epic poetry that keeps breaking off before narrative or the lyric can betray. And individual permutations from some of the more successful concrete poems in the earlier collections often read like premonitions of the Deleuzian aspects of the longer poem:

> o i am a pen open man or happener

as 'Pomander' puts it (*CP*, 173). 'Opening the Cage', also from *The Second Life*, may also be read instructively in relation to the Divan's poetry of immanence and absence (*CP*, 178):

> And that nothing is poetry I am saying and I have to say it
> Saying poetry is nothing and to that I say I am and have it

Take your pick! Significantly, however, *The New Divan* closes with a sequence of 'Unfinished Poems' dedicated to Veronica Forrest-Thomson, who had died at an early age in 1975. When Morgan came to pen a brief contextual introduction to this sequence for his *Collected Poems* in 1990 he mentioned 'the French structuralists, Wittgenstein, John Ashbery and J. H. Prynne' as influences on the younger poet and they certainly shared an interest in what has come to be known today as 'innovative, language' poetry (*CP*, 373–80). Morgan's own interest in this approach is confirmed by a heavily annotated copy of Rosemary Waldrop's study *Against Language?* contained in his personal library.[14] In 1989 he gave a lecture on language poetries at the University of Liverpool:

> Much language poetry has neither image clusters nor a recognisable syntax [...] this makes it harder, but does it make it worse? If there is no human situation, do we switch off, or on the contrary do we bend closer? Whether or not all this will stay in the mind is perhaps less important than whether the reader is going to be forced to bring forward a new kind of short-term attentiveness.[15]

What is striking here is the interest in these poems not as poetry per se, but as experiences for the reader that affect human consciousness and even develop it indirectly. Again, we are not far here from the Deleuzian investment in art as event, affect and sensation.

Concrete verse and language poetry were important points on the compass for Morgan as he tried to work out his own aesthetic. But possibly the most important element was not so much an influence as a practice: the practice of translation. Translation as an experience of breaking down poems in one language to constitute them in another was a constant feature of Morgan's activity and without it he would have been a very different poet. This chapter might be entitled 'Full Flourish', but the fantastic extent of that flourish is only apparent if we acknowledge that while he was creating all this original verse he was also making sometimes highly innovative translations of a vast array of European poetry. Colin Nicholson has ably demonstrated the importance to Morgan's own poetry of the defamiliarisation techniques and principles learned from his translation into Scots of Mayakovsky.[16] Indeed, an entire book remains to be written about these kinds of connection. Yet, if one were to choose a single foreign poet among the forty or so that he tackled between 1959 and 1970 who seems closest to Morgan in terms of sensibility and the complex movement of his verse, it would be Sándor Weöres. Here is a single stanza from his version of Weöres's 'The Lost Parasol', also a long poem, one notes. It could easily be inserted into 'The New Divan':

> A sky-splitting single-sloped precipice,
> its lap a lemon-yellow corrie of sand,
> far off a rosy panorama of mist,
> curly hills in a ragged mauve cloud-band;
> above, the couple stood; below, the sun-wheel stirred;
> in the dawn-flames, so interdependent
> they stood, afraid, at the very edge of fate;
> boulders rolled from beneath their feet,
> they were quarrelling, tearing their hearts,
> each of them deaf before the other starts.[17]

Here again – despite the presence of end-rhyme – is the colourful, lightly orientalised landscape that also displays Western characteristics, a background to unnamed, ambiguous lovers whose quarrel is never defined.

This mention of lovers inevitably prompts one to reflect on the way sexual identity is portrayed in 'The New Divan' and, indeed, if its pattern in the long poem can help us to understand its presentation in the two earlier collections. Elsewhere, I have argued that, although the Divan's trajectory is non-linear and eschews conventional autobiography, the fact that roughly a quarter of the poems that make up the sequence deal with amorous or sexual encounters suggest that the experience and expression of sexual activity is what grounds the poem as a whole.[18] Although some critics have argued that by the stage Morgan came to write 'The New Divan', he no longer felt the need to disguise the references to gay sex, I would suggest that if the whole sequence is read carefully one may trace a deliberate 'outing' of sexual preference as the poem's implicit and most pressing narrative. From the coded world of fragment 4's gay 'bear' and 'passwords' (*CP*, 295–96) we move through a number of middle section stanzas which deploy rather a lot of non-gender-specific pronouns into later fragments where the male love interest is identified by name as the poet's friend Cosgrove and concludes with a fairly graphic description of sex with an anonymous squaddie (*CP*, 329–30). Placed immediately before the stanza quoted above which describes the stretcher party that bears the dead officer away, this fragment further reinforces Morgan's philosophical emphasis on the importance of the human body and his recognition that – as he puts it in 'Glasgow Green' – 'the beds of married love / are islands in a sea of desire' (*CP*, 169). As a whole 'The New Divan' maps those 'seas of desire' from a perspective that is gradually revealed as gay. The gradual nature of this revelation is important and speaks to the difficulty of gay lives in mid-twentieth-century Britain. As the narrator insists in poem 26 (*CP*, 303):

> To take without anxiety the love
> you think fate might have left you is
> hard, when the brassy years without it
> have left an acid on the ease of purpose.

We may interpret this as a clear explanation for the poem's formal difficulty as the Divan seeks to account for the difficult, sometimes fleeting, erotic encounters of its protagonists. Another way to approach this trajectory, however – without dwelling on the vexed issue of nomenclature – would be to describe it as 'queer'. As Sarah Ahmed has pointed out, this term 'comes from the Indo-European word "twist"', adding that 'queer is a spatial term which then gets translated into a sexual term'.[19] 'The New Divan' is a poem 'about' sex and space, one that 'orients' sex *in* the disconnected, unstable, nomadic spaces of the Eastern deserts and the imbrication between the two is fundamental to the linguistic textures and complexities of the long poem.

These spaces may seem distant and rather different from the geographical locations of both the previous collections. Both *The Second Life* and *From Glasgow to Saturn* seem to invest primarily in Glasgow and America. But, as Deleuze recognises, 'there is the rhizomatic West, with its Indians without ancestry, its ever receding limit, its shifting and displaced frontiers. [...] America reversed the directions: it put its Orient in the West, as if it were precisely in America that the earth came full circle; its West is the edge of the East' (Deleuze, 20). It is no surprise, therefore, to discover that Morgan's first major collection, *The Second Life,* opens with an image of mist rolling out of the Pacific, a western mist that moves east obscuring everything in its path, taking 'the flash from the axe', dousing the apparently outdated heroics of the writer Hemingway as he takes his own life (*CP*, 145).

The second poem of the collection is set in Los Angeles; repeatedly, it exhorts the city and America to acknowledge a measure of responsibility for the death of Marilyn Monroe. The exclamations that pepper this strange poem seem simultaneously to celebrate and ironise America's promotion of a movie star to heroic status, a shallowness caught so precisely in Andy Warhol's repetitive screenprint of the actor's seductive surfaces. Caught somewhere between ode and elegy, Morgan's poem seems less decided, formally speaking, than Monroe herself (*CP*, 146):

> 'All I had was my life
> [...]
> There is now – and there is the future.
> What has happened is behind. So
> it follows you around? So what?'

These are lines confident in their materialism, their un-nostalgic obliteration of past and tradition, oriented towards the future. As he makes Piaf say in the next poem, 'Je ne regrette rien', 'I don't keep the past in my pocket' (*CP*, 146–48):

> I strike a match to my memories,
> they light a fire and disappear.

Just as, perhaps, 'a cigarette adventuring' in 'The New Divan' misses 'the swift gaff' (*CP*, 311). Cigarettes, indeed, are signs not simply of – sometimes illicit – desire in Morgan's verse, but of the kind of cruising sexuality foregrounded by the long poem. It is not exclusive to a homosexual world. Even at forty-five, Piaf can see

> the dead cigarette
> in his firm mouth
> he throws it aside
> it begins and
> I regret nothing
>
> We sway in the rain,
> he crushes my mouth.
> What could I regret
> if a hundred times
> of parting struck me
> like lightning if this
> lightning of love
> can strike and
> strike
> again.

The poem tapers to an end just as 'the last spire / trembles up' in 'One Cigarette', winding, perhaps, like an oriental snake (*CP*, 186).

Some might object that 'One Cigarette' in fact records a moment of joy, of togetherness, but the smoke also signals absence and farewell. Indeed it is important to recognise that the short poems which briefly evoke coupledom in both *The Second Life* ('From a City Balcony', 'When You Go', 'Strawberries', 'One Cigarette', 'The Picnic') and *From Glasgow to Saturn* ('In Glasgow', 'Drift') are hedged around by others which express angst and a sense of love's transitoriness. Because the 'happy' love poems are placed next to each other in *The Second Life*, they make a particular impact, but at the gate to this idyll we find the ambiguous 'seas of desire' that wash over 'Glasgow Green', the internalised homophobia of 'The Suspect', the hypostasisation of homosexuality in 'The Second Life' and 'The Unspoken' and the existential mindscapes of 'The Witness', 'Absence' and 'Without It'. Indeed, the love poems in *From Glasgow to Saturn* confirm this pattern and form the dark panel of the diptych. Fewer in number, they make poetry out of what inevitably passes and changes: momentary possible desire ('After the Party'), the responsibilities of shared lives ('At the Television Set'), loyalty and disloyalty ('From the North') and again absence ('The Milk-cart' and 'Estranged'). It is significant, however, that the last poem in this collection to deal with same-sex attraction is not 'Estranged' but 'Christmas Eve', in which a gay man's loneliness when confronted by the heterosexuality of Christmas time is relieved by the come-on made by a veteran of Aden on the top floor of a Glasgow bus. His Glasgow speech, his tattoos, all denote the return of the hardman who introduces us to the underworld/undergrowth of gay trysts in 'Glasgow Green'. The concluding stanza, which reflects on this encounter, points the way forward to the more methodical exploration of the patterns of same-sex concealment and revelation in 'The New Divan'. The experience makes the speaker feel 'as if I was lifted by a whirlwind / and thrown down on some desert rocks to die' (*CP*, 283). Had the censorious bus conductor not got in the way, narrator and soldier would have had a shared experience of the Middle East to talk about as well. The poem ends on a note of regret, but not downright pessimism. As the last line implies, the narrator is still prepared to run the risks of these types of encounter which – when the full flourish of Morgan's love poetry is considered across three collections – seem to form a kind of signature. As Michael Warner has noted of John Ashbery's poetry:

> Contrary to myth, what one relishes in loving strangers is not mere anonymity, nor meaningless release. It is the pleasure of belonging to a sexual world, in which one's sexuality finds an answering resonance not just in one other, but in a world of others.[20]

As 'Glasgow Green' makes clear, that 'resonance' can be dangerous but it does not stop the narrator of that poem reaching for rhetoric and imagery of biblical dimensions to express the compelling nature of his desire, which is seen as but a facet of all human desire (*CP*, 169):

> Longing,
> longing
> shall find its wine.

It is clear, then, that 'The New Divan' can help us to understand both Morgan's celebration and chronicling in *The Second Life* of the rhizomatic, sensation-led Beat culture that emerged during the 1960s as well as his moving, sometimes painful, plotting of the sexual energies that fuelled his new-found creativity. His third major collection as a whole can also clarify the earlier volume's reorientation of the sublime and its inscription in forms that explicitly and implicitly interrogate the possibility of a truly modern epic poetry. God was on the agenda as well as sex.

In *The New Divan*, Morgan's secularism and scepticism are visible in his attack on Platonic idealism in 'The Shadow', one of the 'Ten Theatre Poems', and also in 'Lévi-Strauss at the Lie-Detector', in which the French structuralist's love of system is undermined in a concrete poem which subtly critiques its ahistorical bias. Relying on his method of producing new and contradictory meanings from statements by a process – a system indeed – of vowel and consonantal subtraction, Lévi-Strauss's declaration that 'any classification is superior to chaos' is made to dissolve into an admission that 'any class fiction is superior chaos'. Readers fresh from the 'Glasgow Sonnets' sequence that closes *From Glasgow to Saturn*, with their devastatingly effective exposé of Glasgow slum life, would have cause to grimace ruefully at that. The main point to be made here, however, is that the satirical attack on idealism is couched in the form of concrete poetry. Returning to *The Second Life* we find that one of the most powerful and memorable of the earlier collection's concrete poems is 'Message Clear', in which the monotheism of Christ's 'I am the resurrection and the life' undergoes a similar process of reconstitution. Whereas the Lévi-Strauss poem begins with his bold declaration, however, 'Message Clear' starts haltingly and more movingly with a question: 'am i'. In attempting to answer that question, the speaker inadvertently reveals an identity whose spiritual co-ordinates are pagan and multiple and include the Egyptian deities Ra and Thoth. As Eleanor Bell has written, 'While some of the key critics of concrete have linked the form to its purely formal values, Morgan's experimentations with concrete often contain elements of wit and personality, a presence of some kind within the text'.[21] Indeed most of Morgan's concrete verse could be described as 'off concrete', to adopt the subtitle he added to 'Canedolia' (*CP*, 156). This is precisely what makes the concrete poems of this collection so readable, whether they take the form of the minimalist 'Siesta of a Hungarian Snake' (*CP*, 174) or the tongue-twisting 'The Chaffinch Map of Scotland' (*CP*, 179). In both these poems sound and vision are disposed in perfect balance, the wit is worn lightly but is not without point and depth and it may be that it was in this form that Morgan created some of his most distinctive and memorable achievements.

The expression of 'personality', to adopt Bell's term, is crucial to understanding both the limits and the opportunities of Morgan's experimentalism. Although both *From Glasgow to Saturn* and *The New Divan* draw quite heavily on surrealist principles and practice in many poems and often gesture towards the language-led poetry of American contemporaries such as Charles Bernstein and Michael Palmer, he was never prepared to fully embrace an aesthetic that abandoned the lyric subject, however fragmented and challenged it might appear in his verse. In his copy of Rosemary Waldrop's book *Against Language* he underlined a passage that noted how André Breton 'does not want to destroy the cognitive aspect of language of which he is very aware'.[22] Indeed, when one stands back from these three central collections, it is possible to see that the strand weaving through each of them – despite Morgan's legitimate disavowals of homogeneity – is the attempt to match experiment and tradition, to show them to each other and to us. Morgan's remark to Walter Cairns identifying his concrete verse as 'poems in space'[23] gets its most graphic illustration in *The New Divan* when 'Space Sonnet & Polyfilla' (*CP*, 341) presents a literal version of precisely this aesthetic. Here mutilated sonnet form requires the reader to fill the gaps in the structure by 'pasting' in parts of words that have 'dropped' further down the page. When this has been done a vision of a colonised Mars subject to thought control, 'straightjacket form' and – perhaps by extension – 'penal therapy' emerges. Yet that nightmarish vision is simultaneously complemented and undermined by the gappy mirror image printed beneath it on the same page where the 'polyfilla' seems to have a life of its own. The 'parts of words' turn out to be words in their own right, some of which shakily remind the reader of the familiar human story. Here we find 'eve' again, her 'sin', her possible presence in 'me', 'her', 'he' as well as an alternative version in an 'ape' that 'can'. But those stories are also mocked by some of the other fragments: there is a rather Beckettian 'hat on table', somebody or something is 'up it' and the hat is 'all apy / on member'. Perhaps the 'message clear' we are meant to take from this is that ultimately it all boils down to sex – again! Morgan's 'push-me-pull-you' aesthetic is designed to simultaneously invite and frustrate such attempts to make connections and tell stories.

What this and other poems such as 'Spacepoem 1' (*CP*, 194) or the more famous 'The First Men on Mercury' (*CP*, 267) make most clear, however, is the intimate connection in Morgan's mind between his practice of concrete verse and his attempts to create a form of modern epic poetry out of the matter of science fiction. It is in the great so-called 'science fiction poems' which appear in all three collections that his persistent interest in epic and its potential to express a modern sublime achieves its richest expression. There, he presents fragmented narrative forms whose lightly worn experimentalism finds its *raison d'être* in the genre itself.

'The First Men on Mercury' is a poem of multiple ironies, not the least, or the least moving, of which is the emergence among the Mercurians of human speech. Read in conjunction with the longer science fiction poems, it may seem merely an enjoyable entertainment as natives and aliens exchange communicative codes and identities. Yet in its theme and in its final lines it anticipates or recalls the consistently humanist message at the core of 'Memories of Earth' (*CP*, 330–40) in *The New Divan* and 'In Sobieski's Shield' (*CP*, 196–98) in *The Second Life*. The messages implied and exchanged between the Mercurian-voiced humans and the humanely articulate Mercurians at the end of 'The First Men on Mercury' are blunt and uneasy: 'take what you have gained', 'nothing is ever the same'. And much the same conclusions are reached in the two longer poems.

'Memories of Earth' conjures again the desert landscapes of the immediately preceding epic 'The New Divan', but observed this time by a team of visiting, sympathetic human-like aliens. Like the 'Divan', it recalls a variety of historical epochs and incidents whose seeming coexistence is facilitated by the time-bending effects of the visitors' presence. If Morgan is on record as an admirer of Hugh MacDiarmid's scientifically inspired stony landscapes, he also noted that the older poet's interest in stones seemed to preclude much concern for the ordinary human beings who had to live among them.[24] In 'Memories of Earth', Morgan mischievously miniaturises his time and space travellers so that they may 'enter' the stone itself. The remainder of the poem reveals that it has a beating, human heart, the memory of which remains with and changes the visitors despite the authoritarian reprimands of 'The Council' which

> stared as if I was
> an alien life-form, which perhaps I am
> now. (*CP*, 340)

'Memories of Earth' does not shy from a graphic account of the Holocaust, its horror and pathos renewed through the fresh perspective brought by alien eyes. Similarly, in 'In Sobieski's Shield' it is the visible traces of the First World War that provoke some of the most remarkable lines Morgan ever wrote and force the protagonist to value more fiercely and draw close the slowly rematerialising forms of his beloved wife and child. If, as I have argued, Morgan's experience of war is largely sublimated in 'The New Divan', it is displaced to reappear – changed and changing – in these science fiction poems. So alienating, it seems, is the experience of war that it makes an alien of you (that is of course: a real human being) before you can see it clearly for what it is (*CP*, 197):

> I can see a stark hand brandishing nothing through placid scum
> in a lull of the guns what horror that the livid water
> is not shaken by the pity of the tattoo on the dead arm
> a heart still held above the despair of the mud
> my god the heart on my arm my second birth mark
> the rematerialisation has picked up these fragments I have
> a graft of war and ancient agony forgive
> me my dead helper

It is difficult not to gasp when rereading these lines through the prism of the lines and poems that compose the succeeding collections. While it is tempting to say that they 'anticipate' some of the images of 'The New Divan', the effect is more complex perhaps precisely because they occur in a science fiction poem that plays with notions of time travel and rematerialisation. One has a momentary vision of Morgan suddenly able to project himself into the future and be present at the composition of the final stanzas of 'The New Divan', for here, undoubtedly, are images of the tattoo and the dead soldier that mark so movingly the concluding stanzas of the later poem. The emotional effect is all the greater, too, for the way these lines pull the concept of a 'second life' or poetic 'rebirth' into the mix and for the perfect judgement Morgan displays as the speaker's syntax becomes correspondingly more breathless, less grammatically or poetically 'correct'.

What these lines also suggest is that while Morgan's 'breakthrough' collection, *The Second Life,* is so often seen as a forward-looking, optimistic renewal of energies and potentialities, it should not be thought of as a collection that closes the door on the past. 'In Sobieski's Shield', 'From the Domain of Arnheim' (*CP*, 198), the ironies of some of the concrete poems, all show a writer who was profoundly marked by his personal experience of war, who was, in fact, in his own coded manner, constantly thinking about it and attempting to find contemporary ways of speaking its impossibility. In 'In Sobieski's Shield' the phrase that remains with one is 'there's a new graveness of the / second life' (*CP*, 197) and it is possibly in the science fiction poem's filtering of vision and emotion through its fictitious personae that the true gravitas of the poet's rebirth may be measured. The collection's title poem, 'The Second Life' (*CP*, 180), while it is a famous and compelling poem, does not manage to find quite the same convincing balance between rhetoric and subject matter.

It is indeed at the 'microscopic' level of individual lines that the connections between the apparently disparate aspects of Morgan's range become most visible. The emotional power contained in the phrase 'a new graveness of the / second life' is extended by the line it runs into: 'a new graveness of the / second life that phrase again we go up together'. '[T]hat phrase again' refers to the necessarily reiterated idea of rebirth but – for those who have been listening carefully to the collection – it also refers to the concluding phrase which echoes a line – itself repeated – that marks the climax of 'In the Snack-bar' (*CP*, 170), one of Morgan's most moving poems about Glasgow life. This is an aspect of Morgan's work in these three collections that I have not really touched upon until now, yet it was an important part of his work in these years. 'In the Snack-bar' (*The Second Life*), 'Stobhill' (*From Glasgow to Saturn*), many of the Glasgow Sonnets look unflinchingly at the underbelly of big city life and, taken together, one might well claim an 'epic' dimension for these poems also. This is clearest, perhaps, in 'In the Snack-bar' when the narrator accompanies a blind tramp to the toilet down flights of stairs and back up again (*CP*, 171–72):

> He climbs, and steadily enough.
> He climbs, we climb. He climbs
> with many pauses but with that one
> persisting patience of the undefeated
> which is the nature of man when all is said.
> And slowly we go up. And slowly we go up.

That image of a tramp, shuffling painfully across and up through space, reminds one inevitably of Beckett, yet it is a mark of Morgan's originality that we should also be able to recognise in this figure the contours of space-travelling aliens who are none other than our very selves, but changed in the ascent.

Edwin Morgan's poetry voyages bravely over the surfaces of a culture that – due to the experiences of war and holocaust – had become suspicious of any claim to depth, to roots. This is the aesthetic of post-war Europe, typified in the experiments of the 'nouveau roman' and the films of Antonioni. Anti-authoritarian, often hedonistic, it nevertheless performs extraordinary acts of brinkmanship as it collages formal experiment and tradition. The concrete poems that aspire to forms of expressivity, the continual return of the sonnet, the prevalence of ode and elegy within his oeuvre, these are all gestures that Morgan's more surreal work, his subversion of epic poetry's established narrative drive, implicitly critique. There is a sense in which this incredibly ambitious writer simply wanted to make all poetry's possibilities and potentialities simultaneously present to us. If, for a moment, we imagine that the world visited by Tromro and his companions in 'Memories of Earth' is also Planet Poetry then the end of the poem's first 'tape' presents a moving and amusing simulacrum of Morgan's poesis (*CP*, 333):

> we know now what we might have guessed: our time
> and this world's time can never be in phase,
> its images, its messages, its life
> must come to us like an eternal present,
> and by our very meagrest interfering
> we trigger fragments of the vanished prints
> but have no key to make the sequence clear.
> Tromro will have to ...

CHAPTER FOUR

Edwin Morgan's Poetry from Scotland

Cairns Craig

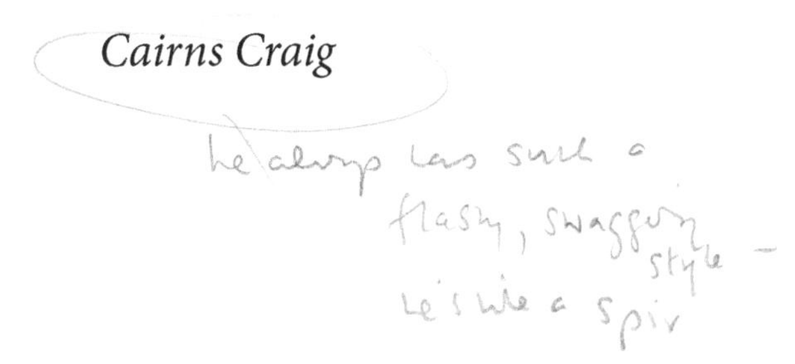

The publication of Edwin Morgan's *Sonnets from Scotland* in 1984 was to prove as decisive a turning point in his career – and in the public's perception of him – as had *The Second Life* in 1968. That earlier volume established Morgan as the 'international' Scottish poet – fellow-traveller with the Beats (in poems such as 'The Death of Marilyn Monroe'), experimenter with 'concrete' ('French Persian Cats Having a Ball') and 'sound' poetry ('Canedolia'), playful constructor of typographic witticisms ('Siesta of a Hungarian Snake'), almost more famous for his translations of European poets such as Montale or Mayakovsky than for his own writings. 'Seven Headlines' said it all in many variations:

absolu   t   e
        m   odern
        men
Il faut être absolument moderne
(*CP*, 176)

Morgan was the 'absolute modern' and the modern was 'international' – as evidenced in his editorial role on the journal *Scottish International* from 1968. Though many of his poems were about local subjects – 'Glasgow Green', 'The Starlings in George Square' – or local encounters – 'Good Friday', 'In the Snack-bar' – they were framed by a style that declared its international affiliations, that saw Scotland anew through the medium of elsewhere (the 'Chinese moment' in 'Aberdeen Train'), or celebrated modernity in Scotland ('The Opening of the Forth Road Bridge, 4.IX.64'). Implicitly, Morgan's poetry was the answer to the failure of Scotland to be fully part of the modern world: Scotland had to be made modern, because Scotland was a place resistant to modernity, resistant to renewal, left out of the technological transformations that were reshaping humanity's relationship with the cosmos:

> Vostok shrieks and prophesies, Mariner's prongs flash –
> to the wailing of Voskhod Earth sighs, she shakes men loose
> at last –
> out, in our time, to be living seeds sent far beyond
> even imagination. (*CP*, 199)

The 'living seeds' of the future go forth from Russia and America, two of the cultures whose most important poets Morgan imitates or translates, as though, through him, Scotland might itself at least mimic the trajectory of a history it cannot itself perform, a history projected into a future that makes the past, the national past, the weight of past tradition, irrelevant to modern creativity. On this basis, for instance, Morgan would distinguish himself from the 'modernists' of the preceding generation: as compared with Pound or Eliot, he would prefer a poetry

> relying less I think on earlier literature. I've the feeling of wanting to get away from that, I think; I'm a pretty strongly anti-traditionalist in that sense. I really on the whole dislike history and tradition. I'm interested in what is happening, and I'm interested in what will happen, more than I'm interested in what has happened, I think, so that my long poem, if ever it comes out, will be rather different from existing ones. It will perhaps be 'now' plus the future, rather than 'now' plus the past. (*NNGM*, 33)

'"Now" plus the future' suggests that Scotland, Scotland as a past, is irrelevant to Morgan's conception of poetry. As late as 1990, when the magazine *Cencrastus* published a special issue on Morgan,[1] it linked him with Alexander Trocchi and William Burroughs, both of whom had been contributors to the 1962 Edinburgh Writers' Festival where Trocchi had famously challenged the relevance of Hugh MacDiarmid's work to contemporary Scotland. By framing Morgan with Burroughs and Trocchi it suggested that Morgan might be, like Trocchi, a poet of resistance to the traditions of Scottish literature – perhaps even a writer in 'exile', with Glasgow, where he had lived continuously since returning from service in the Second World War, as much a place of exile from the rest of Scotland as Paris or New York. It was as a native Glaswegian rather than a native

Scot that he had described himself in a letter to Michael Schmidt in 1972 – 'I am really a very native Glasgow-loving root-clutching person'[2] – and his preference for Glasgow as distinct, and as distinctly different, was a view which Morgan retained even late in his life: he was reluctant, for instance, to attend the celebration of the opening of his archive at the Scottish Poetry Library in Edinburgh because he thought it ought to be housed in Glasgow, and was only convinced to attend when he could defiantly wear a T-shirt with a picture of a Tunnock's Caramel Wafer on which was inscribed, 'Glasgow Takes the Biscuit'.[3]

Certainly many of those who interviewed Morgan in the 1970s regarded 'Scottishness' as something he would want to distance himself from: the assumption was that Morgan was part of 'a cosmopolitanism' that would necessarily be opposed to the rise of the Scottish nationalism that had taken psephologists aback by its successes in the 1960s. Morgan's response to such implications clearly came as a surprise to his interviewers:

> I think I am actually [a nationalist]. I think I would probably call myself that, though I don't feel very much attracted to the SNP. I'm not a member of any of the political parties, but I think in a sense that I feel Scottish and not English, and feel also that [there] is still a meaningful sense in which you could call yourself a Scottish writer, even though it's very hard to define this. In that sense I would still feel that there is enough that is distinct for it be defined and developed, and, if possible, carried forward as a kind of tradition. I think there must obviously be a good deal of overlapping, both with English and with foreign international cultures – this is inevitable. But I would still feel quite strongly enough conscious of Scotland as an entity or the Scots person as being different from the Englishman, to want to keep this. In that sense I would call myself a Scottish nationalist. (*NNGM*, 40)

It was as modernist from Scotland that Morgan established his reputation: that he was a Scottish 'nationalist' was not evident to those who admired his adoption of innovative modernisms from around the world.

This widespread emphasis on Morgan's achievement as an internationalising modernist tells us much about the nature of the culture by which he was surrounded from the 1950s to the 1970s; it may also tell us much about how different was the Scotland of the 1980s from those earlier decades, and explain how Morgan the 'Futurist', cut off from 'history and tradition', became by 2004 – however reluctantly he himself accepted the term – the nation's 'Makar'.[4]

Nostophobia

In 1968, the year when Morgan's first collection of poems, *The Second Life*, was published, his sometime colleague at the University of Glasgow, Kenneth White, sixteen years his junior and in the French rather than the English department, decided that there was no future for creativity in Scotland, or indeed, in Britain more generally. He left for Paris and a literary and academic career in French and in France, declaring,

> in recent times, many of the poets with the life-desire and intellectual demands that go with the production of the most powerful poetry have found it impossible to go on living within British precincts at all. We need only think of D. H. Lawrence, with his loathing of the 'pettyfogging narrowness' of England – and if Dylan Thomas, another exemplary figure, remained, who would deny that it was the British set-up and cultural atmosphere that obliged him to turn himself into a kind of Divine Clown, playing incessantly a tragic-comic role and perhaps never reaching anything like his full development as a poet. And there is Yeats, considering that London is the enemy of all real culture, trying to ground a more fundamental culture around that lonely tower in Galway; and Joyce who, if he took the trouble to criticise Ireland, felt that England was *beneath* criticism; and MacDiarmid, who has been raging now in vociferous Anglophobia and hatred of 'grey Englishry' (the cause, as he sees it, of what we might call 'grey Scottishry') for half a century.[5]

The specifically Scottish context of his revulsion at the dead-end nature of British culture is perhaps captured in his little poem 'Rue d'Écosse, Hill of Sainte-Geneviève, Paris':

> There's nothing much in the rue d' Écosse
> that dark little cul-de-sac –
> just the full moon and a stray cat.[6]

Scotland as a 'dark little cul-de-sac' is a dominant theme of Scottish writing in the 1950s and 1960s. The country as cultural entity had no future and, in a commonplace of the time, 'anyone who had get up and go, got up and went'; if there was, in American parlance, some creative 'cat' in the cul-de-sac, it was a 'stray' – there by accident and on its way to somewhere else.

Despite the fact that, except for the war years, he had never lived anywhere else but Scotland, Morgan contributed his own share to this bleak account of the Scottish inheritance. In the second issue of *Scottish International* he published 'The Flowers of Scotland', a poem later included in the *Penguin Modern Poets* volume he shared with Alan Bold and Edward Brathwaite and which set out clearly the failings of his native land:

> Yes, it is too cold in Scotland for flower people; in any case who would be handed a thistle?
> What are our flowers? Locked swings and private rivers –
> and the island of Staffa for sale in the open market, which no one questions or thinks strange –
> and lads o' pairts that run to London and Buffalo without a backward look while their elders say Who'd blame them –
> and bonny fechters kneedeep in dead ducks with all the thrawn intentness of the incorrigible professional Scot –
> and a Kirk Assembly that excels itself in the bad old rhetoric and tries to stamp out every glow of charity and change, most wrong when it thinks most loudly it is most right – (*CP*, 203)

Ten verse paragraphs of the ailments of Scotland are contrasted with the powerlessness of those who resist its repressions: 'and dissidence crying in the wilderness to a moor of boulders and two ospreys'.

The editorial of that issue of *Scottish International* declares that 'Much of what we struggle against is summed up by Edwin Morgan's poem on the facing page'.[7] What the poem expresses is, in effect, a deep revulsion from the actual nature of the 'homeland', and revulsion which was characteristic not only of many responses to Scotland in the early issues of *Scottish International* but of the cultural environment in which Morgan had grown up. In the 1950s and 1960s the achievements of Hugh MacDiarmid and the Scottish Renaissance movement of the 1920s and 1930s were only beginning to be appreciated, but that achievement was a double-edged sword as far as contemporary responses to Scotland were concerned, since its creative potential was matched by a deeply antipathetic stance towards previous Scottish cultural achievements. If Hugh MacDiarmid, founding figure of the Renaissance, listed 'anglophobia' as one of his interests in his entry in *Who's Who*, much more significant in terms of the development of Scottish culture was what I will call his 'nostophobia', his hatred for the institutional world of Scotland, his recoil from the reality of modern industrial Scotland, his rejection of its cities, its bourgeoisie, its culture since as far back as the Union, or, perhaps, as far back as the Reformation. In 1945, following the announcement of a festival in Edinburgh to help in the reconstruction of Europe, and to which 'every distinguished composer and executant might be attracted', MacDiarmid responded in *The Voice of Scotland* that such an occasion would only 'emphasise the absence of their peers in Scotland itself and the better the programmes the more ghastly would yawn the abyss between them and the utter inability of the Scottish people to assimilate and profit by anything of the sort, let alone be stimulated even to try to produce anything of comparable worth on their own part'.[8] Even though 'Scottish internationalism' is to be preferred to and asserted against 'English insularity', the literary content of the Scottish tradition is minimal: 'Literary critics in Scotland have always been as rare as snakes in Iceland – that's one of the reason for our creative poverty.'[9] Though Morgan carefully distanced himself from those – the poets of the so-called 'second wave' of the Renaissance – who thought that only poetry in Scots could carry forward MacDiarmid's achievements, 'nostophobia' was a distinctive thread in the magazine of which he was first an editor and then an 'editorial advisor'. In an 'Open Letter to Archie Hind', for instance, published in *Scottish International* in October 1971, John Lloyd challenged the implicit nostalgia of Hind's support for the workers of the Upper Clyde Shipbuilders, of his nostalgic desire to identify himself with the 'authenticity' of working men:

> The cutting edge is the guilt Scots often appear to feel that they are writers/artists/intellectuals at all, and not part of the nitty gritty of boots and shovel, pick and piece-bag. It's as though they develop a mental castration fear. Having dared to develop the mental organ until it stands up above those of his fellows, the one thing the Scot wants to do is to disguise it, in case someone takes a chop at it.[10]

By contrast, Lloyd explained how

> I like living in London much of the time. It was in London that I learned various pleasures like, for example, LSD (the drug), wearing my hair long, that I began to gain a measure of sexual freedom and feel a gradual loosening of the tightness of my own inhibitions. Now all these things could have happened in Govan, perhaps, but in London it was easier.[11]

Scotland is the place where intellectuals are mentally castrated, London where they are sexually liberated. Eighteen months later, the April 1973 edition of the magazine advertised a forthcoming conference on 'What Kind of Scotland?' but the issue was introduced by a piece of 'reportage' which underlined the effect of arriving in Scotland from that metropolitan London that Lloyd had evoked:

> Step straight from the middle-class ghetto – well-dressed, well-mannered children, Saturday morning coffee in Louis's *patisserie*, Sunday lunchtime drinks in the *Horse and Groom* – into Glasgow now, and the effect is … well, shattering is not too strong a word. Surely it wasn't as bad four or five years ago? On my way to stay with friends near Drymen, I drove through Glasgow at night, just as the pubs were skailing. A dying place, murdered by neglect. Crumbling peeling stonework, boarded-up shops, slogans sprayed everywhere. Children clustered aimlessly on street corners. I stopped twice at phone boxes, both vandalised, the floors covered in spew and piss. I couldn't believe it.[12]

The journey towards the debate about 'What kind of Scotland?' begins in nostophobia; little wonder that the nostophobic haunts its discussions: 'The relevance of what was being said about fear, guilt and lack of confidence was sharp and tangible to this kind of Scottish audience.'[13] John Herdman's report on the conference in the April 1973 issue of *Scottish International* begins by recounting psychiatrist Aaron Eesterson's idea that 'people are often driven mad directly by the behaviour towards them of members of their own families', and muses on how, for the audience, this must have raised the question of 'how far the tensions of a small, cramped national society like that of Scotland, not dissimilar to a family in many ways, may help to induce various kinds of corporate madness in the Scottish people'.[14] Only the nostophobe can see through the 'corporate madness' that blinds the national psyche of those who live within the boundaries and traditions of the nation.

The political and historic ironies of the situation are caught in an 'Open Letter' from Tom Nairn, who challenges 'the romantic-nationalist' conception of the nation and notes 'How unpropitious the terrain has always been in Scotland for such imagined "nationalist phases", whether in music or anything else! And hence the true nationalist's irrepressible gloom in our land'[15] – a gloom that is evidenced by a quote from Morgan's 'The Flowers of Scotland'. Nairn has, however, his own nostophobic conception of Scotland as a culture whose past failure gives it a kind of advantage over the failings of other countries like England and France:

> It was natural, inevitable, that the great age of European nationalism triumphant (1848–1945) should have produced such responses everywhere in Europe, even in those marginal areas which did not and could not 'make it' like the bigger states. Nor is it surprising that the ideology lives on into the days of the Common Market. However, I believe that attention to 'what is really there' shows that the long winding road was never in fact traversable by the Scots. Their major cultural talent is the shortcut. *Not* having 'roots' of the requisite kind has been their chief advantage in life, at least during modern times. It is why they were so important in the brief era of cosmopolitanism before nationalist cultures were entrenched everywhere; and also why they have put up such a desperately poor performance during the age of *Nationalstaat* itself. It was not their element – nor is it ever likely to be now.[16]

Scotland's advantage in the modern world is the failure of its national and nationalist culture: those who succeeded in creating a nineteenth-century nationalism are now the sclerotic leftovers of a historical epoch of no contemporary relevance. Failure may be the basis of modern Scottish culture, but it failed earlier and differently than England or France – and that is its only hope.

In this context, Morgan's celebration of the modern can be read as arising from a similar rejection of his inherited environment: the game playing of much of Morgan's poetry in *From Glasgow to Saturn* (1973), for instance, with its various escapes into alternative worlds and alternative languages, cannot avoid confronting, in the end, the fact that

> stalled lives never budge.
> They linger in the single-ends that use
> their spirit to the bone, and when they trudge
> from closemouth to launderette their steady shoes
> carry a world that weighs us like a judge.
> ('Glasgow Sonnets x', *CP*, 292)

'Glasgow Sonnets' invokes a world in which

> No deliverer ever rose
> from these stone tombs to get the hell they made
> unmade. The same weans never make the grade.
> The same grey street sends back the ball it throws.
> ('Glasgow Sonnets ii', *CP*, 289)

Poetry's alternative realities, however powerfully imagined, cannot challenge a world trapped in apparently permanent decay: it is the lesson of MacDiarmid's futuristic 'Glasgow, 1960' (published in 1935), in which football-sized crowds produce a 'record gate' at Ibrox to hear 'a debate on "la loi de l'effort converti" / Between Professor MacFadyen and a Spainish pairty',[17] but

> Hugh MacDiarmid forgot
> in 'Glasgow 1960' that the feast
> of reason and the flow of soul had ceased
> to matter to the long unfinished plot
> of heating frozen hands. We never got
> an abstruse song that charmed the raging beast.
> ('Glasgow Sonnets iv', *CP*, 290)

By framing this vision of a stalled history in sonnets Morgan underlines the enclosure that is modern Scotland, its entrapment in a form whose essence is repetition, even when the poet is disporting his most outrageous flights of fancy:

> Let bus and car
> and hurrying umbrella keep their skill to
> feed ukiyo-e beyond Lochnagar.
> ('Glasgow Sonnets viii', *CP*, 291)

Glasgow may be Morgan's launch-pad to poetic Saturns but it, like the Scotland around it, remains relentlessly saturnine.

For a poet who disliked 'history and tradition', however, Morgan expended considerable energy from the 1950s to the 1970s in coming to terms with the poetic past of Scotland. In the early years of his time as a lecturer at Glasgow he published, in 1952, 'Dunbar and the Language of Poetry', an essay which identified 'energy' as itself the key feature of Dunbar's work – 'What is immediately noticeable [...] is the *display* of *poetic energy* in forms that have considerable technical and craftsmanly interest' (*CB*, 46) – and between then and the late 1970s he had published essays on Gavin Douglas, William Drummond, Robert Fergusson, Robert Louis Stevenson, Hugh MacDiarmid, Edwin Muir, as well as general essays that reflected on 'Scottish Poetry in English' and 'The Resources of Scotland'. This continuous engagement with the Scottish poetic past had none of the obliterative intent behind MacDiarmid's 'Back to Dunbar' agenda in the 1920s: instead, Morgan patiently teases out what might still speak to contemporary readers as, for instance, when he compares Stevenson with Gerard Manley Hopkins:

> of course it is impossible not to see the difference between a man who was a poet to his finger-tips and one who like Stevenson was an occasional poet whose main work lay elsewhere, in prose. But Hopkins is dazzling and it is important to give Stevenson his due. His verse is a genuine part of the tradition of Scottish poetry, which it extends in more than one direction, and in addition to that it holds out a range of poetic effects and pleasures which is, I believe, a good deal wider than we have been accustomed to assume. (*CB*, 156)

Stevenson is to be understood in terms of what he contributed to 'the tradition of Scottish poetry', and if, for many, it is difficult to relate 'to traditions that may seem more like locks than keys' ('The Resources of Scotland', *CB*, 19), Morgan nonetheless wants to open up those traditions and test what is usable: 'There comes a time when out of respect for itself a country must collect its resources, and look at its assets and shortcomings with an eye that is both sharp and warm: see what is there, what is not there, what could be there' (*CB*, 23–24). It is also the time to evaluate what Scottish writers have contributed to 'world literature', a term invented by Goethe, the literary figure who dominated the early years of Thomas Carlyle's writing career, and it is Carlyle's truly international – and transdisciplinary – influence that Morgan seeks to emphasise:

> Engels admired Carlyle; so did James Joyce. To Engels, it was necessary to penetrate through the surface of Carlyle to find the serious and important social analysis. To Joyce, Carlyle was one of the great liberators of language and style, which is why he uses Carlyle so much in *Ulysses*, both in the Yes, the Everlasting Yea, of the conclusion, and in the remarkable parody of Carlyle which he brings in at the crucial moment of the

> birth of Mrs Purefoy's baby in the maternity hospital, again taking Carlyle as a celebrator, an anti-Malthusian, a yea-sayer to life.
> ('Carlyle's Style', *CB*, 140)

The 'international', in other words, not as an escape from Scottishness but as its fulfilment: for in Carlyle's style, with its mixture of the biblical with the Germanic, of Scottish with English, 'there are many parallels to be found in Scottish literature – Sir Thomas Urquhart, and the long satirical and flyting traditions, to say nothing of Scottish preachers or Scottish speech habits' (*CB*, 35). Reintegrating into Scottish traditions the figure whose departure for London was often taken to be indicative of the death of those traditions, folds internationalism back into the national, as does reinterpreting MacDiarmid's late poetry in the context of the American long poem or Hans Magnus Enzensberger's *Mausoleum*, in which 'each poem is printed as a very clear collage of original poetry and documented writings or utterances of the great man in question' ('MacDiarmid's Later Poetry', *CB*, 193). Far from being nostophobic, Morgan's criticism of Scottish writers from the 1950s to the 1970s bespeaks a generous inclusiveness of those writers about whom something is known and a desire to discover more about what is unknown or known only partially: 'It is no use shying off from Macpherson's Ossian or Henry Mackenzie as if they were beneath serious concern. The history of drama in Scotland may be the blank it seems to be, and then again it may not; the fact is that until a complete history of it is written we are talking about it from insufficient knowledge' ('Towards a Literary History of Scotland', *CB*, 12). If the internationalism of Morgan's poetic experiments suggested the nostophobe's belief that creativity could only be fulfilled by escape from the constrictions of the national past, Morgan the critic and teacher was diligently attempting to recast that national past into one which could contribute to a creative future for the nation.

Theoxenia

> But the gods have their own
> undying life, and Heaven, if it needs anything,
> needs heroes, needs
> humanity, needs
> all things mortal. For
> spirits of Heaven can in themselves feel nothing,
> and therefore someone else (if I may say this)

> must surely feel, show sympathy
> for the sake of the gods
> who need him.
> (Friedrich Hölderlin, 'The Rhine', *CT*, 258)

Hölderlin's 'The Rhine', as translated by Morgan, insists that the gods wander among humanity, seeking what their godly status would deny them – emotion, sympathy, identification. In ancient Greece it was believed that Zeus might appear at the door of any household at any moment, disguised as a stranger: one therefore had to be hospitable to strangers, since one never knew when the stranger might be a god:

> Demigods besiege my thoughts now
> and I must seek them out, dear as they are,
> for their lives do often stir
> any heart in its longing.
> But what can I call him, the stranger
> like you, Rousseau, who with a soul
> unconquerable, strong to
> endure, a firm understanding,
> a sweet talent for listening
> that he gave out the speech of the purest
> like the wine-god, from divine abundance.
> (Hölderlin, 'The Rhine', *CT*, 259)

Hölderlin's encounter with 'the stranger' who comes like a god across his threshold re-enacts that moment of meeting between man and god, man and god-in-disguise-as-man, that the Greeks denoted by the term *theoxenia*, the hospitality which was due to a stranger because it might also be hospitality to a visiting god: '– Then gods and men celebrate their union / it is a celebration for all the living'. Morgan's translation of Hölderlin's poem may have been inspired by the fact that it is addressed to his friend Izaak von Sinclair, who was from a Scottish-German family that had been resident in Germany for two generations. Those who cross borders, like Rousseau and like Sinclair, those who come as strangers but are friends and inspirers, bring with them the possibility of encountering the gods:

> Sinclair my friend! God may appear to you
> on the sultry path under the fir-trees or
> in a dark oak-wood sheathed with steel or

> in clouds, you know him, since you know in your own youth
> the strength of his goodness.
> (Hölderlin, 'The Rhine', *CT*, 261)

Such unexpected encounters with the stranger is a key theme in many Morgan poems, whether in the banal environment of 'In the Snack-bar' – and how differently, in this context, might we read its final line, 'Dear Christ, to be born for this!' (*CP*, 172), with its possibility of God made flesh – or the science fiction encounter in 'From the Domain of Arnheim' in which time travellers visit their primitive precursors: 'There are no gods in the domain of Arnheim', the speaker asserts but of course he is one who is godlike, or at least spirit-like, in his absent presence:

> I know you felt
> the same dismay, you gripped my arm, they were waiting
> for what they knew of us to pass. (*CP*, 198)

A comic inversion of that encounter is dialogically presented in 'The First Men on Mercury' (*CP*, 267) and a celebratory version in 'Trio', when ordinary human beings on a Christmas shopping trip become visitors from the gods:

> the guitar swells out under its silky plastic cover, tied at the neck
> with silver tinsel tape and a brisk sprig of mistletoe.
> Orphean sprig! Melting baby! Warm chihuahua!
> The vale of tears is powerless before you.
> Whether Christ is born, or is not born, you
> put paid to fate, it abdicates
> under the Christmas lights
> Monsters of the year
> go blank, are scattered back,
> can't bear this march of three. (*CP*, 172)

A secular *theoxenia* can take place even in Buchanan Street.

For Morgan, the work of translation opened up poetic possibilities that had been closed down in the narrowing expectations of poets and poetry that had come to dominate poetry in English in Britain in the 1950s: as he put it in the 'Introduction' to *Sovpoems* in 1961, 'every "advance" in formalism is a further withdrawal from human relations and confidence – it snaps another link of trust between man and man' (*CT*, 31). Soviet poetry, he asserts, offers a counterpoise to this diminished sense of how the poet relates to his social world: 'without the one big thing that the Soviet artist does have – interest, care, and positive confidence in and for man and society – there is too little to build on, and the arts become a sort of fascinating marginal fantasy, where talent and effort (and money) are devoted to convincing a sceptical world that the materials used are more interesting than the mind that shapes them or the end it shapes them to' (*CT*, 31). Translation provides the opportunity to bring alternative conceptions of poetic purpose into one's own cultural sphere: by being hospitable to strangers one can find flights of poetic inspiration that take you in alternative directions.

The very first issue of *Scottish International* in January 1968 offered an essay by Morgan on the theme of metamorphosis in the work of Andrei Voznesensky, prefaced by the assertion that a 'poetry which wants meaningfully to interlock with this age must be prepared to be vulnerable, fluid, various, adventurous and searching'.[18] The poem on which Morgan focuses and for which he provides his own translation is 'Wings':

> The gods are dozing like slummocks –
> Clouds for layabouts!
>   what hammocks!
>
> The gods are for the birds.
> The birds are for the birds.
>
> What about wings,
> all that paraphernalia?
> It's too weird, I tell you,
> What did the ancients see in these things?
> Nearer
>   and nearer
>   to the fuselage
> clouds press them in,
>   to a vestige-
> ality of winginess on our things,
> our marvel-machines, strange
> to them. Men have unslung
> something new, men don't hang
> out wings, men are with it, bang.
> Man, men are winged![19]

The theme of the translation of men into (technological) gods is enacted in the translation into English of a Russian avant-gardism, inspired by the Soviet spaceflights, that gives new 'wings' to poetry in Scotland. Technological progress allows a Russian poet to consort with the gods – 'men become the gods they once adumbrated'[20] – but the hospitality of translation allows those gods to be guests in a previously flightless Scotland: a poetic *theoxenia* allows the godlike spirit of the Russian poet to offer creative nourishment to the Scottish domestic environment.

It was with precisely this aim that Morgan translated the Russian poet Mayakovsky into Scots: could Scots be 'hospitable' to a Russian modernist whose manifesto declared that poets should 'feel an insurmountable hatred for the language existing before them' (*CT*, 108)? Was Scots in the 1970s still capable of the kind of fusion with modernity that MacDiarmid had achieved in the 1920s? *Wi the Haill Voice: 15 Poems by Vladimir Mayakovsky* invited the moving spirits of modernism in Russia and in Scotland to be (godlike) guests at the (writing) table of Edwin Morgan:

> There is in Scottish poetry (e.g. in Dunbar, Burns, and even MacDiarmid) a vein of fantastic satire that seems to accommodate Mayakovsky more readily than anything in English verse, and there was also, I must admit, an element of challenge in finding out whether the Scots language could match the mixture of racy colloquialism and verbal inventiveness in Mayakovsky's Russian. I hoped Hugh MacDiarmid might be right when he claimed in 'Gairmscoile' that
>
> > ... there's forgotten shibboleths o the Scots
> > Hae keys to senses lockit to us yet. (*CT*, 113)

Wi the Haill Voice exploits in its title the potential of Scots to create those effects which Mayakovsky's Russian contemporary, Alexei Kruchonykh, focused in the phrase 'the word is broader than its meaning' (*CT*, 110): '*Broad* Scots' creates a potentiality of meaning absent from English, so that 'Haill' is not only a translation of what is rendered in English as 'full', but 'haill' in the sense of 'whole', thereby challenging the prevalent assumptions that the very language of Scots is symptomatic of a fragmented culture, incapable of wholeness;[21] at the same time, it punningly invokes 'hail', to call from a distance, which is effectively what Morgan's translations allow Mayakovsky to do – to call from the distance of Russian and through the distance of Scots to a contemporary English-speaking audience. The theoxenic implications of this process are made manifest in the poem 'Vladimir's Ferlie' (rendered in English as 'An Extraordinary Adventure', the only poem, as Morgan notes in his introduction, of which there is an extant recording of Mayakovsky reading): it is a poem in which the poet rails at the sun for its summer heat, only to discover the sun descending to enter his cottage:

> It burst door, winnock, and winnock-frame:
> it brasht and breeshlt
> till it wan
> its pech, it spak fae the pit o its wame:
> 'Thon bleeze had never been retrackit
> Sae faur as this sin I was makkit!
> Ye caad me, poet?
> Whar's yir trackie?
> I like my jeelie guid and tacky.' (*CT*, 123)

The modern god of an atheistic philosophy, the sun, comes to tea ('trackie') like the gods of old in their wanderings among mankind: a theoxenic celebration allows the poet to accept the sun's recommendation that he should 'gang furrit shinin gowd and shair!' ('go forward shining [like] gold and sure'), despite fatigue and criticism, and having been hospitable to the gods makes the poet himself godlike:

> To shine ay and shine aawhere, shine
> to the end o endmaist days –
> that's aa!
> This is the sun's
> slogan – and mine! (*CT*, 125)

Morgan's translation helps Mayakovsky achieve his ambition 'To shine ay and shine aawhere', an ambition that would be impossible without the hospitality that welcomes the stranger into the vernacular of another culture. Translation as *theoxenia* is the necessary prelude to, or accompaniment of, the enrichment of one's cultural resources. An essay from 1977 on 'Gavin Douglas and William Drummond as Translators' focuses on translation as the necessary route to a new national identity: 'we can see Douglas as indeed an exemplar of Renaissance vernacular revival, when country after country in Europe seized on translation of established classics as an act of linguistic independence and maturity, implying at the same time a culturo-national independence and maturity' (*CB*, 68).

For Morgan, translation was not the verbal equivalent of exile or of joining a 'colourless or promiscuous internationalism',[22] it was a way of infusing the national territory, the national psyche, with virtues, with literary opportunities that it might not have had – it might not have happened to have had – within its own cultural evolution. That a Russian Futurist could be comfortably entertained within Scots was proof that Scots was an integral part of European modernism, that MacDiarmid's achievement was not an isolated event of no significance to the 'wholeness' – indeed to the 'haleness', in the sense of 'health, fitness' – of Scottish culture. If the gods of modernism can come and take tea in Scots, then Scotland is indeed a fitting home for modern poetry.

Scotland Began to Move

Nostophobia in Scotland reached its peak in the years after the referendum on a Scottish Assembly in 1979. It was, in part, an explanation of why the country had failed to deliver the parliament it had been offered, even taking into account the fact that the Westminster government had gerrymandered the result by insisting that forty per cent of the electorate, rather than just a majority, had to vote in favour. The tone was set by Murray and Barbara Grigor's exhibition 'Scotch Myths' in 1980, and by the follow-up film of the same title in 1983, which mocked the romantic representations of the nation and the kitsch which passed as Scottish 'culture'. Those against the establishment of a parliament could use such material as evidence of why Scotland was better governed from London; those in favour could use it as an explanation of why so many Scots had no confidence in their ability to govern themselves. Scotland was a country whose cultural achievements, from James Macpherson's Ossianic poems to J. M. Barrie's novels and plays, from Walter Scott's historical novels to the 'Celticism' of Hugh MacDiarmid, were founded on fraud, falsehood and escapism – 'sham bards of a sham nation', as Edwin Muir had summed up the situation in his poem 'Scotland 1941'.

For Edwin Morgan, 1979 produced 'a sense of political numbness'. In an interview with Colin Nicholson he commented: 'I had been hoping that there would be an Assembly, and the sense of let-down was very strong.'[23] His reaction, however, was not to retreat but to become more assertive: he told Nicholson that he had 'felt impelled to write a lot', because such writing 'represents both a determination to go on living in Scotland and a hope that there might be some political change'.[24] If politics cannot change Scotland then art must, and *Sonnets from*

Scotland, published in 1984, is Morgan's first statement of his refusal to submit to the political realities of the 1980s, an insistence that there are alternatives, that there have been and will be alternative Scotlands than the one produced in 1979 when 'A coin clattered at the end of its spin' ('Post-Referendum', *CP*, 449).

Sonnets from Scotland also brings to a culmination Morgan's presentation of poetry as *theoxenia*, as the meeting place of gods and men, the intersection of the timeless with time, and of Scotland as a place hospitable to such minglings. The theoxenic frame of the sequence is a series of encounters with Scotland by unnamed visitors, space or time travellers, who encounter fragments of real or possible Scotlands from its earliest formation –

> We saw Lewis
> laid down, when there was not much but thunder
> and volcanic fires ('Slate', *CP*, 437)

– to the time when, by the building of 'The Solway Canal', Scotland is separated from England and becomes its own 'northern island' (*CP*, 455). Through the eyes of these visitors we glimpse the history of Scotland from its emergence from the Ice Age and the arrival of the first human beings to the coming of the Romans and of Christianity, and the first map-makings of the late Middle Ages. The poems play on the intersections of time and the timeless: 'The Ring of Brodgar' (*CP*, 438), for instance, envisages that the standing stones on Orkney may be recording devices that retain the sounds of the sacrifices to which they were witness –

> It filled an auditorium with pain.
> Long was the sacrifice. Pity ran, hid.
> Once they heard the splintering of the bones
> they switched the playback off, in vain, in vain

– while Pontius Pilate, witness to the sacrifice of God among men, is presented as having returned to Fortingall in Perthshire, mythically the place of his birth, where

> He crawled to the cattle-trough
> at dusk, jumbled the water till it sloshed
> and spilled into the hoof-mush in blue strands,
> slapped with useless despair each sodden cuff,

and washed his hands, and watched his hands, and washed
his hands, and watched his hand, and washed his hands.
('Pilate at Fortingall', *CP*, 439)

Far from the fructifying effects of the meeting with gods, as envisaged by Hölderlin, here the events of time can have no meaning for those who have been in touch with the gods; history, and its sufferings, are mere spectacle to those who live beyond time:

There is a mirror only we can see.
It hangs in time and not in space. The day
goes down in it without ember or ray
and the newborn climb through it to be free.
The multitudes of the world cannot know
they are reflected there. ('The Mirror', *CP*, 440)

Equally, however, to those who have grasped the scale and scope of the geological time frame within which human history is situated and which makes irrelevant the geographical territory by which the nation is shaped, the time of human history can only have the briefest significance. Thus 'Theory of the Earth' connects Robert Burns, the nation's bard, with James Hutton, the great Enlightenment geologist who suggested the volcanic origins of rocks. Burns's song 'A Red, Red Rose' seems to set love in the geological time frame of Hutton's theory,

And I will luve thee still, my Dear
  Till a' the seas gang dry. –

Till a' the seas gang dry, my Dear,
  And the rocks melt wi' the sun

and Morgan's poem sets both in that vastness in which the Scotland that one celebrated and the other explored will have dissolved into nothingness:

            They died almost
together, poet and geologist,
and lie in wait for hilltop buoys to ring,
or aw the seas gang dry and Scotland's coast
dissolve in crinkled sand and pungent mist. (*CP*, 443)

With such godlike knowledge what remains of mere human love? And what consolations can there be from the workings of the imagination if only 'imagination could have read / granite boulders back to their molten roots'? *Theoxenia* allows humanity a godlike perspective on the universe but one which merely reveals how insignificant is human life in the scale of that universe – and yet the gods continue to come, searching for a contact and purpose that is denied them in their own endlessness.

Into these theoxenic interminglings are introduced a cast of characters, often themselves visitors to or sojourners in Scotland – such as 'G. M. Hopkins in Glasgow' (*CP*, 445) – whose lives reveal humanity's attempts to defy time, or the limits imposed on them by their historical circumstances, or the limits of their biological origins: each is a symbol and a symptom of humanity's aspiration for a godlike transcendence that may itself be no more than an evolutionary accident:

> the force that could inter
> such life and joy, in fossil clays, for apes
> and men to haul into their teeming heads.
> ('Carboniferous', *CP*, 437)

Thus 'At Stirling Castle, 1507' recounts an incident to which Morgan had already alluded in his essay on 'Dunbar and the Language of Poetry', noting how Dunbar, in the 'Fenyeit Freir of Tungland', 'can hardly wait to describe the charlatan aeronaut's "flight" from Stirling Castle, pursued and mobbed by all the birds of the air, attacking and crying alliteratively and cumulatively according to their characters' (*CB*, 47); in Morgan's sonnet the focus, however, is on the aeronaut's effort to fly when there is as yet no technology that can make flight possible:

> He frowned, moved back, and then with quick crow struts
> ran forward, flapping strongly, whistling cuts
> from the great heavy space with his black gear
> and on a huge spring and a cry was out
> beating into vacancy, three, four, five,
> till the crawling scaly Forth and the rocks
> and the upturned heads replaced that steel shout
> of sky he had replied to – left, alive,
> and not the least key snapped from high hard locks. (*CP*, 442)

Here human ambition outstrips itself but prefigures in its very failure the 'wings' of Voznesensky's celebration, 'Man, men are winged!' It also, however, prefigures the failure of Scottish politics in 1979, which is imaged in 'Post-Referendum' as a damaged, fallen angel, incapable of flight:

> We watched the strong sick dirkless Angel groan,
> shiver, half-rise, batter with a shrunk wing
> the space the Tempter was no longer in.
> He tried to hear feet, calls, car-doors shouts, drone
> of engines, hooters, hear a meeting sing. (*CP*, 449)

For both the flying man and the fallen angel, the time has not yet come when human control, whether in technology or in politics, can match the possibilities of the imagination, but if the technology and circumstances conspire, can imagination remake the world?

> The universe is like a trampoline.
> We chose a springy clump near Arrochar
> and with the first jump shot past Barnard's Star.
> ('Travellers (1)', *CP*, 447)

The universe, perhaps, is made for the human spirit – 'Immensities / are mind, not ice' ('Post-Glacial', *CP* 437–38). Thus 'Poe in Glasgow' celebrates Edgar Allan Poe's presence in the dockyards of Glasgow as the inspiration of his 'The Domain of Arnheim', a story projecting the future of man's relationship with nature as one in which nature is re-formed and reshaped in a way that 'shall convey the idea of care, or culture, or superintendence, on the part of beings superior, yet akin to humanity', who can create 'nature in the sense of the handiwork of the angels that hover between man and God':[25]

> 'Wake up!' a sailor coiled with bright rope cried
> and almost knocked him off his feet, making
> towards his ship. 'You want to serve your time
> as cabin-boy's assistant, eh?' The ride
> and creak of wood comes home, testing, shaking,
> 'Where to?' He laughed. 'To Arnheim, boy, Arnheim!' (*CP*, 443–44)

Arnheim is the place where humanity becomes godlike, and the gods can consort with humanity as equals: Poe's Arnheim is the unlikely destination that industrial Glasgow makes possible.

The theoxenic aspiration to an interaction between gods and humans, of godlike humans and human-like gods, is the theme on which *Sonnets from Scotland* plays many variations – comically expressed in 'Caledonian Antisyzygy' (*CP*, 446), with its invocation of 'Doctor Who', the constantly metamorphosing Time Lord of the BBC children's programme, or in 'Gangs' in which Glasgow's famous past of gangland fights is transformed into a struggle between the working classes and the language of that god of the 1980s, economics:

> Whit's that? *Non-Index-Linked!* Did ye hear it?
> Look! *Tiny Global Recession!* C'moan then,
> ya bams, Ah'll take ye. *Market power fae Drum!* (*CP*, 449)

Or it is represented tragically in De Quincey's laudanum inspiration that cannot escape the depression that descends on his room in 'Rottenrow', where

> He looks out east to the Necropolis.
> Its crowded tombs rise jostling, living, thronged
> with shadows ('De Quincey in Glasgow', *CP*, 444)

– but no longer with gods.

Since gods do not live in time they are not trapped in the unilinearity of history or, indeed, on a grander scale, in that unidirectional determinism of the physical universe known as the 'arrow of time'. In any present moment, many futures are possible: with each decision most are silently annihilated. For the gods, all of those futures may be equally real, but for human beings only one track leads from the present to the future – a singularity only too painfully borne in on the supporters of devolution in 1979. It is this contradiction between the openness of the imagination of the future and the closed nature of historical reality that *Sonnets from Scotland* dramatises, in part by redistributing the elements of the past to question the history of which we are the inheritors – did Pilate actually come from Fortingall? – and in part by recounting various futures, from the point of view of his time travellers, as though all were equally real, equally realised from out of the numberless possible futures at any particular moment in time. In 'The Ticket' Morgan dramatises this existential splitting of the paths of existence through another man-god, Gurdjieff, propagandist for the spiritual awakening of mankind:

'There are two rivers: how can a drop go
from one stream to the next?' Gurdjieff was asked.
The unflummoxable master stretched, basked,
'It must buy a ticket,' he said. A row
of demons dragged the Inaccessible
Pinnacle through the centre of Glasgow,
barking out sweaty orders, pledged to show
it was bloody juggernaut time, able
to jam shrieking children under crushed spires.
But soon that place began to recompose,
the film ran back, the walls stood, the cries died,
the demons faded to familiar fires.
In New York, Gurdjieff changed his caftan, chose
a grape, sat, smiled. 'They never paid their ride'. (*CP*, 446)

On the one hand this narrative plays with alternative versions of Eastern religion in the Western imagination – those that rise to a transcendentalism of which the West is incapable, such as Gurdjieff's 'The Work' or Zen Buddhism's 'satori', or those like the 'juggernaut' that celebrates the Hindu god Krishna, which crushes human beings under its wheels. The 'Inaccessible Pinnacle' – both a spiritual ambition in Gurdjieff's philosophy and the name of a Munro in Skye – turns into a machine to crush the populace of Glasgow under its wheels, exactly as the Industrial Revolution had done, but that destructive flow of the energy, that possible future as the continuation of a destructive past, is, in defiance of physics (and therefore, implicitly, as a justification of a non-materialist conception of the world), reversed: imagination, which has conceived one future, annuls it, reconceives another.

The possible Scotlands that *Sonnets from Scotland* envisages are all commentaries on the decision that determines the nation's future. In 'The Norn (1)' (*CP*, 451), the nation is wrapped in plastic and, though still recognisably Scotland-shaped, is, like Scotland after the referendum, invisible; it is an occasion, however, to assert how art may be the means to the recovery of lost values:

For all they've been made art, they've not lost face.
They'll lift the polythene, be men again'. (*CP*, 452)

An equally possible future for a Scotland which has not achieved independence is one in which it is obliterated in a nuclear war (since the British nuclear fleet is stationed at Faslane, close to Glasgow):

> Then they were running with fire in their hair,
> men and women were running everywhere,
> women and children burning everywhere,
> ovens of death were falling from the air ('The Target', *CP*, 452)

or in which the systems that control the nuclear weapons fail:

> No one was left to hear the long, All Clear
> Hot wind swept through the streets of Aberdeen
> and stirred the corpse-clogged harbour.
> ('Computer Error: Neutron Strike', *CP*, 453)

Or, indeed, the nation may be consumed by a geological catastrophe, as in 'Inward Bound', where the country is sucked down into the earth in a reverse geomorphology –

> Flapping, fluttering, like imploding porridge
> being slowly uncooked on anti-gas,
> the Grampians were a puny shrinking mass
> of cairns and ski-tows sucked back to their orig-
> ins. Pylons rumbled downwards; lighthouses
> hissed into bays; reactors popped, ate earth (*CP*, 454)

– or it may become the desert in which so many of its most important poets fought in the Second World War: 'Why did the poets come to the desert?' ('North Africa', *CP*, 446), Morgan asks, and answers, why might the desert not come to Scotland and its poets:

> There was a time when everything was sand.
> It drifted down from Findhorn, south south south
> and sifted into eye and ear and mouth
> on battlefield or bed or plough-bent land.
> ('The Desert', *CP*, 454)

Sonnets from Scotland is the meeting place of real and imagined Scotlands, of Scotlands striving towards a higher potentiality – a godlike perspective in which human life achieves the condition of 'A Golden

Age': 'That must have been a time of happiness. / The air was mild, the Campsie Fells had vines' (*CP*, 457) – or Scotlands subject to political, military or ecological catastrophe:

> We stood in what had once been Princes Street.
> Hogweed roots thrust, throbbed underneath for miles.
> The rubble of the shops became the food
> of new cracks running mazes round our feet,
> and west winds blew, past shattered bricks and tiles,
> millions of seeds through ruined Holyrood.
> ('The Age of Heracleum', *CP*, 453)

Imagination can envisage, can project, and can present as real all these possible futures – but which will we choose? We will choose the world in which humans become gods only if we imagine a world that can change, and change radically:

> – That was the time Scotland began to move.
> – Scotland move? No, it is impossible!
> – It became an island, and was able
> to float in the Atlantic lake and prove
> crannogs no fable. ('Outward Bound', *CP*, 456)

In *Sonnets from Scotland* redemption and disaster are carefully balanced but the thrust of the sequence is towards redemption: it sets aside nuclear and ecological destruction to envisage a Scotland capable of restoring itself as a place of civic virtue and human creativity:

> It was so fine we lingered there for hours.
> The long broad streets shone strongly after rain.
> Sunset blinded the tremble of the crane
> we watched from, dazed the heliport-towers.
> The mile-high buildings flashed [...] ('Clydegrad', *CP*, 456)

The gods may be closer to us than we think; we may be closer to the gods than we imagine – if only we allow our imagination of Scotland to be one in which

> in thistle days
> a strengthened seed outlives the hardest blasts.

The Nation's Makar

With *Sonnets from Scotland* Morgan found a subject matter to which he could bring all the experimentalism of his earlier poetry, all its play of sound and display of typography, while remaining focused on a topic of profound seriousness both to his conception of poetry and to his commitment to Scotland as an 'entity'. Morgan the 'clever internationalist' became Morgan the serious nationalist – a poet who liberated his nation by reshaping it on the lines of a modernist poetry that refused the orderly progress of history and that celebrated disjunction, displacement, and the potential of a spiritual reality to overcome the juggernaut of a merely material existence. Scotland is a country like the 'Colloquy in Glaschu' (*CP*, 440), in which different languages, different traditions, different histories are in constant dialogue:

> God but *le son du cor*, Columba sighed
> to Kentigern, *est triste au fond silvarum!*
> *Frater*, said Kentigern, I see no harm.
> *J'aime le son du cor*, when day has died,
> deep in the *bois*, and oystercatchers rise
> before the fowler as he trudges home
> and *sermo lupi* loosens the grey loam. (*CP*, 440–41)

The multiple languages of this dialogue are testimony to the many traditions that went into the making of Scotland, but '*le son du cor*' is actually an allusion to a nineteenth-century poem by Alfred de Vigny – the allusion reveals that the literary reconstruction of a Celtic past is actually the foretelling of a future art which will itself be past to the author who quotes it: literary traditions travel both backward and forward in history, defying the arrow of time. And lurking in the sixth line, the 'fowler' furtively indicates the William Fowler whose sonnets Morgan took to be a central case of Scotland's multilingualism:

> Prest pour m'eloigner from this monde, madame,
> I leave my sins to it, to heaven mon ame,
> my sight aux vents, mes pleurs unto the seas,
> my flames to feu, mes gazings unto your ees. (*CB*, 14)

In the world of physics and the world of history there is only one path: as in Calvinist predestinarianism, the singularity of the future is made certain by the foreknowledge of God. But in the world that Morgan invokes in *Sonnets from Scotland*, the gods share with humanity a world of many possible futures, of many alternative realities which, in their comings and goings, they turn from possibilities into realities:

> The boat was grounded, she walked past him singing.
> To her, he was a man of forty, reading.
> Within him the words mounted: 'Sing for me,
> dancing like Wisdom before the Lord, bringing
> your mazy unknown waters with you, seeding
> the Northern Lights and churning up the sea!' (*CP*, 445)

In Scotland the 'mazy unknown waters' – celebrated in 'A Place of Many Waters' (*CP*, 450), 'true / as change is true' – defy direction. The past is infused with the future, the future with the past. Scotland resists the unilinearity of history, recreates itself and survives, however destructive the environment through which it has to pass:

> Scotland was found on Jupiter. That's true.
> We lost all track of time, but there it was.
> No one told us its origins, its cause.
> A simulacrum, a dissolving view?
> It seemed as solid as a terrier
> shaking itself dry from a brisk black swim
> in the reservoir of Jupiter's grim
> crimson trustless eye. (*CP*, 456)

Scotland survives, even in a world where the gods 'were gone' and there only remained 'a sea of doubt' (*CP*, 456): Scotland survives in the imagination of its poet, a poet who had remade himself and his own poetic trajectory as a challenge to the apparent dissolution of his country's future. Morgan became the nation's 'makar' by confronting so resolutely a situation in which the country's creativity seemed to be about to be annulled, yet again, by a history which did not include it among the future nations of the world: 'The Coin' discovers a Scotland which has existed, sometime, as

> *Respublica Scotorum*, sent across
> such ages as we guessed but never found
> at the worn edge where once the date had been

and where as many fingers had gripped hard
as hopes their silent race had lost or gained.
The marshy scurf crept up to our machine,
sucked at our boots. Yet nothing seemed ill-starred.
And least of all the realm the coin contained. (*CP*, 454)

From a far-distant future Scotland is discovered to have realised itself, to have become not one of the potentialities that history has cast aside, but one of those made real by human choices: the Scotland that is a future imagination in the early 1980s becomes a reality of the history of those theoxenic travellers who come, many centuries later, to make its acquaintance. In *Sonnets from Scotland*, Morgan found a form in which his resistance to Scotland as a non-entity, his commitment to Scotland as an entity, could, through many metamorphoses, reveal Scotland as a nation full of potential awaiting realisation, rather than a nation in apparently terminal decline. To envisage, in 1983, that Scotland might still be a place of godlike aspiration was a gift to the nation, and when Jack McConnell, then First Minister, came to present Morgan with his citation as the nation's first Makar, he might have rephrased Morgan's translation from Hölderlin as an address to Morgan himself:

But what can I call him, the stranger
like you, Morgan, who with a soul
unconquerable, strong to
endure, a firm understanding,
a sweet talent for listening
that he gave out the speech of the purest
like the wine-god, from divine abundance.

CHAPTER FIVE

Cold War Morgan

Adam Piette

Och, och, there's a monster in the loch
And we dinna want Polaris.

On 4 March 1961 the Scottish CND (SCND) and Direct Action Committee Against Nuclear War (DAC) organised a series of mass protests against the introduction of American nuclear submarines with their Polaris submarine-launched fleet ballistic missiles (FBMs) into Scotland, specifically to the submarine refit facility – known as FBM Refit Site One – at the Holy Loch near Dunoon.[1] The submarine tender USS *Proteus* had arrived on 3 March with its store of reserve missiles. Submarine Squadron 14 welcomed in USS *Patrick Henry* on 6 March, escorted into position by the *Proteus*. Later that year, the floating dry dock USS *Los Alamos* was towed into the Holy Loch, fully operational by November. Harold Macmillan had announced the deal in November of the year before, the government arguing that this was not a base, just a refit facility – yet, as Alan Dobson has argued, 'for all practical intents and purposes, a squadron of nine submarines operated from the Holy Loch with six on station and a maximum of three at any one time by the tender ship anchored in the loch'.[2] On 21 May, the DAC sent boats out to try to board the *Proteus*, whilst on land a vigil was held on the pier at Ardnadam. In September, the Committee of 100 organised sit-ins, a 12,000-strong mass rally at Trafalgar Square, marches at Dunoon and Greenock. The protests had no effect, and harsh punishment was meted out to activists (Pat Arrowsmith, who led the September campaign, suffered three months of solitary confinement, hunger strike and forced feeding).[3] This encouraged the authorities to go ahead with plans to create their own Polaris fleet. At Nassau in December 1962, President Kennedy and Macmillan signed the Polaris Sales Agreement whereby the US sold the missiles minus warheads to be housed in British-built submarines with British warheads. In 1963

HMS *Resolution* was built, and launched in 1966. Three other Resolution-class subs, HMS *Renown*, HMS *Repulse* and HMS *Revenge*, were built by Vickers at Barrow-in-Furness over the next two years, each with an American-designed missile section, British Rolls-Royce pressurised-water nuclear reactors, and carrying sixteen Polaris A3 missiles. Naval facilities at Faslane were refitted to create a nuclear submarine base, with an armament depot at Coulport. HM Naval Base Clyde (HMS *Neptune*) at Faslane on Gare Loch even had its own Polaris Weapon System School, commissioned in 1966.[4] So by the end of the 1960s, the heart of the British Cold War was in Scotland, with a half-American atomic heart. Concealed within the tranquil sea lochs west of Glasgow was this lethal technology designed by Lockheed, tested at Cape Canaveral, capable of striking targets 2,800 miles away, each missile having three warheads with a collective power of one megaton, roughly eighty times the yield of the Trinity test. The maths of megadeath force a pause for thought: sixteen times eighty – so each sub could theoretically inflict sixteen megatons of yield, notionally 1,280 times the force inflicted on Hiroshima.

In Edwin Morgan's 1968 collection *The Second Life*, he plays a Hamilton Finlay kind of game with the names of boats and shoreline places. 'Boats and Places' ends with this short section:

> VII
> Ardnadam
> Polaris Eve
> mother-felucca.[5]

The pier at Ardnadam was the pier used by the crew of the *Proteus*, and was the scene of the vigil against the base by the DAC protestors. Morgan picks out the 'Adam' from the Gaelic placename (*Àird nan Damh*, meaning 'the headland of the ox') and links it psychosexually to the missile on the submarines. This generates a third line through association with the boatyard at Ardnadam, conjuring a more peaceful, ancient and wind-powered vessel to counter the nuclear machine out there in the Holy Loch. It also happens to sound a little like 'mother-fucker': an appropriately American cursing of the American FBM technology that is screwing up the world. The three lines re-enact the DAC protest, the felucca resembling the 'pacifist navy' that tried to disrupt the *Proteus* in 1961 (sixteen DAC canoes matching the sixteen missiles), feminising the male phallic technology at the same time as countering its lethal seriousness with direct action wit.[6] There may also be an environmental edge to the triplet:

Adam and Eve represent the human species threatening mother Earth with the twisted retooling of Holy Loch as submarine death trap.

Earlier in the decade, Morgan had thought through the nuclearisation of Scotland with *The Whittrick* dialogues. The last in the series, written in 1961, features a futuristic dialogue between cybernetic robotician Grey Walter and Jean Cocteau, representing science and poetry respectively. The 'whittrick', Scots for weasel, has by this stage come to mean anything imaginary that enables truths to enter into dialectic. In the Walter–Cocteau dialogue, we see the 'turtle' robots Walter had developed in the 1940s, which in the 1960s he has developed (in the world of the poem) into a mind-reading robot, named 'Whittrick'. The poem ends with a rather predictable Faust reference, and it is difficult to see much real seriousness in the dialogue beyond a rather louche comparison between cybernetic programming and the leaps of intuition of the poet; that is, except for the fact that the whole dialogue takes place not in Walter's lab in Bristol, but at Hunterston nuclear power station on the Ayrshire coast. Building of the complex had begin in 1957 and it was finally opened by the Queen in 1964, so the GEC Magnox power station was being built whilst Morgan was writing the dialogues. At one point in the poem, Walter invites Cocteau onto the balcony to survey the nuclear scene:

> Out there are the huge cooling-towers;
> The grid of power that strides off across the moors;
> The blaze of laboratories like a city;
> And those lights moving slowly down the greying firth –
> The great atomic tankers, looking like islands.
> You hear their horns?[7]

Atomic tankers were being discussed in 1961. General Electric, the company that designed and built Hunterston, had been contracted by the Atomic Energy Commission to install reactors in tankers, though the plans were eventually shelved.[8] Walter's vision of nuclear energy is Faustian and merges with Satan's temptation of Christ, the display of power transforming the Scottish landscape into a technologised super-metropolis of the future, 'like a city', 'like islands'; the National Grid become a network of colonising energy across the Scottish moors. GEC, the state's electricity board – and, with Walter's voice, modern technology itself – have 'atomised' the environment with a totalising and Satanic relish here. The atomic tankers on the firth link up to Hunterston and then into the future through the Whittrick robot, which is also nuclear-powered.[9] The speculative fiction here imagines a near future of Faustian nuclear ambitions; but feeds off the post-Windscale anxieties of Cold War Scottish culture.

For out there in the greying firth in 1961 there were no atomic tankers. But there were nuclear submarines, looking like islands, each with a horn, booming out famously in the 1959 nuclear submarine movie *On the Beach*. The horns frighten the seagulls in Morgan's dialogue ('The seagulls hate it: there they go, shrieking') – and gulls are troped as protest poetry by Cocteau ('Poetry's like a gull, protesting'). The gulls are 'warmer than the grid, / More vocal than the booming tankers' (*CP*, 115). Their allies are the secretly subversive poet, like a spy in the new nuclear state: 'The poet is invisible, he speaks in code' (*CP*, 115). Morgan is taking into the orbit of the Hunterston civil nuclear reactor the protest movement further up the firth, the vocal protests of the DAC and SCND activists, and relating them to his own creative practice as activist-poet and anti-nuclear invisible code-breaker and 'spy'. The targeting of gulls is not just some Romantic identification of the poet with the natural (and with the gullible?) – there were real concerns after the 1957 Windscale disaster that radioactive waste disposal was polluting the coasts. In a 1959 technical report for the United Kingdom Atomic Energy Authority, for instance, H. J. Dunster discusses his studies of 'five years of experimental discharges of dilute liquid waste' from the nuclear reactor, the need to 'estimate the maximum permissible rates of discharge from Windscale works', and mentions experimental testing of coastline environment: 'measurements of the resulting radioactivity of fish, seaweed, sea bed, and shore sand'.[10] Gulls shriek at the sound of the nuclear technology since it signals waste pollution of their environment and bodies through the food-chain, just as the human species had been irradiated by strontium 90 and the massive curie discharge at Windscale. When Walter begins his tour of his lab with Cocteau, he distinguishes his space from the Hunterston reactor: 'This Hunterston station's mainly for atom men. / [...] this building here, where I work, is different. / It's a Cybernetic Unit' (*CP*, 111). Cocteau's reaction is sarcastic: 'Ah! / Much more interesting than the disposal of / Radioactive waste' (*CP*, 111). The strange troping of poets as gulls issues from the pollution cycle of radioactive waste products that is written into some of the deepest fears of nuclear technology.

But there is another link between Grey Walter, Scotland and the nuclear which may account for the strange stress on seagulls. In 1956, Grey Walter published a science fiction novel, *The Curve of the Snowflake*, which features a group of scientists who set up a project to design a flying submarine using nuclear fusion for fuel. The submarine is based on the flying fish, and rises, as one of the scientists on its first test flight remarks, '"from the depths to the heights, from a rush of dark water to white surging foam and the sudden lift into the free view of sky and sea and mountain!"'[11] Many of the scientists involved have worked on H-bomb development, and there is a Cold War plot of sorts when Moscow uses a leak of information about the new technology to pretend it has it too. The second phase of the project is manned spacecraft, using satellite launch technology based on Wernher von Braun predictions (and curiously itself predicting the 1957 *Sputnik 1*). But what makes the novel pertinent here is the fact the testing of the new flying sub takes place on the Clyde, managed by a Scottish engineer. This Scottish Los Alamos is based near Gourock on the firth. Morgan's playful link between nuclear power, atomic tankers and seagulls on the 'greying firth' recalls Grey Walter's fantasy of nuclear-powered sea–air technology, a technology only actually realised by submarine-launched ballistic missiles. For what really rises from the depths to the heights, from a rush of dark water to white surging foam, suddenly lifting into the sky, is a missile launched from a nuclear submarine. That Grey Walter is reimagining Polaris as his *Flying Fish* is not only confirmed by its nuclear fuel, but by its development into a satellite rocket, as if designed by von Braun. The seagulls fear the horn of the tankers because they signal the 'flying fish' nuclear sublime as Polaris apocalypse.

There is another dimension to the Grey Walter SF novel – it contains a letter from the far future, as one of the scientists is projected there by time travel.[12] As the scientist looks back at 1956, he sketches out the terrible truth about radiation fears of the late 1950s – that mutation rates might rise and only appear in the population in the next generation. 'As soon as the various government authorities started to blow off really big (FFF – fission-fusion-fission) thermonuclear bombs in the nineteen-fifties, the question of influencing human genetics arose' (177). Grey Walter's own fears of nuclear technology clearly motivate the dream of a de-weaponised Polaris, a post-FFF nuclear fuel, and a projection of a future surviving mutational contamination of the species by 1950s radiation. Morgan's own replay of Grey Walter's fantasy is streaked through with post-Windscale anxiety about the nuclear industry, its 'grid of power', 'blaze of laboratories' and Faustian ambitions for controlling land, sea, sky. The rivalry between Cocteau and Walter in the poem turns on the fear that cybernetics might generate an imaginative robot ('the flash of imagination has been built in', says Morgan's Walter (*CP*, 116)). That science-fictional question disguises a darker speculation, there in the resemblances between irradiated seagulls and *Flying Fish* Polaris missiles: that a cybernetic dream of nuclear power might sacrifice animal genetics to the thermonuclear god in the loch.

'sputsputsputsputsputsputsputsputsputsputsputsputsputsput'

If UK nuclear culture is far too Scottish for Morgan's liking, then it is odd how difficult it is to unpack the subversive comedy of the patches of countercultural anti-nuclear lines in his work. That may have something to do, perhaps too simply, with the mixed allegiance to Soviet matters through attachment to both socialism and Soviet poetry. For at the same time as Morgan pitches poet against nuclear scientist, he also seems to betray companionable awe at the sputnik-inspired space race of the same Cold War. His space poems read at first as admiring of the plucky, crazy space-expanding ambitions of the Soviet Gagarin cult, as 'Spacepoem 1: from Laika to Gagarin' makes pretty clear on its sound-surface. There is great energy and exuberance to the poem as a display of language, as firecracker word-pyrotechnics, as lovable verbal nonsense. Colin Nicholson admires the verve of this and relates it to Dada: the poem 'pushes syllable-repetition over the edge of sense to connect technology with Dadaist subversion – from "dada" to "dagaga"'.[13] For Nicholson, the sustained sound-repetitions in the poem signal computer as well as space technology releasing strange language forces, and elsewhere connects 'Spacepoem 1' to Russian poetry; so the sustained sound play signals a Khlebnikovian 'technical exuberance' and 'ingenious unintelligibility' (Nicholson, 63). Yet at the same time, Morgan, in the 1950s at least, thought an absolutely disorderly poetry was not poetry at all. In his 1952 essay 'Dunbar and the Language of Poetry', he distinguishes between ordered energy and energetic orderliness. Poetry should be the former, and should not relinquish order as such:

> Energy without order usually gives us the feeling that we are in touch with a poet but not with a poem: the forges clang, the air is thick with the spark and fume of production, but in the end nothing is made, no object is presented to us that we can grasp and appraise.[14]

So it might be useful to turn again to the seeming nonsense of 'Spacepoem' and see if beyond its clanging music and thick sound-repetitions, there might not be something concrete we can grasp and appraise.

The poem is about Gagarin, but it is in Laika's voice, as the epigraph tells us. What linguistic comedy there is needs to take this essential fact on board: we are in a dog's brain, communicating beyond death, across technologised spacetime from animal to human, from Laika's *Sputnik 2* to Gagarin's *Vostok 1*. The scene is automatically set, given the huge impact of Gagarin's spaceflight: Gagarin is hearing Laika over his headphones whilst on the first manned spaceflight in April 1961. But what he seems to be hearing is simply the sound of the spaceflight as mechanical noise: 'ra ke ta ra ke ta', the first line says, over and over: we seem to be hearing the engine rumble of the cockpit, the sound of *Vostok 1* itself. Yet with a little Russian we know what Gagarin is hearing is the word for 'rocket' repeating, broken into phonemes. The next line has 'sputsputsputsput' etc. Again, it may be just the put-put-put of a childish engine on its way. Yet it is also the first phoneme of 'sputnik'. What is being signalled to Gagarin is a message from another Russian space-race orbiting vehicle, not *Vostok 1*, but the first satellite, the satellite that ignited the space race in the first place. 'Sputnik' means 'fellow traveller' and indicated that a satellite is earth's fellow: yet it also signals fellow travellers in another sense, those who went along with the Stalinist agenda in the 1930s. Again, phoneme-splitting is occurring – we just have 'sput', so just the travelling not the 'nik' of the agent. Something about dissolution of the human within the 'put-put-put' of space technology may be at the back of this. Things becomes stranger with the third line.

The third line does read as sheer nonsense, un-machinic, gibberish – poetry without order, indeed:

> nik lai nik bel nik strel nik pchel nik mush nik chernush nik zvezdoch.

Yet closer attention reveals order in the verbal energy. The missing phoneme from 'sputnik' is ticking through the line, alternating with single phonemes which evolve into what look like Russian words or names. But we will need the fourth line to make sense of these. The fourth line is 'kakakakakaka' etc. – if the 'nik' of 'sputnik' has fallen down into the line below, then we ought to connect the stray phonemes and words/names to the 'ka' phoneme. That is what the little code seems to suggest we do. And if we do, we get 'laika', 'belka', 'strelka' 'pchelka', 'mushka', 'chernushka', 'zvezdochka'. The first in the series gives us the clue. Lai + ka = Laika, the dog speaker and signaller of the poem, first earth-born creature to be sent into space in November 1957, the Muttnik of *Sputnik*. Belka and Strelka were sent into space on *Korabl-Sputnik 2* in

August 1960. Pchelka went up for a day in December 1960 on *Korabl-Sputnik 3* along with Mushka. Chernushka did one orbit on *Korabl-Sputnik 4* in March 1961, Zvezdochka (named by Gagarin himself; it is the name of a nuclear submarine shipyard on the White Sea) on *Korabl-Sputnik 5* in March 1961, so a month before Gagarin's flight. Laika, in other words, is barking out the names of her fellow travellers, the space dogs of the flight tests that gave the Soviets confidence to put a man in space.

So it is all about names, dog names – the sound-surface turns out not to be machine-made, but dog-made, Russian projected through the airwaves onto the strange spacetime of Morgan's poem. And the names get translated, speaking of the silent Morgan orbiting round this space chatter, barking signal traffic. Later in the poem we have 'barker whitie-arrow beespot blackie star'. Laika means 'barker' in English. 'Strelka' means 'arrow' and 'Belka' 'whitie' (the 'ka' being a diminutive), so 'whitie-arrow' translates Belka and Strelka, the famous space dog double act. 'Pchelka' means 'little bee', 'Chernushka' translates as 'blackie', 'Mushka' meaning 'little spot'. And 'Zvezdochka' means 'little star'. So the names are translating into English for our benefit, fellow travellers in the 'sputnik' of the spacepoem.

We have not, however, got really any further once we have discovered just this first thing: that Laika is communicating dog names related to the Soviet space programme. What emerges is that knowing these are fellow dog travellers does invite us to read the lines less with abstract Dadaist exuberance devoid of content. It invites us to read them with feeling, and to ask in particular what kind of feeling. Is Laika simply enjoying barking those names across spacetime to Gagarin? Just as Dunbar's 'glancing and headlong jugglery' of rhyme and alliteration is not simply a 'delight in itself' but also enables the poet to 'work up the fiery poetic object' (Morgan, 'Dunbar', 147), so it is the impetus of Laika's feeling which works up the fiery poetic object which is the spacepoem as fusion of sputnik/Vostok and organic animal voicings.

The first section of 'Spacepoem' reads as an insistent iteration, a beating repetition of name – but it end with barks, with Laika beginning to sound desperate at not being understood – thus the shift to English:

> barkbark! whitewhitewhite! blackblackblack!
> star! spot! sput!

And so she goes on, fusing names ('starrow!' = star and arrow, crossing Zvezdochka with Strelka), linking the 'sput' of the space rocket with 'spot' of the dog name, confused to indicate something else: 'sput! stop!' – Laika's barks may be barks of alarm.

After a silence, she begins again, with a quieter iteration of the 'sput'-motif – but curiously altered. We have 'putputputput' etc. So again, this may just be her imitating engine noise. But with the other insistent phoneme 'ka' still in our ears from the first section, is it crazy to hear 'kaput', especially as the form invites us to link up phonemes falling from line down to line? The next line is as eerie: just the 'niknikniknik' we had heard tracking through the third line, but here without the dog names. The 'kaputnik' has put paid to the dogs, eliminated them from the record. It is also speaking another name, the 'Nik–' of 'Nikita Khrushchev', and this is confirmed with the next line of the section which fuses the missing '–kita' with the '–keta' of the Russian for rocket and the 'K' of 'Khrushchev': 'ka kra keta ka kra keta' etc. The last line achieves the fusion neatly with 'nikitaraketa!' The section has moved on from the dog names desperately barked, shadowed by death, to the male human mastermind behind the whole project, curiously fused with the rocket he launched – and the section begins to riff on other figures, 'Vladimir' of the biomedical expert in charge of the space dogs, Vladimir Yazdovsky, and 'Yuri', Gagarin's first name. Vladimir summons Vladivostok, fusing Yazdovsky with the Vostok rocket (whilst also bringing to the foreground 'Vostok' meaning 'East'), as well as leading eventually, and poignantly, to 'yurimirny', a portmanteau of Yuri Gagarin's name and the word for peace (some hope). Again, this section ends with desperate barks:

> vladimirny! yurilaika! nikitaraketa! balalaika!
> raketasobakaslava! vladislava!

'Slava' is a nickname ending like the diminutive 'ka'; but it also is a greeting, a hailing, a praising. 'Raketasobaslava!' breaks down in translation to 'Rocket-Dog-Hail!' But with the desperate hailing of the lines before, especially the hopeless barking of the dog names, we are left with a curiously unsettling affective mishmash: at once the dog imitating the rhetoric of Soviet propaganda (all hail the Soviet rocket dog!), and signalling that the 'sobaka' is slave to the rocket, slave to the hailing of Vladimir Yazdovsky, Yuri Gagarin, victim of a balalaika-kitsch drowning out of animal reality. 'Slava' meaning 'glory' drowns out the 'mir' of peace, just as the shouting match of Cold War propaganda renders invisible the victims and servants of the space race project.

The two sections seem to split into animal and human names as tribute to the glory of the progress from dogs in space to man in space. But that glory is only won through the ruthless translation of Laika into space dog into dead dog into Yuri Gagarin. Laika has great difficulty getting to say the name Gagarin. Line after line tries first to shake off the noise of the rocket, which fuses with the 'da' from 'Vladimir' whilst generating 'Vladivostok' as fusional joke (appropriately, since Vladivostok hosted the relay station that sent radio propaganda out of the Soviet Union). She manages to mutate from this cluster to 'Gagarin' by first indulging in Dadaist numbing repetition of 'da' 'dadadadada' etc., recalling rather pitifully the 'kakakaka' of Laika's last phoneme. She can then move to first phoneme with 'daga daga daga' etc., which is reinforced in the next line by repetition ('dagaga dagaga' etc.), enabling a fitful breakthrough finally after ten lines of the section: 'dakakgaga rin dakakgaga rin' etc. Note how even here 'Gagarin' is corrupted by the insistent 'dakak' phonemes, a mutational growth out of 'Ni**k**it**a**', 'Vl**ad**imir', 'Vosto**k**' and 'Vl**ad**ivosto**k**', and that this mutational tic splits Gagarin in two, revealing a stupified 'gaga' and a 'rin' like a ghost remnant of Rin Tin Tin. The mutational punning here is feverish, betraying again an affective energy behind the desire to communicate with Yuri across the borders of death, spacetime and species. With the brief interlude into English at the end of the first section, we are also invited to cross the language barrier, generating a hint at the burden at work: 'dada' + 'daga' = dead dog; 'dagaga' = dog gaga. And what is it that has done the harm – the answer comes with the first of the barked names: 'vostok!' – culminating in man–machine hybrids ('nikitaraketa!') and animal-enslaving propagandised technologies ('raketasoakaslava!').

These dark intimations come across the Vladivostok-airwaves as noise and chaos; but betray dissentient ordered energy in the animal feelings about the space programme hype and scientism. For the spaceflight in 1961 took place months after Eisenhower's warning on leaving office in January about the military–industrial complex. The same year as Gagarin visited the UK on a victory tour, President Kennedy announced the moon landing as a ten-year project, visiting Wernher von Braun's Rocket City facility at Huntsville, Alabama. Behind both the Soviet and US space programmes was Nazi rocket science – the Americans had hoovered up the Peenemünde V2 scientists headed by von Braun in Operation Paperclip in 1945; the Soviets had gathered plans and assembly details when they overran Eastern Europe. The 'raketa' that launched Laika and Gagarin from Baikonur Cosmodrome in Kazakhstan had been developed for missile systems, and most dangerously the intercontinental ballistic missiles that by 1961 both sides had developed. Baikonur Cosmodrome was first a test site for the first ICBM, the R-7 Semyorka, from which the Vostok rocket was derived.

Morgan's poem, then, speaks to the dark suspicions in the air in the 1960s about the new machine–man hybrids of cybernetics, rocket technology, missile systems: Yuri, Laika warns, may become swallowed up in the military–industrial combines, the 'nikitaraketa' racket in the Soviet Union that mimics Eisenhower's military–industrial complex. What space does poetry have when space itself has succumbed to the *slava*-propaganda of the superpowers? That question is part of the point of 'Spacepoem': maybe the poet under Cold War compulsions is like a dog caught up in a racket, a complex, a machine, whose only freedom is to bark at the noise breaking down identities into components or data for its military–industrial progression.

But something more occurs across and between the lines: the wit crosses over from Russian into Scots, as when the line-endings of the first section riffing on the '–nik' and 'sput' of sputnik, the 'nik–' of Nikita, the '–ka' of the diminutive generates 'kana sput', which with enjambment over to the next line reads 'kana sput / nikka'. The following matching enjambments read: 'kana stup / nikka', 'kana pust / nikka', 'kana psut / nikka', 'kana tusp / nikka', 'kana tsup / nikka', 'kana upst / nikka'. Hidden in this weird repetitive cluster is the Scots phrase 'cannae stop Nikita', i.e. nothing can stop Khrushchev's space programme from chewing up all the dog-citizens of the Cold War world. But the mutational energy and the shift to Scots together reveal a counter-energy to that depressing statement. Just as the line-break does put a stop there where the voice says there can be no stop, so the language mutation becomes, at the level of the political unconscious, a demonstration that the language of the world is local, is the people's, is Morgan-Laika's, and it is the street and the strays and the poets of the people, not the complex and its Vostoks and Vladivostok propaganda, which decide when and how to say stop. The mongrel street dog Laika, part Russian Laika, part terrier, has a bark that is worse than sputnik might and main: for as a poem, Laika can satirise, express affect, communicate across spacetime, survive death, move, warn, resist and challenge all power systems, all at the same time. The 'kana'-canine stops Khrushchev, stops the absorption of dog's 'ka' by sputnik's 'nik', breaks the line of power from state to pet citizen in the military–industrial machine and its propellant language.

'"Civilians" are not really, truly, people'

Morgan's engagement with the Cold War was complicated, as we have seen, by his commitment to a socialist politics inspired by the Russian avant-garde, and kept alive through his spirited translations of Mayakovsky, Khlebnikov and others. He wrote about this attachment in his 2004 essay 'Flying with Tatlin, Clouds in Trousers: A Look at Russian Avant-Gardes'.[15] There he reminisced about working in the late 1980s with Chris Carrell and the Glasgow Third Eye Centre, whose *New Beginnings* exhibitions featured Hungarian and Russian art, and celebrated *perestroika* and *glasnost*. He published his poem 'New Beginnings and Old Memories' in the essay for the first time. The poem recalls the excitement of 1930s pro-Soviet enthusiasm, his compassion for his friend George on the Murmansk convoys during the war when the Soviet Union was an ally, and then fast-forwards to 'Perestroika skimming her troika / like Mungo's mother across the old badlands' (Carruthers *et al.*, 95), leading to a celebration of the new beginnings of the *glasnost* thaw in the Cold War. The memoir goes on to remember the ways his study of Russian at Glasgow University was inextricably linked to 'the sense of modernity in early twentieth-century Russian arts, [...] a left-wing modernity not devoted to rearranging the past, but rather to adumbrating the future' (Carruthers *et al.*, 97). This enthusiasm drew him to Russian poetry, particularly Blok and Mayakovsky; and through vigorous Scots translations, MacDiarmid and Sydney Goodsir Smith made the Russian avant-garde Scottish. Morgan's own translations retained contact with this ecstatic revolutionary moment when belief in 'the possible transformation and betterment of society' (Carruthers *et al.*, 100) could coexist with adventurous and daring modernist experiment. Morgan goes on to praise Russian Futurist work too, for the same reasons, and includes in his essay one of his sound-poem translations of Khlebnikov's 1908 'Incantation by Laughter' into Scots as 'Gaffincantrip'. The translation work makes clear how Mayakovsky's celebration of the new urban energies of modernity, the new world of '[s]treets, cars, trains, subways, skyscrapers', enabled him to begin to celebrate Glasgow in high spirits, and 'daring, shock, hyperbole' (Carruthers *et al.*, 103).

That exuberant celebration still marks everything Morgan wrote. At the same time, his poems also sensed, throughout his long career as a poet, the darker collective-machinic energies that tyrannised over the Cold War consciousness on both sides of the Iron Curtain. An early poem about Korea recreates on the page the terrible landscape of the Cold War's hot wars, imagining the modern soldier 'at the threshold of death, / Or worst this side of the atom / To be caught in the awful napalm / And wrapped in that inquisition / And blanket of secular fire'.[16] The weird and uncanny 'The World' of 1977 tries to defend technology, at some unknown science-fictional future, but the result is a twisted Audenesque self-cancelling rhetoric:

> I don't believe that what's been made
> clutters the spirit. Let it be patented
> and roll. It never terrorized
>
> three ikon angels sitting at a table
> in Moscow, luminous as a hologram
> and blessing everything from holograms
>
> to pliers at a dripping nail. (*CP*, 346)

What is being made here is a re-creation of the contortions of those who tried to defend Stalinist terror in the name of technocratic progress and ideological blessings. Two of the 1984 *Sonnets from Scotland* imagine nuclear holocaust: 'The Target' scenes 'women and children burning everywhere, / ovens of death falling from the air', and zooms in on Rhu become a 'demon's pit', 'Faslane a grave' (*CP*, 452). 'After Fallout' imagines mutant gulls flying above the globe 'hatching genes' (*CP*, 452). 'Computer Error: Neutron Strike' tries to picture a world where all organic life has been zapped leaving nothing but machines and buildings (*CP*, 453). And right to the end of his life, with poems like 'Urban Gunfire' from the 1990 *Hold Hands Among the Atoms* collection, a left-liberal conscience speaks out against the fanatics with guns:

> 'Civilians' are not really, truly, people.
> As regimes fall, they're only 'caught in crossfire'
> [...]
> too feeble to be seen by psyched-up fighters.
> Their cries are in another world.[17]

Beyond partisan politics, and beyond the left/right opposition of traditional systems, Morgan was intent throughout his writing life on the more sinister opposition between military–industrial 'psyched-up fighters' with their war machines (in their Soviet, American or tyrannical regime versions) and the ordinary world of civilians. The stance of non-combatant conscientious objector in the Second World War is sustained into the world of the Cold War and beyond.

In his 'The World' meditation, it is striking that Morgan moves to dramatic monologue to be able to ask the big question: 'Technologies like dragonflies, the strange / to meet the strange; and at the heart / of things, who knows what is dependent?' In the new world that Cold War technologies of death and transformation created, the war networks, the information revolution, the globalisation of mediatised control, who has access to knowledge sufficient to even raise the question of the dependence of the estranged subject on the strange regulations and regimens being generated by Cold War systems? Going against the grain of his own attachment to left-wing modernity, Soviet avant-garde art and poetry, against the grain of his natural scientism and progressive optimism, against even the localising humanitarianism of his Scottish sense of the Cold War, Morgan's best work touches on this tricky, maddening, dragonfly question, swarming at his ear and at the margins of his multivocal art.

CHAPTER SIX

Morgan and the City

Robyn Marsack

To think about a city is to hold and maintain its conflictual aspects: constraints and possibilities, peacefulness and violence, meetings and solitude, gatherings and separation, the trivial and the poetic, brutal functionalism and surprising improvisation.

Henri Lefebvre[1]

I feel very strongly about the *immediate* environment of Glasgow, you see, and have often written about that. I suppose this is partly natural because I live there, but there is probably also a little slice of the deliberate about that too, to let people in London or wherever know that here is someone living in and writing about Glasgow of all places!

Edwin Morgan[2]

Edwin Morgan belonged to Glasgow, then Scotland, and after that, the universe: from Glasgow to Saturn the line was fairly direct. Sitting amidst his peers in Alexander Moffat's *Poets' Pub* painting, Morgan is at a slight angle to the rest and one reason must be the comparative indifference he showed to the rural Scotland that nourished most of the others in various ways. Even two poets (not in the painting) with whom Morgan shared a modernist sensibility – Ian Hamilton Finlay and W. S. Graham – were on the whole more concerned with their natural surroundings than he was: Finlay in his garden, and Graham on the Cornish coast.

The city where he was born in 1920, lived all his life (except for his war service) and died provided Morgan with the multitude of contradictions that Lefebvre summarises, which inform and energise his poetry. In 1920 Glasgow was still a great manufacturing city – second city of empire – with the yards on the Clyde producing 672,000 tons of shipping that year.[3] At the same time, the MP James Stewart described the city as 'Earth's nearest suburb to hell',[4] with over sixty-six per cent of Glasgow families living in one- or two-room dwellings. The years of Morgan's childhood were a massively unstable period in Glasgow's history, responding to the see-saw of international relations: in terms of shipbuilding, a drop to 175,000 tons in 1923, back up to 600,000 in 1928, with a dizzying decline through the years of the Depression to a mere 56,000 tons in 1937, when unemployment levels reached thirty per cent of the insured population.[5] Morgan's father worked for the iron and steel merchants Arnott, Young and Company, and the family also registered some ups and downs. They never owned a car, and thus Morgan recalled from his earliest days travelling by public transport, where 'your ear is attuned to the broadest kind of Glasgow speech as well as what you're using yourself. I always liked listening to what I heard being spoken in the streets, in buses, and so on.'[6] Long afterwards he set down a rare childhood memory, of being on a tram with his mother and offered a sixpence:

> 'Ur ye a good boay?
> Sure ye're a good boay.'
> I was not so sure.
> My mother hissed
> 'Take it, take it,
> always take
> what a drunk man gives you!'
> I remember how nicely
> he clasped my hand around the coin.[7]

The chance encounter and the touch of a working-class man are recurrent elements of Morgan's Glasgow poems, sometimes benevolent, sometimes menacing.

Morgan was a student at the High School of Glasgow from 1934 to 1937, and later suggested that the poetry of the Romantics on the English syllabus 'wasn't the kind of poetry I should have been reading as a person living in Glasgow in the thirties. [...] It took me a while to understand you could write about anything – ugly things, dirty things, painful things.'[8] Studying art at the High School, however, was a different matter: here he came across the architecture of Le Corbusier; he could relate that to his early fascination with Russian art, and it sharpened his observation of Glasgow buildings.[9]

By 1938, now at the University of Glasgow, he had discovered the French Symbolists, and 'Baudelaire particularly … was a kind of revelation':

> I got into [Baudelaire] before I got into Eliot, and it seemed to me that he was one of the few who had, at a very early date really, the sense in poetry of what was going to be a modern city and I liked that tremendously. I think subconsciously I had been looking for that and not finding it, but it seemed to be there in Baudelaire.[10]

It was a significant year for Morgan intellectually, including his first trip to Paris, and for Glasgow too, with the hosting of the Empire Exhibition. There was an element of nostalgia in the Exhibition – greater Glasgow still had one million inhabitants but had been overtaken in the empire by Bombay and Calcutta, even Sydney and Montreal – as well as pride in signs of recovery. Morgan's interest in urban architecture was stoked by the show, and he had a keen sense of Glasgow's innovation in the 1930s, despite the miseries of the Depression:

> The Beresford Hotel, the Odeon Cinema, the Kelvin Court flats, the Lumex lamp factory, the Bennie Railplane, and most of all the Empire Exhibition in Bellahouston Park – all these were not just modern but modernist […] When the Empire Exhibition opened in 1938 (and I had a season ticket), I was studying Russian at Glasgow University and […] I found there […] a left-wing modernity not devoted to rearranging the past but rather adumbrating the future. I found it thrilling.[11]

He compares Tait's Tower at the Exhibition to designs by the Russian Futurist Tatlin, and bemoans the common fate of Scottish inventions, developed elsewhere; in particular George Bennie's 'rocket-like elevated railway system, which you could see for many years slowly rotting away near Milngavie, and which certainly would have worked if anyone had taken it up'.[12]

Looking back in 'Tram-Ride, 1939 (F.M.)', he evoked the loneliness of this modernist city:

> How cold it is to stand on the street corner
> at nineteen, in the foggy Glasgow winter,
> with pinched white face and hands in pockets, straining
> to catch that single stocky gallus figure […]

Stood up, as he thinks, and feeling terribly exposed, 'glanced at / idly by the patient Cosmo queue', the speaker retreats to the top deck of a southbound tram, suppressing tears:

> shameful – shameful – to be dominated
> by such emotions as the busy
> tramful of half indifferent half curious folk would
> mock at if they knew [...][13]

The city provided the opportunity for cinema-going (by 1930 Glasgow had 127 cinemas), for friendship, romances, quick encounters – illicit encounters – and a precious anonymity: all this, as a young man coming to terms with his sexuality, Morgan needed. If he was 'idly' observed, he could also observe, eavesdrop, learn the codes that transcended class, live dangerously if he chose to do so.

> Writers who live in large cities and use urban material develop – instinctively! – a very quick, unstudied, unprying, oblique yet intense and unforgetful way of looking at people and things: it's like using a very good silent automatic camera disguised as a pair of eyes. To look too long at anyone is dangerous (in Glasgow at any rate – I don't know about other places), and so the rapid flickering scan is characteristic of the urban poet.[14]

This observational method is evident already in a poem such as 'Night Pillion', written in 1956, where the night-ride and its exhilaration cannot be neutral, as the *Glasgow Sonnets* could not be. Such camera-vision is inextricably linked to a sense of social being; it is what the Russians had taught Morgan, that modernity need not go the way of Pound and Eliot. While he did learn from Eliot, and poems such as the 'Preludes' spoke to him immediately, the vision of *The Waste Land* was inimical to Morgan: 'What an extraordinary thing to say that London is an unreal city! [...] Can you believe that a man like that existed? Did he actually walk in these crowds?'[15] Riding across Glasgow,

> We lost the shining tram-lines in the slums
> As we kept south; the shining trolley-wires
> Glinted through Gorbals; on your helmet a glint hung.
> A cat in a crumbling close-mouth, a lighted window
> With its shadow-play, a newspaper in the wind –

> [...]
> Perhaps I only saw the thoroughfares,
> The river, the dancing of the foundry-flares?
> Joy is where long solitude dissolves.
> I rode with you towards human needs and cares.[16]

In the middle of Morgan's unhappiest decade, a solitary span, the old Glasgow was beginning to stir and change around him. In the 1950s Glasgow's industrial base, strengthened by the war, was steady because of the Cold War demands: shipbuilding, engineering, metal manufacturing were all flourishing, and in 1951 there were about 17,500 jobless Glaswegians (although that rose to about 83,000 in 1958). There was car manufacture at Linwood, the Ravenscraig steel works at Motherwell, and there was the beginning of the housing revolution.

The 1951 census recorded that over fifty per cent of Glasgow city households had no bathroom, and there were nearly 100,000 families on the waiting list for new housing. The aim was to demolish 97,000 dwellings – in Anderston, the Gorbals, Springburn, Townhead – and to embark on the largest flat-construction programme of any British city.[17] Basil Spence won awards for his Hutchesontown C blocks in the Gorbals, completed in 1965 and inspired by Le Corbusier's tower blocks in Marseilles.

Besides the flats, there was intervention in the mid-1960s in the shipping industry under Harold Wilson's government, with the construction of the *Queen Elizabeth 2* as a showcase for the Upper Clyde Shipbuilders from 1965 to 1967. Morgan was following these developments in his extraordinary series of scrapbooks, which he had begun to compile as early as 1931. His biographer describes them as sort of 'collage, or bricolage, of images, ideas, forms and discourses juxtaposed or contrasted'[18] and this outlet for his visual and verbal imagination seems to evidence a precociously modernist and continuously urban sensibility. As Malcolm Bradbury remarks in his essay on 'The Cities of Modernism', 'Realism humanizes, naturalism scientizes, but Modernism pluralizes, and surrealizes', and this is just what the Scrapbooks do. Bradbury continues:

> Where in much realist art the city is the emancipating frontier [...] in much Modernism it is the environment of personal consciousness, flickering impressions, Baudelaire's city of crowds, Dostoevsky's encounters from the underground, Corbière's (and Eliot's) *mélange adultère du tout* (adulterous mixture of everything).[19]

Not quite *du tout*, because of the maker's process of selection. Greg Thomas has noted some of the prominent images, picking out Morgan's 1938 Exhibition ticket pasted into Scrapbook Three, alongside an image of Tait's Tower.

> In later volumes, images of monolithic functional buildings, constructivist or brutalist, multiply. One colour photograph from Scrapbook 12 presciently surveys a sweep of futuristic city highway in São Paulo (2411); but the most engaging images are of the 1950s–60s renovation of Morgan's home city. The same book features a panoramic shot of a new high-rise council estate at Moss Heights, 1954 (2324); Scrapbook 15 the 'lights of the first multi-storey housing block in the Hutchesontown-Gorbals development scheme reflecting on the river Clyde [...]'[20]

This was a picture from 1962, when Morgan himself moved out of the family home at last, and into a newly built concrete block of flats, Whittinghame Court in Anniesland.[21]

Morgan's breakthrough happened in the 1960s: happiness in a stable relationship, and the publication of *The Second Life* in 1968. The volume includes concrete poems, and in the poem he wrote on his seventieth birthday, 'Epilogue', looking back over the decades, Morgan explicitly links this formal experimentation with what was happening in Glasgow. He 'heard Beats', the poetry of Allen Ginsberg and his San Francisco contemporaries that coincided with the end of 'a rather bleak and tight phase' of his own poetry: 'More and more of "the world" came into my poetry from that time.'[22] He

> sent airmail solidarity to Saõ
> Paulo's poetic-concrete revolution,
> knew Glasgow – what? – knew Glasgow new – somehow –
> new with me, with John, with cranes, diffusion
> of another concrete revolution, not bad,
> not good, but new.

The Second Life collects the first clutch of Glasgow poems that were to establish Morgan's reputation: 'Good Friday', 'The Starlings in George Square', 'King Billy', 'Glasgow Green', 'In the Snack-bar', 'Trio' (all written between 1962 and 1965) – along with the love poems 'From a City Balcony', 'Strawberries', 'One Cigarette'.[23] They are full of 'human needs and cares'.

They gaze straight at the disfigurements of Glasgow: the sectarianism, poverty, alcoholism; homosexuality driven underground, turned violent; and they rejoice in what is resilient and undeterred, from the confused celebration of Easter by the drunk on the bus to the 'sweet frenzied whistling' of the starlings, and in particular the emblematic trio of young people on Buchanan Street, which Morgan chose as his own 'desert island poem' when asked in 1982.

He begins the title poem, 'The Second Life', with an exhilarated comparison of Glasgow with New York, adhering to the long-established preference of the West of Scotland for the view across the Atlantic.[24] Morgan's perspective on New York was partly shaped by the writing he loved, discussed in his 1969 essay 'Three Views of Brooklyn Bridge'. The essay begins with a quotation from Thomas Wolfe's *Of Time and the River* (1935): 'What bridge? Great God, the only bridge, the bridge of power, life and joy, the bridge that was a span, a cry, an ecstasy – that was America.'[25] This vision of singing stone and steel, of possibility, is what Morgan engages with at forty:

> Can it be like this, and is this what it means
> in Glasgow now, writing as the aircraft roar
> over building sites [...]
> green May, and the slow great blocks rising
> under yellow tower cranes, concrete and glass and steel
> out of a dour rubble it was and barefoot children gone –
>
> Many things are unspoken
> in the life of a man, and with a place
> there is an unspoken love also
> in undercurrents, drifting, waiting its time.
> A great place and its people are not renewed lightly.
> The caked layers of grime
> grow warm, like homely coats.
> But yet they will be dislodged
> and men will still be warm.

This is the 'love that dares not speak its name' speaking, but still under wraps. Here the yellow cranes are as much a presage of spring as the daffodils, in 'a place that is quite willing to renew itself in a fairly devastating sort of way'.[26] The ecstasy and the optimism could not be sustained, as the grimmer poems from the same collection show. In his homage 'To Joan Eardley', Morgan writes of the painting on his wall that its brushstrokes

> fix what the pick
> and bulldozer have crumbled
> to a dingier dust,
> the living blur
> fiercely guarding
> energy that has vanished

and this was what his poetry could also do, preserve the energy whether it be positive or negative, the contradictory life of the city.

When Morgan was chosen for inclusion in the popular *Penguin Modern Poets* series in 1969, Glasgow poems dominated the selection. 'For Bonfires' showed the 'happy demolition men' (Morgan marks out an 'Irishman, bending / in a beautiful arc') who 'cheer the tenement to smoke'. But 'The Flowers of Scotland' is driven by a politicised anger before its expression in the *Glasgow Sonnets*, taking its title from Roy Williamson's 1960s song that has become an unofficial national anthem. Morgan's enumeration of the flowers of hypocrisy in Scotland ends with a sharp dig at 'the preservationist societies, wearing their pens out for slums with good leaded lights',

> and by contrast the massive indifference to the slow death of the
> Clyde estuary,
> decline of resorts, loss of steamers, anaemia of yachting, cancer of
> monstrous
> installations of a foreign power and an acquiescent government –
> what is the smell
> of death on a child's spade, any more than rats to leaded lights?[27]

With the publication of *Instamatic Poems* and the *Glasgow Sonnets* in 1972, Morgan returned to the notion of the urban poet as camera, and he related this to the slightly later *Newspoems* (1975) and the impetus provided by 'found' material.

> A busy city street will have its expected intelligible range of meanings … but the eye of the good photographer will isolate, out of the readable flux, some totally unexpected and probably unrelated collocations of

> persons or objects which will then seem more meaningful than all the cut-away and rejected 'meaning' of the general scene. No one else saw what he saw, though it was there to be observed.[28]

The titles are simply places and dates: 'Glasgow 5 March 1971', robbery with violence; another under the same title features a knife thrown in court and 'the striking absence of consternation'; 'Glasgow November 1971' mentions 'the Royston boy / of thirteen murdered by the Blackhill boy / of twelve' – it is the old Glasgow, city of hard men and gangs.

Morgan's *Glasgow Sonnets* catalogued the problems that could not be solved by buildings, and in many cases were exacerbated by the new architecture. The first three blocks of the (in)famous Red Road flats in Balornock were officially opened in 1966; the twenty-eight- and thirty-one-storey towers were to house nearly five thousand people in much better conditions than they had left behind, but on the city periphery, with few amenities and a fracturing of long-established communities that was to prove the worst effect of the rapid slum clearance.

> A multi is a sonnet stretched to an ode
> and some say that's no joke. The gentle load
> of souls in clouds, vertiginously stayed
> above the windy courts, is probed and weighed.
> Each monolith stands patient, ah'd and oh'd.
> And stalled lifts generating high-rise blues
> can be set loose. But stalled lives never budge.[29]

Morgan's optimism about lift-repair, at least, was unfounded: the increasing problems of this and other peripheral housing led to the end of such multistorey building by the mid-1970s, and eventually a demolition programme got under way. Spence's building went in 1993 (the same year as Ravenscraig closed), because it was simply too expensive to maintain and repair. Morgan saw this social promise and architectural boldness disappearing, and wrote in 2004, 'Even today I have a sinking of the heart when I see on TV high-rise buildings being demolished.'[30] The first of the Red Road flats, all twenty-eight storeys, was demolished in a six-second explosion in 2012, and there was huge controversy over the proposal to demolish the last-but-one block as a spectacular part of the opening of the 2014 Commonwealth Games in Glasgow. What would the poet have made of that?

'Human needs and cares' emerge from the desolation of Glasgow when Morgan turns to the days of industrial decline. As the 1960s proceeded, there was little investment in modernising infrastructure and in 1971 the new Conservative government under Edward Heath refused outright to continue support for the shipyards. Where the optimistic early 1960s had seen sit-ins for the civil rights movement in the USA, and love-ins (as in San Francisco) later in the decade, Glasgow in August 1971 staged the 'work-in' that Morgan refers to in the fifth sonnet. Led by the three Communist Party activists Jimmy Reid, Jimmy Airlie and Sam Barr, this demonstration was staged to prevent the government liquidator from entering and dismantling the Upper Clyde Shipbuilders, and was accompanied by a strike of 200,000 workers in the West of Scotland and mass protests at Glasgow Green.[31] The following year Heath's government backed down, and the Govan shipbuilders received thirty-five million pounds in aid, yet there was still no modernisation of the yards. 'But all the dignity you muster / can only give you back a mouth to feed [...] / while distant blackboards use you as their duster.'

The sonnets, just as much as the concrete poetry, had a rigid form that nevertheless allowed the expression of explosive emotions. 'I am very strongly moved by the absolute force of what actually happens, because ... there is really nothing else that has its poignance, its razor edge.'[32] The ten *Glasgow Sonnets*, originally published in an edition of 125 copies by the Castlelaw Press, were widely noticed in Scotland, and the *TLS* reviewer compared them to Siegfried Sassoon's First World War poems in saying 'something intelligent and human about an unbearable situation'.[33] *From Glasgow to Saturn* (1973) collected the *Sonnets* with other poems, including 'Death in Duke Street' and 'Stobhill', the monologues about an abortion, in an edition of two thousand copies. The concrete/sound poems in the same volume, such as 'The First Men on Mercury', demonstrate that Morgan did indeed range from his city to outer space, from realism to modernism, and that the terrible limitations of Glasgow life were not the whole of his theme. But he had established his right to speak for the city, and in 1978 BBC Radio 4 commissioned him to document Glasgow's changes in a feature that combined his poem with the voices of demolition workers, published in the *Collected Poems* as 'The Demolishers'. Here the need for change is acknowledged: 'Due and overdue, so long due / that change is painful when it comes'. Morgan conveys its Janus nature: 'the jaunty and the jaundiced': 'is there no past / they'd weep to lose, exposed and tugged / like the cheap, carefully chosen paper?'

They clear a space for the future.
The city breathes and sighs, settles, is restless, is furious,
is knee-deep in rubble, is renewed.
Buildings are – works of art, tombstones,
machines for living in, punctuation-marks
in history, legends, targets for stones,
pyramids, wonders, too old or too new [...]

As Glasgow crawled out of the 1970s, Morgan's focus on the city shifted. Ian Jack, writing about the 'Repackaging of Glasgow' in 1984, commented:

> Some marvellous and intriguing things have been happening to the city. Epidemics of stone-cleaning and tree-planting have transformed its former blackness into chequer works of salmon pink, yellow and green. Old buildings have been burnished and refitted. Museums, delicatessens and wine bars have opened, and thrive. New theatres occupy old churches. There are business centres, sports centres, heritage centres, arts centres.[34]

It was a long time after the Clean Air Act of 1956, but Glasgow was cleaning itself up. The Burrell Collection opened in 1983, and the huge campaign to change the city's image, 'Glasgow's Miles Better', kicked off that year, with the adoption of 'Mr Happy' as the city's icon.

It was a good year for Hamish Whyte to bring out *Noise and Smoky Breath: An Illustrated Anthology of Glasgow Poems 1900–1983*, published by Glasgow District Libraries and the Third Eye Centre, the Sauchiehall Street arts venue that had been founded by Tom McGrath in 1974 and hosted many poetry readings. Whyte reckoned that this was, perhaps surprisingly, the very first anthology of poems about Glasgow. In the year of relentlessly upbeat marketing, it served to present a much more nuanced version of the city. He rejected the idea of a Glasgow 'school', but admitted the existence of a 'group of individual poets with roots in Glasgow or close connections with the city' and 'an outlook distinctly non-parochial', naming Morgan alongside Stephen Mulrine, Tom McGrath, Tom Leonard, Alan Spence and Liz Lochhead.[35] In his acknowledgements, Whyte thanked Morgan especially for his encouragement: his 'influence on the way we look at and write about Glasgow – particularly as a place to be *celebrated* – cannot be overestimated'.

By the time of the Glasgow Garden Festival in 1988, the number of visitors to the city had increased from 700,000 to 2.2 million.[36] The 1986 designation of Glasgow as European City of Culture for 1990 had stunned people both inside and outside the city. In London, one commentator remarked, Glasgow had historically been regarded as 'the city of mean streets and mean people, razor gangs, the Gorbals slums, of smoke grime and fog, of drunks, impenetrable accents and communists'.[37] In Glasgow, Tom Leonard published 'A Handy Form for Artists in connection with the City of Culture', which asked at its close:

> when am I going to turn on my radio or television and hear honest language*/with the land around Glasgow practically crackling with radioactivity you soon won't even be able to go to Saltcoats for a paddle*/ why do the lamb chops in the butchers glow in the dark*/why don't they put turnstiles on the housing schemes and make them deprived heritage Museums*/with all this Mr Even Happier nonsense*/ [*delete if inapplicable].[38]

Leonard's *Six Glasgow Poems* (1969) had 'honest language' at its heart, and Morgan's essay on 'Glasgow Speech in Recent Scottish Literature' takes Leonard's work as central to this development in poetry, claiming for his own well-known poems simply a desire to use local speech 'in a serious context far removed from the usual music-hall associations',[39] and relying on their being read aloud to supply the authentic pronunciation. Alongside the sounds, structure, political concerns of the younger man's poetry he identified the importance of comedy, 'from the playful to the ferocious', but again very far from 'journalistic and vaudeville stereotyping' that had made it difficult to write seriously – or to be taken seriously – in Glasgow speech.

In the 1980s and 1990s, as Glasgow was 'repackaged', Morgan found other subjects attracted him more: the matter of Scotland in the wake of the failed 1979 referendum on devolution, for example. *Sonnets from Scotland* (1984) included Glasgow, of course, but it appeared in its post-apocalyptic guise, or as background to some remarkable temporary inhabitants: De Quincey, Poe, Hopkins. These were precursors of the series of historical characters invoked in 'Nine in Glasgow' in *Cathures* (2002). In the landmark interview with Christopher Whyte in 1988, published when Morgan was seventy, he admitted that it had become much harder to write about central Glasgow, 'which has had its face lifted; this doesn't give rise to feelings from which poems come': 'Perhaps if you're writing about a place and a city, writing about its problems, it's more productive than just writing a kind of PR job for the new Glasgow.'[40]

The 1980s, following his retirement from the University of Glasgow, were also a period when Morgan was much in demand outside Scotland. He had loved and been moved by Istanbul; struck out again for Albania immediately there was a direct flight available from London to Tirana; travelled to Naples at the invitation of the British Council to read his translations of Leopardi. He wrote to Hamish Whyte about the 'pullulating street life' of Naples, with 'lots of old but peeling buildings rather like Glasgow before the campaign': 'I think it is the sense of a rich, spilling-over, uncontrolled life that attracts me so much about cities like Naples and Istanbul and (looking back) Cairo.'[41]

In these decades Morgan was an increasingly public figure: his dramatic work reached a wider audience; poetry readings were much more common as part of festivals and arts programmes; and his poems of the 1960s and 1970s were part of the school curriculum, 'In the Snack-bar' for example, and 'Glasgow Green' – it still surprised him that the latter was taught in schools, since it centres on an act of homosexual rape. His work had been controversial in some respects: the local press had taken issue with the 'Stobhill' poems being taught in schools even before his coming out had raised conservative hackles; and in 1983 the poster-poems on birds and beasts commissioned for Glasgow's subway had been rejected by the SPTE, on the grounds that there were 'no piranhas in the Underground'.[42] Nevertheless, he was recognised as Glasgow's pre-eminent writer, and his appointment as the city's Poet Laureate in 1999 honoured his achievement.

The collection that came out of his laureateship, *Cathures – New Poems 1997–2001*, begins with a set of historical monologues of which the first, 'Pelagius', is a kind of anticipatory farewell, a benediction on the city. Morgan was nearly eighty, his health was failing, and this poem – in the voice of the fourth-century theologian – expresses his credo 'man is all' and his deep-seated optimism about the works of man (although the same volume contains his 'Trondheim Requiem' for the victims of the Nazi death camps). He turns sometimes lightly, often satirically, to 'Changing Glasgow 1999–2001', but also returns to the notion of the enduring spirit of Glasgow he commented on to Christopher Whyte: 'That was always part of the image of Glasgow in the past, that it was both dangerous and friendly', admitting that he was 'sentimental' about the friendliness.[43] 'Gallus', a sketch of a young man attaching himself to Morgan and a radio presenter in a Glasgow street, has a streak of sentimentality; 'Junkie' proceeds through its ten couplets with compacted compassion. In *Demon*, we glimpse hell in Argyle Street, but

Morgan – who was definitely of the devil's party when it came to *Paradise Lost* – gives to the spirit a verbal energy, a persistence, that is intended to be seductive. And here, in what might have been his last collection, he invents a new form for a set of nine lyrics, 'Cathurian stanzas', that would serve him well as the scaffolding for the autobiographical sequence *Love and a Life* (2003).

That sequence was collected in the Carcanet volume *A Book of Lives* (2007), by which time Morgan was the poet laureate of Scotland, the first Scots Makar. It included 'Old Gorbals', a personification of the area now changed utterly, where you used to feel 'hearts beating and lips meeting / as private twenty storeys up / as in any cottage by the sea'. Old Gorbals, 'in a spirit of something or other / sprayed a wall with DON'T FORGET'. Morgan had not forgotten: he evokes old loves rather than old places in *Love and a Life*, but a hidden Glasgow peeks through, in the mention of an encounter in 'the Biograph (peace to its long-lost rubble!)' and in the cleaning and repair of his own apartment building: 'so now that we are so scoured and open and clean, what shall we do?'

In writing terms, there was not much more that Morgan could do, but Glasgow offered his own work back to the poet. Back in 1996 he had been commissioned to write four poems that were incised on stone paving slabs outside the restored City Halls in Candleriggs, so he was already underfoot. *His City Speaks to the Poet*, a double CD of readings of his poems by a wide range of participants, was brought together by Benno Plassmann and played across the city on 27 April 2005, saluting the poet's eighty-fifth birthday. In 2008, Jim Carruth and others from the St Mungo's Mirrorball poetry network arranged a twenty-four-hour 'Morganathon' in Glasgow. It was based on the anthology *From Saturn to Glasgow: 50 Favourite Poems by Edwin Morgan*, of which fifteen thousand copies were distributed free across the city as part of the Aye Write! book festival that year. 'When we asked Edwin Morgan himself what he thought of the idea he said "Daft!" – and then changed his mind – "But good!"'[44]

Morgan's lifetime, then, coincided with Glasgow's heyday, decline, 'desperate renewal', reinvention. In his poetry the city is chiefly, but not exclusively, the site of masculine lives: builders and demolishers; men encountering other men with violence or tenderness, cheerful or insulting, drunk and defiant; inspirational figures such as John Maclean, Kossuth, Fox, St Mungo himself. He saw it alongside the great cities of the world – Istanbul, New York, London, Leningrad[45] – and championed its modernity over its heritage, relished its capacity for change. His idea of modernism in poetry was entwined with his interest in new architecture, but his notion of 'concrete' was, he supposed, at the 'warm end' of the spectrum.[46] A love of formal experimentation coexisted with endless, non-judgemental curiosity about human activity and potential, and those are the heart of his urban poems: the inhabitants of the 'sonnet stretched to an ode', the 'uncontrolled life' within the grid of the streets.

CHAPTER SEVEN

Edwin Morgan and European Modernism

Ernest Schonfield

Morgan's *Collected Translations* (1996) is one of his most substantial achievements. This chapter looks at the trajectory of his translations from, and use of, poets of European modernism, in various forms, in a range of political contexts and languages, and in the continuing dialogue, or open conversation, of Morgan's poetic practice. Amongst the dozens of poets Morgan has translated, five stand out – Eugenio Montale, Sándor Weöres, Vladimir Mayakovsky, August von Platen and Attila József – because Morgan has dedicated a separate volume to each one. This chapter will show that by engaging with modern European poetry, and with these five poets in particular, Morgan was able to develop his voice in a number of important ways.

What did Edwin Morgan get from European modernism? It provided him with a set of models which shaped his poetic practice, and a sense of interconnected traditions which shaped his own identity. The blurb on his *Collected Translations* makes these points very clearly: 'his own work nourishes itself from the poetry of other lands and ages'; his work as a translator 'is also part of the mechanism that Morgan, as a Scot, employs to define his place as a European'. Morgan anticipates this in an essay of 1977 on Gavin Douglas and William Drummond as translators, where he invokes 'the subtleties of the communion of European writers, a vast web of ideals and traditions shading off in each country into finer and finer distinctions and measures of vernacular or personal variation'; and he adds: 'Drummond relished these European blueprints.'[1] Peter McCarey suggests that the same could apply to Morgan himself when he states that Lorca's 'Asesinato' could be seen as a 'blueprint' for Morgan's poem 'The Barrow'.[2] So, European modernism gave Morgan a set of 'blueprints' and a sense of 'communion', of belonging to 'a vast web of ideals and traditions'.

Through translating, Morgan found a number of poets with whom he could identify. His requirements for a worthwhile translation are 'a devotedness towards the task in hand, and a certain empathy between the translator and his chosen poet [...] it is only when he can project himself confidently and happily into the mind of the target poet that his work gains the lift and fluency we all want to see'.[3] Morgan has 'always enjoyed the use of many different voices and personas'.[4] For Morgan, translation involves a process of imaginary identification and projection, but one which is rooted in empathy and genuine affinity. Marco Fazzini once asked Morgan: 'what moves the genuine translator is not a mimetic urge, but an elective affinity [...] Do you believe in what Goethe called "elective affinity"?' Morgan responded: 'Yes [...] I think it is an important idea!'[5] The reference is to Goethe's novel *Elective Affinities* (1809), which explores relationships in terms of chemical reactions between couples who find themselves irresistibly drawn together. These statements indicate that translation for Morgan is far from being an intellectual exercise; instead it is an emotionally charged process. In the evocative essay 'The Translation of Poetry' (1976), Morgan suggests that translation is 'like strangers moved to embrace across a fence'.[6] It can be transformative, too: 'A good translation, like a good original poem, has the effect of slightly altering the language it is written in [...] as regards the available potential of that language'.[7] Not only does the translation transform the target language by 'shaking its shibboleths', it also transforms the translator too: 'When he moves, he is no longer himself'.[8] Therefore, Morgan uses translation for practical purposes: to test the expressive limits of English and Scots, and also to modulate his own identity by assuming different poetic personae.

Morgan's scrapbooks from the 1930s and 1940s contain many excerpts from French Renaissance poetry (Maurice Scève, Saluste du Bartas); French classical drama (Racine's *Phèdre*) and French modernism (Jean Ajalbert, Albert Samain, Marceline Desbordes-Valmore, Victor Kinon, Germain Nouveau, Arthur Rimbaud, Paul Valéry, Jules Supervielle). He also begins to include numerous extracts from Russian poetry. His first translations were from Verlaine, in 1937; his last published translations in 2007 were from Paul Valéry and Tristan Tzara.[9] Despite Morgan's enduring interest in French modernism, in his translations of the 1950s, his focus is not French at all, but Italian and particularly Russian poetry.

Morgan's turn to Eastern European and Russian poetry puts him in the company of the Scottish modernist Hugh MacDiarmid, and more recent Northern Irish poets such as Seamus Heaney and Tom Paulin, who have engaged with the work of Eastern European poets in order to negotiate their own aesthetic and political positions.[10] According to Heaney, 'the surest way of getting to the core of the Irish experience' is to contemplate the country from outside, e.g. from the perspective of Warsaw and Prague.[11] The turbulent history of Eastern Europe and Russia in the twentieth century means that poets have produced their work in testing political circumstances. As Morgan puts it in a textbook called *East European Poets* which he produced for the Open University:

> Under circumstances like these, if there was any lesson European poets had to learn, and did learn, it was the lesson that patience, irony, deliberation, cunning, and an anti-hysterical and even anti-indignant art were more likely to make their points than a romantic or rhetorical grasping of lapels, poets' or readers'.[12]

Both Morgan and Heaney are drawn to the same poem by the Polish poet Zbigniew Herbert (1924–1998), 'A Knocker'. The poem contains these lines: 'my imagination / is a piece of board / my sole instrument / is a wooden stick / I strike the board / it answers me / yes – yes / no – no'.[13] Heaney interprets this poem as saying: 'Enjoy poetry as long as you don't use it to escape reality.'[14] Morgan's commentary is worth quoting in full:

> The poet is to be wary, precise, concrete, hard, impersonal, unlyrical, unpretentious. [...] It is almost as if life had taught the poet no longer to trust anything beyond immediately tangible objects and necessities, above all not to trust the heroic gesture, the flamboyant claim, the fanatical or obsessional path. To survive, even unheroically, may be the heroism of our times.[15]

Morgan, it seems, has tried hard to learn his lessons from the Eastern European poets he has encountered, and it is certainly true that his poetry is tangible, material and (mainly) unpretentious.

Translation is, on one level, a form of appropriation. The translator takes another person's voice and makes it their own. Amongst Morgan's many translations, there are five single volumes: Montale (1959), Weöres (1970), Mayakovsky (1972), Platen (1978) and József (2001). This suggests that these five poets were particularly significant to Morgan. Let us now consider them in chronological order.

Poems from Eugenio Montale (1959)

Why did Edwin Morgan turn to the work of Eugenio Montale (1896–1981) in the fifties, when he was trying to establish himself? What drew EM to EM? Perhaps the Italian poet gave Morgan an opportunity to work through his 'difficult relationship'[16] with Hugh MacDiarmid (1892–1978), the dominant literary figure in Scotland at this time. Harold Bloom has argued in *The Anxiety of Influence* (1973) that younger poets are often troubled by the influence of their famous precursors, and that they must struggle to resist this influence if they are to develop. In *The Whittrick* (1961), Morgan tried to negotiate his relationship with MacDiarmid by staging an imaginary encounter between MacDiarmid and James Joyce. In my view, Morgan's translations of Montale can also be seen in this perspective. There are uncanny parallels between Morgan's relationship with MacDiarmid on the one hand, and Montale's relationship with his precursor Gabriele D'Annunzio (1863–1938) on the other. MacDiarmid was an admirer of D'Annunzio: *In Memoriam James Joyce* (1955) uses a quotation from *Alcyone* (*Halcyon*, 1903) as an epigram. *Alcyone* is the third volume of the series *Laudi del cielo, del mare, della terra, degli eroi* (1903–1918). It is a dithyrambic, Nietzschean tour de force which celebrates the ecstatic fusion between the self and the landscape. Montale's first collection, *Ossi di Seppia* (*Cuttlefish Bones*, 1925), has been seen as a direct response to D'Annunzio's *Alcyone*, 'an attempt at wringing the neck of its overweening eloquence'.[17] D'Annunzio's ecstatic fusion with his environment was predicated on the rejection of a moral conscience, which would act as a brake to physical sensation. In Montale, 'this ecstatic fusion is more often sought after than achieved, defeated by an almost paralyzing self-consciousness'.[18] It seems possible that much as Montale countered D'Annunzio's heroic vitalism with his own troubled self-consciousness, so too did Morgan turn to Montale's poetics as a means to counter the dynamism of MacDiarmid. Montale's dislike of fascism led him to cultivate coded messages of resistance. Both Montale and Morgan try to keep partisan politics at a remove from their work, preferring allusion to directness.

Jonathan Galassi explains that a Montale poem is typically a 'catalogue in which objects pile up on each other in an allusive accretion of signifiers'.[19] This is the quality which Morgan appreciates in Montale's verse. As Morgan puts it: 'long before one fully understands a difficult poem by Eugenio Montale, his world stirs and reveals itself: there is a shimmer, a play of light on water and on crumbling buildings, a face glancing in a mirror [...]'.[20] For Montale, a glimmer of light can signify life. One example of this is Montale's poem 'Eastbourne' (1933/35) where the revolving doors of the hotel are 'All flashing leaves and facets'; the door is 'a roundabout that traps / And sweeps up everything it whirls' (*CT*, 18). Commenting on these verses by Montale, Morgan argues that poets should reserve their deepest receptivity for reality in its undefined, material state: 'a poet may find himself committed to a flash of glass' (*Essays*, 71).

Did Morgan have the stubborn materiality of Montale's verse in mind when he wrote *The Cape of Good Hope* (1955)? A brief comparison with Montale's *Mediterranean* (1924) may be useful here. In Montale's poem, the sea reveals to the poet the law of his own existence: 'to be as various / As vast, yet fixed in place' (*CT*, 9). At the same time, though, the poet stands outside this natural world. The poet wishes he could have been 'rugged, elemental' like the sea, but he does not have its 'uncaring, unrelenting will'; instead, he is a reflective human being, a man who can follow one path and regret not taking the other: 'The track of one path taken, I had still / The other soliciting my heart' (*CT*, 10). Morgan's *The Cape of Good Hope* begins by renouncing love, and launching out 'Over matter alone, and into the sea of matter' (*CP*, 61). In mid-ocean, we encounter 'A gleam, an inhuman shimmer' (*CP*, 64); this gleaming light, familiar to the reader of Montale, is still the symbol of a 'Mindless, meaningless' world (*CP*, 64). But by the end of the poem, the lyric 'I' finds his way back from this wilderness; he turns 'Through the great world of matter to my heart' (*CP*, 73). He concludes that materiality must learn love, and love must appreciate materiality (*CP*, 75). After contemplating the inhuman will of the ocean, the lyric 'I' concludes, like Montale in *Mediterranean*, that he is inextricably bound to his own human heart, and that he cannot abdicate this painful/precious burden. In this way, *The Cape of Good Hope* performs a similar ideological move to *Mediterranean*; it toys with the Nietzschean idea of complete immersion in the blind will of nature, only to step back from this abyss, concluding with a hard-won affirmation of humanist values. It seems that Morgan's engagement with Montale led him to appreciate what Éanna Ó Ceallacháin calls Montale's focus 'on the timeless miracle of individual human experience.'[21]

Sándor Weöres: Selected Poems (1970)

In the Hungarian poet Sándor Weöres (1913–1989) Morgan found a kindred spirit, a poet as versatile as he was. Like Morgan, Weöres is known for experimenting with a wide variety of verse forms, and for his work as a translator (in Weöres's case, from Ukrainian and Georgian into

Hungarian). Like Morgan, Weöres is difficult to categorise. In terms of lyric intensity, William Jay Smith ranks Weöres with Blake, Rilke, T. S. Eliot and Dylan Thomas, but points out that his work is more playful than those poets.[22] Morgan met Weöres at an international poetry conference in Hungary in 1966 and they soon became friends (*BTLD*, 176–80). According to Shona M. Allan, both poets share the desire 'to explore everything and give anything and everything a voice'.[23] Morgan seems to have particularly liked the fact that Weöres has 'a deep sense of the interconnections of human and non-human life' (*CT*, 60). This sense of organic interconnection is displayed to full effect in 'The Lost Parasol' (1953; *CT*, 72–81), a long poem about the gradual disintegration of a discarded red parasol. Morgan calls it 'an astonishingly fertile, original, and thought-provoking work [...] fundamentally awesome in its revelation of nature as relentless metamorphosis' (*CT*, 61). Indeed, the poem is a haunting tour de force which evokes the quality of Rimbaud's 'Le Bateau ivre' (1871) and Brecht's 'The Drowned Girl' (1919). As an epigram for 'The Lost Parasol', Weöres chose a quotation from St Teresa of Avila: 'I think there is much more in even the smallest creation of God, should it be only an ant, than wise men think' (*CT*, 72). This would have appealed to Morgan, whose Scrapbook Three quotes the Puritan writer Philip Stubbes: 'And although they be bloody beasts to mankind, & seeke his destruction, yet we are not to abuse them, for his sake who made them, & whose creatures they are'.[24] 'The Lost Parasol' is a rich ecological compost-heap of a poem that celebrates the wonder of biodegradation.

An earlier poem by Weöres, 'The Underwater City' (1942), would have struck a chord with Morgan, who appreciates decaying cities. Here, an entire city is placed underwater and covered with seaweed. There is a sense of utter devastation about this poem that fits well with its time (1942), as if pre-war Europe had been utterly submerged by a wave of destruction. The sunken city is also a woman, and so on another level this poem may be about an unhappy love affair, as the poet tries to recuperate his memories in the wake of some personal disaster. Much of Weöres's work achieves a delicate balance between utopia and dystopia. This interest in the past and the future of humanity is expressed in a television interview in which Weöres hopes that humankind can 'leave history behind'.[25] What he means here is 'history' understood in terms of continual power struggle and warfare; in terms of a process which divides humanity into winners and losers. As Weöres puts it in 'Difficult Hour' (1960; *CT*, 98–99): 'It was always others man conquered in the past; but – oh tremulous hope! – in the future he conquers himself' (*CT*, 99).

Wi the Haill Voice: 25 Poems by Vladimir Mayakovsky (1972)

Morgan felt a strong affinity with the Russian revolutionary poet Vladimir Mayakovsky (1893–1930). The final poem in his *Collected Poems* begins: 'At ten I read Mayakovsky had died, / learned my first word of Russian, *lyublyu*' (*CP*, 594) (*lyublyu* means 'love'). Most of the Mayakovsky translations were done in 1959–60,[26] and Mayakovsky is also a key presence in *The Cape of Good Hope* (1955). In an interview in 1999, Morgan stressed his sense of personal involvement with Mayakovsky: 'I found him a fascinating, complex, eventually tragic figure with whom I could readily empathize' (*BTLD*, 115). Why? The portrayal of Mayakovsky in *The Cape of Good Hope* suggests three reasons: (1) Mayakovsky's love affair was forbidden by the authorities; (2) he loved the workers; (3) he disciplined his own poetry. Let's start with (1). *The Cape of Good Hope* portrays Mayakovsky in his room in Moscow on 14 April 1930, just before his suicide. Mayakovsky had fallen in love with Tatiana Yakovleva (1906–1991), who had fled Russia in 1925 to live in Paris. In 1929 Mayakovsky was denied a visa to visit her, and in December of that year she married a Frenchman. The lyric self of Morgan's poem asks: 'Who forbids our love?' (*CP*, 71). The sense of shared suffering is clear: Morgan, like Mayakovsky, suffered from forbidden love. (2) 'I turned my love / To millioned scapegoat man' (*CP*, 71). Mayakovsky became a socialist aged fourteen, for which he was arrested and spent several months in prison in 1909, where he started writing poems. His last poems reaffirm his belief in communism. Morgan, although his political engagement was more modest, clearly sympathised. (3) 'To myself hard' (*CP*, 71). Although he belonged to the Russian avant-garde, Mayakovsky satirised the pretentions of his Futurist colleagues. He put his creative talent in the service of the revolution, stifling his own lyric excesses. From 1920 to 1922 he worked for ROSTA, the Russian State Telegraph Agency, producing agitprop posters and slogans for a mass audience.[27] In the preface to *Wi the Haill Voice*, Morgan quotes an American critic who labelled Mayakovsky's populist activity a 'waste of talent'. Morgan disagrees, pointing out that Mayakovsky was 'proud of the fact that he was able to mould himself in accordance with the demands of a Revolution he wholeheartedly believed in' (*CT*, 105). Morgan is impressed that Mayakovsky made the transition from a 'largely subjective futurism to a more outward-looking, more comprehensible [...] yet not self-compromised poetry' (*CT*, 106–07).

Morgan chose to translate Mayakovsky into vernacular Scots, an appropriate choice since Mayakovsky preferred the language of the street.[28] Morgan states that in Scottish poetry (e.g. Dunbar, Burns and MacDiarmid) there is 'a vein of fantastic satire' that suits Mayakovsky, and he also enjoyed 'the challenge in finding out whether the Scots language could match the mixture of racy colloquialism and verbal inventiveness in Mayakovsky's Russian' (*CT*, 113). Morgan refers twice to MacDiarmid here, and there is a sense that in the Mayakovsky translations, Morgan is attempting to match MacDiarmid's *A Drunk Man Looks at the Thistle* (1926). That landmark poem opened up a dialogue between Scots and Russian modernism because it included translations from Aleksandr Blok (1880–1921). Translating Blok's colleague Mayakovsky was a way for Morgan to emulate MacDiarmid, and specifically to mine the 'vein of fantastic satire' he saw there. Mayakovsky has a wild, elemental, cosmic quality, which is most evident in 'Vladimir's Ferlie' (*CT*, 122–25) and 'The Atlantic' (*CT*, 137–41), where the poet encounters the sun and the ocean, respectively, and recognises them as friends and comrades. The confidential, familiar tone of the Scots helps to create a sense of the poet's intimacy with these elemental powers. Morgan has also shortened the title of 'Vladimir's Ferlie' to only two words compared to nine words of the Russian original.[29] We find a similar sense of communion with the sun at the end of Morgan's 'From a City Balcony' (*CP*, 184).

'Wi the Haill Voice' (*CT*, 38–41), written in January 1930, is Mayakovsky's last major poem and it has a testamentary quality. It addresses 'comrades o posterity', as the poet wonders what future ages will make of him. He imagines a happier age in which words like 'prostitution' and 'tuberculosis' will belong to a forgotten past. One day in that distant future, if 'archeological scaffies seekin licht / on oor benichtet days' (*CT*, 38) come searching, then they might inquire about him, what kind of a man he was. And so the poet announces that he will 'shaw ye the age, and gie ye my ain credentials' (*CT*, 38). The idea of researchers coming from the distant future can also be found in Morgan's long poem 'London', when he writes: 'Now bury this poem in one of the vaults / of our civilization, and let the Venusian / computers come down, and searching for life / crack our ghastly code' (*CT*, 251). Turning back to 'Wi the Haill Voice', Mayakovsky describes himself as a 'sanitary' and a water-carrier who made posters during the Russian Civil War, telling people to boil water in order to prevent the spread of infection. He has walked in the 'gairden' of 'Poesy' but the demure gardener speaks English, not Scots. He would not want a statue of himself in such a place, if outside the streets are full of whores and TB sufferers. He is tired of creating propaganda, and nothing would be more lucrative than writing 'True Romances':

> and naethin
> wid be nicer—
> or mair profitable—
> nor I sud screeve ye True Romances,
> hen.
> But och,
> I've maistert myself therr,
> I've stapplt
> the hass o my sangs
> wi my ain pen. (*CT*, 39)

The brief absence of Scots for 'True Romances' shows the poet's disgust for romantic clichés. It might be profitable to write such things, but he will not do it, because he has mastered himself, he has stopped the 'hass' (throat) of his own songs. If he speaks now with his whole voice, this is because he has trained his voice not to speak in rosy clichés. His poetry is like an army, weapons in service of 'the planetary proletariat' (*CT*, 40). And he does not want a marble statue, it is 'sleekit' (*CT*, 40) – the word means 'smooth', 'slippery', but also 'hypocritical'. All he wants is the shirt on his back: 'Lea me a clean-launert shurt to my back / and to tell ye the truith, I dinna need anythin' (*CT*, 41).

Mayakovsky's later poems use a staircase structure (*lesenka*), in which words are indented and shared out across successive lines. Morgan reproduces this structure in 'Brooklyn Brig' (*CT*, 142–46), Mayakovsky's generous tribute to American engineering. In 'Comrade Teenager!', the final poem in Morgan's Mayakovsky collection, the staircase structure is especially significant. The first half of the poem describes the obedience of young children, and this theme of obedience is also evident in the regular verse lines; there are only two 'steps' in this section. The second half of the poem calls on the teenager to disobey and fight for the Commune. As the poem moves from obedience to disobedience, the lines loosen up, becoming bold, sweeping staircases:

> Comrade teenager,
> ye arna a babby-boo;

be a bonny fechter—
a committit man,
ye ken. (*CT*, 155)

In the last two words – 'ye ken' – the poet appeals directly to the audience for their assent ('you know what I mean'). The Scots 'ye ken', half-rhyming with 'man', and with the alliteration of the consonants 'c' and 'k', sounds better and is much more inviting than its English equivalent could have been in this context. Moments like this fully justify Morgan's choice to render Mayakovsky into Scots.

Platen: Selected Poems (1978)

August Graf von Platen-Hallermünde (1796–1835) is a precursor of German modernism. He was a homosexual German poet whose reputation suffered when he was publicly outed by his rival Heinrich Heine. Platen had mocked Heine's Jewishness; Heine retaliated with a homophobic tirade against Platen in *The Baths of Lucca* (1830). The two bitter rivals came from entirely different worlds: Heine was an impoverished urban Jew from the Rhineland and Platen was a Bavarian aristocrat. Morgan has translated both. For Heine, Morgan uses the vernacular Scots (appropriately, since Heine is a more demotic poet); for Platen, he uses English, with the notable exception of 'Forfairn's my hert' (*CT*, 314), an intense poem of heartbreak. Platen and Heine are both nineteenth-century poets, but their outsider perspectives give a distinctly modern sensibility to their works. Morgan's renderings of Heine's Romantic lyrics and Platen's sonnets show his interest in both poets, but it is clear that he has a special affinity with Platen, and particularly with Platen's *Venetian Sonnets* (1824), which have been called 'the most perfect sonnets in German'.[30] James McGonigal points out that there are several 'psychological similarities' between Morgan and Platen: they were both gay; they both served in wars but did not see any action (Platen enlisted against Napoleon in 1813 but his regiment was not at Waterloo), and they were both erudite, multilingual poets with an interest in foreign poetic forms, particularly the work of Hafiz, a fourteenth-century Persian poet who appears in Platen's *Ghasalen* (1821) and Morgan's *The New Divan* (*BTLD*, 213–14).

The most important affinity between the two poets is in their use of the sonnet form. Morgan became fascinated by the sonnet form in the early 1970s: his translations of Petrarch date from this time (*CT*, 164–66).

Morgan began his translations of Platen's *Venetian Sonnets* around 1970 (*BTLD*, 212), only two years before he published his own *Glasgow Sonnets* in 1972 (incidentally, both works were published by the Castlelaw Press in West Linton). McGonigal suggests that 'it may be that revisiting the strict rhyme scheme of the Platen sonnets influenced EM's choice of this same form for his own *Glasgow Sonnets*' (*BTLD*, 213). The two sonnet cycles are similar in theme: Platen's *Venetian Sonnets* celebrate the faded glory of Venice; Morgan's *Glasgow Sonnets*, too, features a city which has seen better days, littered with derelict buildings 'condemned to stand, not crash' (*CP*, 289). Morgan's sonnets are set against the Clyde Shipbuilders' work-in of 1971–72 led by Jimmy Reid, when the British government tried to close down the shipyards. The sixth sonnet begins: 'The North Sea oil-strike tilts east Scotland up, / and the great sick Clyde shivers in its bed' (*CP*, 290). In Platen's sonnets there are similar scenes of desolation. In Sonnet V the marble walls are 'Now turned to sinking, slowly crumbling things' (*CT*, 318); in Sonnet VIII 'The harbour's derelict, few boatmen call' (*CT*, 319). The connection between Glasgow and Venice becomes even clearer in Morgan's seventh Glasgow sonnet, which portrays the conservationists' efforts to turn Glasgow into a museum piece: 'riverside walks march off the lists', and 'the sandblaster's grout / multiply pink piebald facades to pout / at sticky-fingered mock-Venetianists' (*CP*, 291); 'mock-Venetianists' suggests both the Italianate architecture of Victorian Glasgow and Platen himself. However, these renovations fail to conceal the sense of decline: 'Prop up's the motto. Splint the dying age' (*CP*, 291). Indeed, they hasten Glasgow's transformation from industrial centre to cultural destination.

In both sonnet cycles, form (sonnet) and content (nostalgic emotion) are opposed. It is almost as if the strict form of the sonnet has been chosen in order to resist the theme of decay. Siegbert Prawer argues that Platen uses Venice as a symbol for his own personal problems, in order to contemplate his own emotions from the outside.[31] Venice was humbled by Napoleon; Platen was humbled by the stigma of his own sexuality. Morgan's translations are well attuned to this homoeroticism, e.g. in Sonnet III: 'Gay all around is the dear swarm of souls / Moving in idleness, as if freed from care; / A queer soul can feel free here as he strolls' (*CT*, 318); and in Sonnet XIV, which concludes with the cry of the gondoliers. In the German original, the poet hears the gondoliers but remains silent; in Morgan's translation, he addresses them directly: 'Ah, gondolier!' (*CT*, 321). There is a similar layering of desire in Sonnet IX of *Glasgow Sonnets*, when the city is anthropomorphised:

It groans and shakes, contracts and grows again.
Its giant broken shoulders shrug off rain.
It digs its pits to a shauchling refrain.
Roadworks and graveyards like their gallus men. (*CP*, 292)

In this way, Morgan's sonnets to Glasgow derive their force from the poet's profound identification with Glasgow, which means that the damage done to the city affects him personally. On another level, the *Glasgow Sonnets* are a love song addressed to the 'gallus' (brash, cheeky, bold) men who inhabit the city and dig its roads and pits.

Attila József: Sixty Poems (2001)

Morgan first encountered the poetry of Attila József (1905–1937) in an Italian translation that had been published in 1952. In 1959 Hugh MacDiarmid asked Morgan to help him translate József's work (*BTLD*, 113). Morgan's translations of József bring his career as a translator to an impressive close. József is one of the few poets who are both world class and genuinely working class. Morgan and Mayakovsky are for the people, but they are not – as József – of the people too.[32] József bears comparison to Mayakovsky: both are powerful political poets who address their poetry to working people. Both express the utopian impulses of their turbulent times, the 1920s (Mayakovsky) and the 1930s (József). Both invoke their kinship with primal natural forces: the sun calls Mayakovsky his brother (*CT*, 124), and József calls the forest his comrade.[33] Both question the validity of art and culture: compare Mayakovsky's 'Mandment No. 2 to the Army o the Arts' (*CT*, 126–28) with József's 'Culture'.[34] Both suffered from unrequited love. Both committed suicide. Sometimes reading József is like reading Mayakovsky in a minor key.

József's father was a soap-maker who ran off when he was three; his mother was a washerwoman. He was expelled from university in 1925 because of his poem 'Heart-Innocent' (*CT*, 341), and his third collection of poetry was banned for subversion in 1931. In 1930 he joined the Communist Party of Hungary but was soon expelled from there too. Peter Sherwood states that 'one important reason for this must have been his belief in the importance of sex and love', which made him 'attempt to synthesize Marx and Freud'.[35] József became schizophrenic and he fell in love with his analyst. He died in 1937 and was only rehabilitated by the Communist Party in 1954.

What drew Morgan to the work of József? József's central themes

– urban poverty, love, sex and politics – clearly resonate with Morgan's own work. According to Tom Hubbard, who is translating József into Scots, Morgan and József write 'a poetry of struggle as opposed to a poetry of contentment, a poetry for alert citizens rather than for passive consumers'.[36] Hubbard points out that both poets are alert to cats, dogs and derelict buildings.[37] Morgan said that the József poems which moved him most were those on the poet's mother – József's mother died of cancer when he was only fourteen.[38] The closing lines of Morgan's *Glasgow Sonnet* X with the 'stalled lives' who trudge to the launderette (*CP*, 292) can be compared to József's poem 'Mother'. The poet describes his mother as she carries 'the creaking basket / of clothes, without pausing, up to the attic' (*CT*, 341). Her short life was one of constant toil. In 'My Mother', we read: 'a washerwoman's lot is to die early' (*CT*, 344). Cancer may have killed her, but it was capital that crushed her:

> She pauses with the iron: I see her.
> Her brittle body was broken by
> capital, grew thin, grew thinner –
> think about it, proletarians – (*CT*, 344).

It is this fusion of the personal and political which makes József such an important poet.

József's two great themes are love and politics. His poem 'The Woodcutter' celebrates revolution, as the axe cuts down a tree representing the feudal order (*CT*, 353). His central focus is not revolutionary violence, though, but the work of love. In 'Fly, poem …' we read: 'Love and liberty don't show / tumblers of blood, but living springs'.[39] In 'It isn't me you hear …', the poet suggests that love and politics are intertwined. The answer to the poor man's predicament is to engage with others, or, as the poem puts it: 'To plunge your face into yourself – wasted labour, / you are only washed in the waters of others' (*CT*, 345). There is a sense here that only by loving others can we reveal our true being. This idea is expressed most powerfully in 'Ode', a love poem in six sections (*CT*, 345–49). 'Ode' begins with the poet sitting on a wall, as he inhales the summer wind. In section two he addresses his lover and he tells her:

> You have been able to force
> speech from the universe –
> and from solitude, weaving its fitful deceits
> in the heart's deepest place. (*CT*, 346)

Solitude here is portrayed as a form of deceit. Only in love do we hear the whole universe speak. The poet bears the imprint of his lover's existence, and she has become engraved on his mind 'like acid on metal' (*CT*, 346), so there is a searing, agonising quality to this love which mingles with the poet's joy. The poet feels that he is 'moulded and carved' by her 'simplest glance' (*CT*, 347). Her love makes him into what he is. Then the poem segues into a biological mode, admiring the cells, the lungs and the kidneys of his lover. She seems to contain the entire universe within her body. 'Here, in your huge essence, / the eternal unconscious wanders' (*CT*, 348): this is perhaps a reference to C. G. Jung's concept of the collective unconscious. This experience of love leads to the insight that 'Existence stammers: / only law has a clear voice' (*CT*, 348). Just as solitude is deceptive, so too is clear speech, plain speaking that tries to set itself up as a law. The truth of existence is stammering, erratic, fragmentary, and this is why we need poetic speech to take the measure of the universe. In the final section of the poem, the poet leaves in search of his lover, and he imagines that – if he finds her – then perhaps she will say to him:

> The water's lukewarm, go and try it!
> A towel for your body, dry it!
> The meat is baked, end your hunger!
> In my bed forever linger. (*CT*, 349)

In this way, 'Ode' takes the reader on a brief cosmic odyssey, and, like the *Odyssey*, it ends with an evocation of sensual domestic bliss. The poet's deepest desire is to share the water, the food, and the bed of his beloved. The locus of love is 'the common rumpled bed', as Morgan puts it in Section 12 of *The New Divan* (*CP*, 298). The hidden centre, for both poets, is this shared space.

As we conclude this brief survey of Morgan's translations of European modernists, we can see how this was an essential aspect of Morgan's poetic practice. By engaging in dialogue with other poets, Morgan could work through his own concerns. With Montale he appreciated how an intense consciousness could be expressed through material images. With Weöres he admired the formal virtuosity, the utopian strain and the sense of a big picture. With Mayakovsky he enjoyed the revolutionary swagger but also respected the poet's self-discipline and his social engagement. With Platen he valued the way in which the expression of sexual desire is embedded within an urban cityscape. With József he recognised the interconnections between self and others, between politics and love.

CHAPTER EIGHT

Concrete Realities

John Corbett

This chapter traces the influence of the poetry and manifestos of the international avant-garde of the 1950s on Edwin Morgan's concrete poems of the 1960s. Morgan's committed experimentalism in this period was shaped in great part by his direct engagement with fellow writers, in particular the de Campos brothers in Brazil, through the exchange of letters and the processes of translation.[1] In the correspondence between Morgan and the de Campos brothers, and in the versions he made of their work, we find the Scottish poet trying out techniques that would inform his original poetry in this mode. The Haroldo de Campos archive in São Paulo contains copies of his pamphlets and books sent from the mid-1960s to the late 1990s, usually with a handwritten inscription to either Haroldo or Augusto. For example, a copy of Morgan's selected translations, *Rites of Passage* (1978), is dedicated to Augusto de Campos, acknowledging, in Morgan's Portuguese, that the Brazilian's '*esperimentalismo incentiva a poesia se transfigurar em novas formas*' ('experimentalism encourages poetry to transform itself into new forms'). The aesthetic merits of the new forms of poetry as practised by writers such as Morgan and Ian Hamilton Finlay were fiercely contested in the 1960s, but Morgan's championing of them remained firm and the growing acceptance of experimental verse signalled a new kind of internationalism in Scottish literature.

Poetry that draws attention to the materiality of its medium – the raw sound of the voice and the shapes of the characters on the page – has an ancient pedigree, but the early decades of the twentieth century saw a series of largely independent moves to revolutionise conventional ways of reading and writing poetry by foregrounding the aural and visual substance of language.[2] Bohn traces the outcomes of this radical aspiration through the 'literary cubism' of Spanish Ultraist poets, led by the

Chilean Vicente Huidobro; Mexican poets, such as Luis Quintanilla and Salvador Novo; French poets and artists like Guillaume Appollinaire and André Breton; and Italian Futurist 'aeropoetry' as practised by Ignazio Scurto, Pino Masnata and Tullio Crali.[3] All of these poets sought to break with tradition by using, in particular, the visual substance of their compositions – diagrammatic or iconic designs, varied typefaces – to signify in unconventional ways that, in many quarters, both courted and provoked ridicule. Most of these nascent movements had little wider impact until the 1950s, when disparate clusters of poets who were all experimenting with visual and sound poetry became aware of each other's work and began sharing ideas and offering mutual support. Among these poets were Eugen Gomringer, born in Bolivia but raised in Switzerland, author of a volume called *Constellation* (1953), and a Brazilian trio, Augusto and Haroldo de Campos and Décio Pignatari, who had published the first volume in a series of experimental poetry pamphlets, *Noigrandes,* the previous year. It was the 'Noigrandes' group that popularised the term 'concrete poetry', one of the first recorded uses of the phrase 'poesia concreta' being the title of an article written by Augusto de Campos in 1955. The epithet 'concrete' alluded to then current avant-garde work in the domains of music and the visual arts; it might be noted, however that the Swedish writer Oyvind Fahlström independently published his 'Manifest for konkret poesie' in 1953.[4]

In 1955, the same year that Augusto de Campos published 'poesia concreta', Pignatari and Gomringer met in Ulm, in Germany, and began planning an international anthology of concrete poetry. Although their proposed volume did not finally materialise, Gomringer did support, publish and write about the 'Noigrandes' group, and he adopted the name 'concrete poetry' to describe his own work. One of the more influential documents that set out the ethos of the new form of poetry was the Noigrandes group's 'Pilot Plan for Concrete Poetry' (1958).[5] Alluding to the then-topical *Plano Piloto de Brasília* (1957), which was architect Lucio Costa's model for the construction of a new, modernist Brazilian capital city, the 'pilot plan' was later translated by the authors as follows:

> Concrete poem, by using the phonetical system (digits) and analogical syntax, creates a specific linguistical area – 'verbivocovisual' – which shares the advantages of nonverbal communication, without giving up word's virtualities. With the concrete poem occurs the phenomenon of metacommunication: coincidence and simultaneity of verbal and

> nonverbal communication; only – it must be noted – it deals with a communication of forms, of a structure-content, not with the usual message communication.[6]

The portmanteau term 'verbivocovisual', at the heart of the quotation, is taken from James Joyce's *Finnegans Wake* – it indicates that the concrete poem relies on a heightened perception of the verbal sign in relation to its aural and visual signifiers.[7] The other key term in the quotation is 'metacommunication', sometimes expressed as 'isomorphism', whereby the distinct visual and verbal forms converge into a single whole. Rather than the visual or aural substance simply acting as carriers of a verbal message, the substance contributes to the communicative expression. Or, as Marshall McLuhan was later to say more concisely, 'the medium is the message'.[8] A simple but eloquent example of this principle is Morgan's own concrete poem, 'Archives', in which the phrase 'generation upon' is repeated in a column down the page. As the column grows longer, letters begin to be lost, thus revealing expressions that were 'hidden' in the main phrase; for instance 'erat' (Latin, 'was') and 'era' and, eventually, the hesitation marker 'er', followed by unintelligible grunts, like 'grnn'. The poem, thus, does not describe but enacts the process of entropy, the corruption of signification over time. Although the original sense of the phrase 'generations upon/generations upon' is lost, there is the consequent release of unexpected, yet oddly apposite, meanings.

As international interest in the concrete poetry movement developed through the 1950s, correspondences blossomed, and a widely dispersed group of poets began collaborating on projects across national borders. As James McGonigal's biography relates in some detail, in June 1962, Morgan, then a lecturer in English at Glasgow University, noticed a letter on concrete poetry in the *Times Literary Supplement* by Ernesto Manuel de Melo e Castro, a Portuguese poet who had gained his doctorate in São Paulo.[9] Morgan wrote to de Melo e Castro, who put him in touch with the de Campos brothers, just as Augusto de Campos was contacting Morgan via Ian Hamilton Finlay. This correspondence was to prove influential as Morgan developed his ideas about concrete poetry. His ideas on concrete poetry, developed in talks in the 1960s, parallel in many respects those expressed by Haroldo de Campos in a later essay on Ernest Fenollosa, 'Ideograma, anagrama, diagrama: una lectura de Fenollosa' (1977): Morgan and de Campos both built on the ideas of Fenollosa and Ezra Pound in seeing the Chinese ideogram as a means of fusing meaning and visual structure; and they followed the formalist linguist Roman

Jakobson in paying attention to the phonic structure of poetry. McGonigal (2013) notes that Morgan's enthusiasm for computers also resonates with Haroldo de Campos and others' later use of digital technology in the making of concrete poems.[10]

Looking back in his autobiographical poem 'Epilogue: Seven Decades', Morgan later reflected on this period:

> At forty, I woke up, and saw it was day,
> found there was love, heard a new beat, heard Beats,
> sent airmail solidarity to São
> Paulo's poetic-concrete revolution.

A sense of solidarity with fellow poets who were promulgating new ideas in poetry was evidently important to Morgan. In Scotland, he began collaborating with Ian Hamilton Finlay, who was also enthusiastic about developments in North and South American poetry, and who had begun publishing the avant-garde pamphlet *Poor.Old.Tired.Horse.* through his Wild Hawthorn Press in 1962, as an outlet for original poetry and translation. Morgan contributed work from the Russian of Fyodor Tyutchev to the inaugural issue of *P.O.T.H.*, and the sixth issue of the pamphlet, published in 1963, featured an issue on the de Campos brothers, Pignatari and other Brazilian *concretistas*, such as Pedro Xisto. Morgan's version of Xisto's 'Seaweed' appears in his *Collected Translations*. Finlay and Morgan became the standard-bearers for concrete poetry in Scotland, although one of Finlay's letters to Hamish Henderson, written in April 1966, testily remarks on what he perceived as undeserved attention being accorded to Morgan:

> There's to be an Arts Council show of 'concrete poetry' during the Festival. They have asked Edwin Morgan to arrange it; I feel very strongly that it should have been jointly edited by Morgan and me, since – so far as the world is concerned – the Wild Hawthorn Press IS Scottish concrete poetry.[11]

However, if there was to be tension in the small world of Scottish concrete poetry, it paled in comparison to the strident opposition to the would-be revolutionaries from the circle of established literary and cultural figures who circled the then elder statesman of Scottish letters, 'Hugh MacDiarmid', who celebrated his seventieth birthday in 1962. The background to the polarisation of attitudes to the avant-garde in the early 1960s has been surveyed in detail by Roderick Watson and the role played by MacDiarmid and Morgan in shaping the direction of the 'Macavantgarde' has been thoroughly discussed by James McGonigal.[12] The present discussion draws, in part, on these accounts.

In response to complaints that the literary establishment was blocking younger poets with new ideas, MacDiarmid characterised Finlay and Morgan as 'hopeless mediocrities, ganging up against their betters' on the second page of a polemic entitled *the ugly birds without wings*.[13] A war of words ensued, conducted on the letters pages of the *Scotsman*, and in August 1962, it found a dramatic public platform on the stage of the Usher Hall in Edinburgh, at an International Writers' Conference organised by the publisher John Calder, with the bookseller Jim Haynes, the photographer Alan Daiches, and Sonia Brownell, George Orwell's widow. On an afternoon devoted to 'Scottish Writing Today', and before the no-doubt bemused eyes of fellow writers like William Burroughs, Mary McCarthy, Norman Mailer, Henry Miller and Stephen Spender, Morgan and MacDiarmid participated in a whisky-fuelled panel discussion that quickly deteriorated into a flyting between the old guard, represented by MacDiarmid and Douglas Young, and the new guard, represented by Alexander Trocchi and Edwin Morgan.[14]

While Morgan seems to have regretted the tone of animosity on public display, and the predictably gleeful reporting of the literary spat in the press, he also came to value the airing of views that the conference afforded. The transcription of his contribution to the debate reveals an anxiety about the dominance of 'tradition' in Scottish letters:

> There has been far too much tradition in the last fifty years and we want to wake ourselves up and to realise that things [that] are happening at the present time, and are in the consciousness of everybody, are the things that a writer ought to be feeling and writing about. Things that are perhaps expressing one's reaction to world events, to international events, to atomic power, to space exploration, to the whole world, cybernetics, all this ought to be reflected not only in literature but in the whole intellectual life of Scotland and it is not being reflected, and this is what I want to see.[15]

While Morgan's concern here focuses on the content of Scottish literature and its perceived lack of engagement with modernity, the main bone of contention, as the conference progressed, seems to have been not so much what to write about, but how to write about it. On the final day of the conference, in a discussion on the theme of 'The Novel and the Future',

William Burroughs explained his mode of writing by way of cutting up and folding in his texts to produce non-linear, almost serendipitous combinations of phrases. Morgan was sufficiently fascinated by Burroughs' explanation to produce a report of the conference that is part parody, part homage.[16] It was published in the Edinburgh University magazine *Gambit* in 1962; an extract reads:

> Put Sorley MacDiarmid in your pipe and smoke Young Adam. Mind the carafe. Audience stirred air charged statues blush presbyterian junkie cameras shorthand races next morning's column. MACDIARMID furious international on the quick contacts Scotland not provincial Scottish Renascence writing international outlook translations on the quick Mister Trotchee typical IGNORANCE own Scottish traditions furious contact charge shout bang table. Mind the mike. TROCCHI chairman you want me out you'll throw me out. Pass the whisky. Pass the water.[17]

Morgan's account of the conference, however tongue-in-cheek it might have been, again suggests his openness to experimental literary techniques in exactly the period he was encountering concrete poetry for the first time. MacDiarmid's sustained hostility to the new avant-garde is evident in a letter to Maurice Lindsay, dated April 1965, which touches on the subject of Lindsay's co-editorship of a new poetry journal with Morgan and fellow poet George Bruce:

> I had heard with delight about the EUP Poetry Scotland and will of course be glad to send stuff when I know the date by which you should receive it. There is one thing however about which I must be absolutely frank. I deplore Edwin Morgan's association with you and George Bruce in the editorship. Morgan's prominence in connection with 'Concrete Poetry' and with Ian Hamilton Finlay rules him out completely as far as I am concerned. I will not agree to work of mine appearing in any anthology or periodical that uses rubbish of that sort, which I regard as an utter debasement of standards but also as a very serious matter involving the very identity of poetry. These spatial arrangements of isolated letters and geometrically placed phrases, etc. has nothing whatsoever to do with poetry – no more than mud pies can be called a form of architecture.[18]

The key to the animosity that informed the International Writers' Conference, and to Morgan's adherence to the value of 'these spatial arrangements of isolated letters and geometrically placed phrases, etc.', lies in MacDiarmid's assertion that matters of technique involve 'the very identity of poetry'. Watson notes that Maurice Lindsay had also written a stinging review of Ian Hamilton Finlay as lacking 'in wit and cultural seriousness'.[19] Although Morgan and Trocchi framed their debate with the old guard as internationalism versus parochialism, the actual debate was, as has been widely acknowledged, more to do with the kind of internationalism that Scottish writers wished to be affiliated with. By the 1960s, MacDiarmid's internationalism had long sought to fuse Scottish traditions with European high modernism, in the service of what he called 'a poetry of fact'. His major poetic achievement in the 1950s was, arguably, the long poem *In Memoriam James Joyce* (1955), in which he attempted to synthesise a compendium of arcane human knowledge, from ancient to modern times. Little about that endeavour could easily be dismissed as 'parochial', but neither could it be considered whimsical. Much of MacDiarmid's work from the 1920s onwards is conventionally read as a high-minded, earnest reaction to the perceived sentimental couthiness of earlier 'kailyard' poetry and prose. His and Lindsay's condescending abhorrence of the work of the upstart avant-garde in Scottish letters seems in part driven by their dread of a relapse into triviality, and, to use MacDiarmid's term, the 'debasement' of hard-won standards of intellectual seriousness.

For Morgan and Finlay, the rejection of the aesthetic merits of concrete poetry undervalued the seriousness that informed the apparent artlessness of the poems. Morgan in a letter to Augusto de Campos, dated 8 August, 1963, comments favourably on the range of effects concrete poetry is capable of, a range that extends to political critique:

> It is good to keep the concrete method capable of doing different things, from effects of pure place, relation, and movement to effects of satire, irony, and direct comment. The American poet Jonathan Williams, who has been in this country recently, has done some interesting work (you may know it) which uses certain aspects of concrete technique to comment on the Negro problem in the American South.[20]

Morgan's most obvious attempt to realise the political potential of concrete poetry, perhaps influenced by Williams's work, is 'Starryveldt', which memorialises the massacre of sixty-nine black protesters at a police station in the township of Sharpeville, South Africa, in 1960. Morgan alternates compound words beginning with the fricative consonants 's'/'sh' and 'v' with strident monosyllables that begin and end with the same sounds. It begins:

starryveldt
slave
southvenus
serve
SHARPEVILLE
shove

It is one of Morgan's few concrete polemics, as he acknowledges later, in 1968, in a letter to a Swiss scholar:

> [...] there is a great range of effects in concrete poetry from 'warm' to 'cold'. Some of it is outgoing, joyous, humorous, witty; some of it is stark, hermetic, forbidding; some is political; some is religious; some is mathematical; some is sculptural; some is two-dimensional, some three-dimensional; some abstracts concrete forms such as animals, some concretises abstract forms such as grammatical relationships. I myself incline to the 'warm' rather than the 'cold' end, but I realise that there are other points of view.[21]

To what extent, however, was Morgan's work shaped by his encounter with that of the *concretistas*? It is fair to suggest that Morgan's engagement with 'São Paulo's poetic-concrete revolution' furthered tendencies that were already present in his work, most obviously perhaps in his 'Verses for a Christmas Card' in *The Vision of Cathkin Braes* (1952), which shares the love of Joycean wordplay that inspired the 'verbivocovisual' Brazilians:

Respour this leidyear Phoenixmas
With starphire and restorying dazz.

In some respects the playful compounding of contemporary and archaic, standard and dialectal terms, corresponds to a key strategy also used by the *concretistas*, namely the half-playful, half-earnest concatenation of words to release new senses. One of the earliest series of poems by Augusto de Campos was entitled *Poetamenos* (1953), which compounds 'poeta' ('poet') and 'menos' ('less' or 'minus'), indicating the absence of the conventional author. The poems, in six colours, rearrange their letters in sequences whereby one possible set of expressions merges into another and multiplicities of interpretations are made possible. The apparent abnegation of authority is at odds with the role of the poet as understood by MacDiarmid and his circle; the poetry of fact, as conveyed by the learned 'makar', is usurped by a poetry of inference, one that demands that the active reader shoulder the responsibility of making meaning from the witty traces left by the elusive poet.

The encounter with the *concretistas*, then, spoke to interests already evident in Morgan's early poetry and connected him to a global network of poetic innovation. In his letters to Augusto de Campos, we see Morgan reading and critiquing (with the aid of a glossary and a Portuguese dictionary) the work of the Noigrandes group, sharing observations of the expressive potential of avant-garde poetry internationally, and discussing translations of Ezra Pound, James Joyce and Vladimir Mayakovsky into Portuguese. Morgan also hazarded translations of the poems of the de Campos brothers, with sufficient success for Haroldo de Campos to suggest him as their English translator to Lawrence Ferlinghetti, whose *City Lights* magazine featured work by the *concretistas* in 1965, the year in which the Beats teamed up with the Viennese concrete poet Ernst Jandl to perform before six thousand people in the Albert Hall in London.[22] One of Morgan's poems in his breakthrough collection *The Second Life* commemorates this poetry event. In Jandl's 'phonic concrete' performances, we might see (or hear) the germ of the idea that led to 'The Loch Ness Monster's Song'.

The most ambitious of Haroldo de Campos's poems that Morgan translated was 'Servidão de passagem' (rendered as 'Transient Servitude', *CT*, 286–92); Morgan's handwritten inscription, dated 30 January 1965, in a copy of the pamphlet *Starryveldt* that he sent to Brazil thanks Haroldo de Campos for his '*Admirável* and *Formidável poemalivro de passagem*' ('Admirable and Formidable poembook of passage'). 'Transient Servitude' was translated in close collaboration with the author and first published in a Mexican journal in 1967. McGonigal notes:

> They worked on the detail of this translation from November 1965 onwards. Its blend of concrete techniques and a complex sound poetry of alliteration and assonance with a strong political sentiment was taxing, and EM had to draw on all his translation skills, some of them honed on *Beowulf*'s metric, to express the Brazilian poet's intention.[23]

The literal translation of 'Servidão de passagem' is 'right of way', which might in turn have influenced the choice of *Rites of Passage* as the punning title of Morgan's 1976 collection of translations. However, it is in some of the shorter poems that we can more easily see how the isomorphic techniques at play in the work of the Brazilians influenced Morgan's poetry. Here we look at two short poems, beginning with 'fala/prata' (1962) by Haroldo de Campos, later translated by Mary Ellen Solt as 'speech/silver' (1968):[24]

fala
prata
cala
ouro
cara
prata
coroa
ouro
fala
cala
para
prata ouro
cala fala
clara

speech
silver
silence
gold
heads
silver
tails
gold
speech
silence
stop
silver golden
silence speech
clarity

Haroldo de Campos's source text can be read as a variation on Eugen Gromringer's famous concrete poem 'Schweigen' ('Silence'), which takes the form of a visual block made up of the repeated word 'schweigen', with an empty space at the centre. Both poems comment on the interplay between speech and silence: the word 'schweigen' in Gomringer's text paradoxically articulates 'silence'; however, the empty space at the heart of the block of words equally expresses silence through the absence of the same word. Contemplating the poem, we realise that each element is interdependent: speech on silence, silence on speech. Likewise, Haroldo de Campos's poem plays on a set of explicit and implicit proverbial or idiomatic expressions, 'speech is silver but silence is golden', 'heads or tails' and 'two sides of the same coin'. Folk wisdom, the poem might suggest, argues that silence is more precious than speech, but if speech and silence are interdependent (i.e. two sides of the same coin, heads and tails), then it might be possible to reverse the proverb and argue that silence is silver and speech is golden. Thereby we arrive at clarity. This interpretation, however, is not declared by the poem; again, its isomorphic or metalinguistic strategy is to arrange the elements so that the co-operating reader puzzles out a meaning from both the arrangement of the elements and his or her knowledge of the idiomatic and proverbial expressions alluded to.

It is the form of de Campos's poem – the setting up of the text as a cryptic utterance that is deciphered in the last line – that prefigures a number of Morgan's concrete poems, including 'Message Clear' and 'Dialeck Piece'. In these poems, two of six 'Emergent Poems' (1967) that employ the same technique, and which Morgan sent to Haroldo de Campos, we first see fragments of well-known quotations, namely bits of one-line citations from the Gospel of St John, Burns, Brecht, Rimbaud, Dante and the Communist Manifesto. The fragments offer up contained or hidden meanings, until the full quotation emerges – and we achieve clarity. In 'Message Clear' the quotation is 'i am the resurrection and the life', which offers hidden meanings such as 'i am he / hero / hurt' and 'i am thoth / i am ra / i am the sun / i am the son'. Christopher Whyte has argued that part of the attraction of concrete poetry to Morgan was its cryptic nature; it represented a hidden language that appealed to a poet whose sexual orientation, at the time, required to be concealed from public view and expressed through coded utterances.[25] This acute observation allows for a mischievous reading of 'Dialeck Piece': the quotation is Burns's 'A daimen icker in a thrave', which yields the opening lines 'i / am mick the / dick / i have / me / mate'. Burns's philosophical address to his fellow mortal is thus shown to contain what might be read as a homoerotic boast by a well-endowed Irishman. One can see why MacDiarmid was not amused. Yet, as David Kinloch has observed,

Morgan's concrete poetry does not only encode cryptically: line by line it reveals process, the uncovering of multiple layers of meaning, which Kinloch argues is the key to Morgan's oeuvre. The teasing of meaning from concrete forms dramatises the 'coming out' of clarity from obscurity.[26]

The necessity for taking recourse in cryptic discourse is, of course, not confined to 'secret societies or stigmatised groups' in Whyte's words;[27] it is a mainstream artistic strategy in societies subject to authoritarian control or an oppressive political regime. Morgan's own translation of a Brazilian poem – 'uma vez' by Augusto de Campos – arguably further distances a coded political comment by attending to the sound as well as the sense of the original:

uma vez
uma fala
uma foz
uma vez   uma bala
uma fala   uma voz
uma foz   uma vala
uma bala   uma vez
uma voz
uma vala
uma vez

Read conventionally, left to right and top to bottom, the phrases can be translated literally as 'once upon a time / a ditch / a river-mouth / once upon a time / a bullet / a speech / a voice / a river-mouth / a ditch / a bullet / once upon a time / a voice / a ditch / once upon a time'. However, the poem can also be read as two mirrored diagonals, each following the sequence 'uma vez / uma fala / uma foz / uma bala / uma voz / uma vala / uma vez'. Bohn cites a recording of the poem by four voices, two female and two male. In performance, the poem was read several times.[28] The first reading followed the mirrored diagonals of the visual poem, the second followed the horizontal 'conventional' reading, while the final recitation the four voices began with 'uma bala' ('a bullet') and progressed along the diagonals simultaneously.

As Bohn notes, the different potential readings do not obscure the fact that some kind of narrative is being suggested. There is the storytelling formula ('uma vez / once upon a time'), a mysterious outdoor location ('uma foz', which means a river-mouth), some kind of speech ('uma fala', possibly an altercation or a plea), a bullet, and a ditch. Morgan translates this drama as follows:

once was
one ditch
one beach
once was one whiz
one speech one voice
one beach one ditch
one whiz once was
one voice
one ditch
once was

It will be clear that Morgan's translation is not entirely literal; he was evidently keen to recreate something of the aural correspondences between 'bala / vala / fala' and 'vez / foz / voz' in his 'was / whiz / voice' and 'speech / beach / ditch' semi-rhymes. The result, however, is to make the 'bala' ('bullet') present only through metonymy: the bullet is no longer mentioned but only implied through the 'whiz' of its passing. The original text was composed during the Kubitschek era of government in Brazil, a time of relative political stability and democracy when, after Costa's 'pilot plan' had been approved, the national capital was moved from Rio to Brasilia. However, as the later military coup of 1964 and its brutal aftermath indicate, the threat of personal and political violence remained a constant of Brazilian life, and the prominence given to 'bala' in the original may reflect this fact. But in distancing the reference to the bullet in his translation, Morgan further mystifies the already puzzling meaning of the original, reducing its capacity for political comment even as he strives to maintain the aural echoes of the original's constituent phrases. In Morgan's version, only the mysterious drama remains, as if a film noir had been turned into a concrete poem. Kinloch, again in personal correspondence with me, has suggested that the elision of the bullet in this poem resonates with Morgan's metonymic strategies when representing violence in verse; in *The New Divan,* for example, the conflict of war is also immanent rather than present.[29]

The polyphonic principle of 'uma vez' can perhaps be heard to good effect in Morgan's own 'Spacepoem 3: Off Course', which indicates the Scottish poet's ability to synthesise poetic techniques across time and space. Like 'uma vez' a sequence of noun phrases combines to tell a narrative, this time of a spacecraft being knocked off course by some kind of collision (indicated by an indent at the line beginning 'the crackling somersault'). Thereafter, the epithets that modify each noun are recycled in increasingly bizarre combinations, affording a transcendent view of reality until presumably the spacecraft crashes into 'the growing moon' leaving only 'the floating song'. The debt to 'uma vez' can also be construed in the potential to read this poem in several ways. A horizontal reading of the paired noun phrases recalls Morgan's early and sustained interest in Anglo-Saxon verse (as McGonigal observes in relation to 'Transient Servitude'). Each half-line is often linked by alliteration, as in 'the crawling deltas the camera moon'. However, in a recording made in 1971,[30] Morgan recites the poem 'vertically', by reading the first column of half-lines and then the second column ('the crawling deltas / the pitch velvet'), changing the shape of the narrative and allowing the initially mundane combinations of epithet and noun to become ever stranger. 'Spacepoem 3: Off Course' further demonstrates Morgan's ability to fuse the oldest English verse tradition with the avant-garde principles of concrete poetry.

Translation and experiment – and developing a poetry of inference that invites the active reader to join the game of creating meanings – remained crucial aspects of Edwin Morgan's oeuvre. Ultimately, Morgan's interest in concrete and experimental poetry was in the potential it offered to extend his range as a writer. He confessed to Ian Hamilton Finlay in 1968 that while concrete poetry released in him a 'species of joy', akin to that which he felt when using Scots 'inventively for translation purposes', he also wished to write other kinds of poems, like the narrative 'In the Snack-bar'.[31] And despite his reservations about the dominance of tradition, expressed in the 1962 Writers' Conference, he did not disdain it, and his respect for MacDiarmid's work prompted the older writer to write a warm and candid letter to him in early 1975, praising his *Essays* (1974) as

> [...] indeed among the best things so far written about my poetry – welcome oases on the desert of contemporary literary journalism. That is not as you know, to say that I agree with them – only I am glad to encounter high intelligence anywhere.[32]

In *The Second Life,* a poem dedicated to MacDiarmid faces another dedicated to Finlay – a clearly deliberate juxtaposition that itself indicates that Morgan saw himself in a mediating role, or at least drawing on the traditions that each represented. Morgan infused his understanding of the traditional literary canon – including the modern canon of Scottish literature – with the lessons he continued to learn from the international avant-garde. The writers who offered 'airmail solidarity' to each other did so by extending a global network of contacts whose members interacted through letters and translations – and occasional personal meetings. For example, Ian Hamilton Finlay furnished Morgan with the address of Eugen Gomringer, whose meeting with Décio Pignatari had been one of the defining moments in the development of concrete poetry in the 1950s.[33] Morgan translated a number of Gomringer's poems, including 'worte sind schatten' ('words are shadows'). The translation contains the revealing lines 'words are games / games become words'; together, with the proviso that a game can be a piece of whimsy or a deadly serious endeavour (and sometimes both at once), these lines might sum up Morgan's experimental credo.

CHAPTER NINE

Edwin Morgan's Theatre

Anne Varty

Months after Edwin Morgan's death on 19 August 2010 his memory was honoured by two completely different theatre pieces. In November 2010 students at RSAMD performed a version of his hitherto professionally unproduced *The Play of Gilgamesh* (2005), together with his superbly knowing verse collection 'Ten Theatre Poems'; the following November, Liz Lochhead's *Edwin Morgan's Dreams – and Other Nightmares* was produced at Glasgow's Tron Theatre for the annual Glasgay! festival, weaving together a recollection of his life with his final collection of poetry. These two productions offer twin vectors which carry us to the heart of Morgan's enterprise as a dramatist. The first concerns his practice of intimacy between poetry and drama, and the often noticed theatricality of his verse:

> He has [an ...] elastic relationship to the languages in which he chooses to write, keenly aware of what works best in one poem or another – and this includes his translations. Morgan [...] chooses to write in Scots or Glaswegian only for dramatic purposes, i.e. giving someone or something a particular voice.[1]

The second points to the epic scale and fearlessness of his theatre writing which led to the overwhelming by controversy of *A.D.: A Trilogy of Plays on the Life of Jesus* (2000), and seem to have rendered *Gilgamesh* professionally untouchable.

Morgan's engagement with the stage was long-standing and it took many forms. As a critic he took part in urgent debate about revitalisation of the British stage in 1956, and a decade later he was reviewing Max Stafford-Clark's early work as artistic director at the Traverse.[2] He attended events hosted by the English Stage Company at the Royal Court in London, publishing in their house journal, *Encore Magazine,* in which he called for cool heads to assess the gap between style and substance in the expressions of Angry Young Men. His own excitement was more palpably fuelled by the Berliner Ensemble's 1956 visit to London with *Mother Courage* at the Palace Theatre. Arguing with his friend Ian Dallas he writes:

> Now that I've seen the Berliner Ensemble I am more than ever persuaded that technique and presentation are of the utmost importance. You deny the importance of the revolving stage in your letter; but it is precisely this that stamps the play and its meaning on your memory. The opening scene with the cart going round and the song being sung shakes you right out of the Eliot–Fry–Whiting continuum; it has an astonishing effect, as also have the bare stage and the clear unmelodramatized lighting. Certainly the ideas are important in Brecht, and having the 'world-view' might solve the question of technique, but the point you miss is that without something fairly spectacularly new in technique no world-view whether religious or political is going to revitalize British theatre.[3]

This letter, recently published by Morgan's biographer James McGonigal in *PN Review*, is an important statement of his ambitions for the stage which at the time he was eager for others to carry forward. In it he dismisses much of contemporary practice, not simply poetic drama which could be taken to challenge the 'well-made play' of the era, but also any whiff of the drawing room:

> The Berliners and the Peking Opera can come and go, and people will still be unhappy unless they get their three square walls and half a ceiling – and you, dear friend, what do you do but encourage them? I despair of you.[4]

Morgan's sympathies are expressly with the high artifice of epic theatre and Chinese opera as he firmly rejects collaboration with 'people's' established taste.

A decade later, in his first theatre review for *The Times*, he noted that playwrights had yet to learn to trust their audiences:

> the zany cleverness of the dialogue conceals a fear that serious issues cannot be made interesting to a theatre audience in terms of normal, unhysterical experience.[5]

Much later – thirty and forty years later – Morgan's own plays neither patronise the audience nor compromise substance for style. *A.D.* and *Gilgamesh* find 'normal, unhysterical' modes to convey the most serious of issues. Morgan does this in part by eschewing theatrical realism altogether, embracing the overt artistry of the theatres he welcomed to Britain so wholeheartedly in 1956. This choice is made, however, not simply in light of the critical distance he generates between himself and the style of the angry generation, but it also serves his decision to use the stage for telling primal stories from religious history, legend and myth.

His formal entrance as a writer for the stage is relatively minor and not made until 1982 when, as James McGonigal outlines, he worked with the small touring company Medieval Players. Having been approached by the company's producer, Dick McCaw, and director Carl Heap, who knew of Morgan's poetic interest in revisiting earlier texts,[6]

> Morgan adapted both the late-fifteenth- or early-sixteenth-century Dutch play *The Apple Tree* (1982), the fifteenth-century French farce *Master Peter Pathelin* (1983), and *The Second Shepherds' Play* (1984).[7]

Already Morgan's urge to bring the historically or geographically distant into the foreground is evident, both in his choice of material and in his manner of meeting the challenges posed. In his introduction to *The Apple Cart* he states that he wished 'to make the language itself modern, but set within the structure of a four-stress alliterative line which would hold associations with the earlier English drama and poetry'.[8] From here, a decade later, Morgan translated Edmond Rostand's 1897 heroic comedy *Cyrano de Bergerac* into demotic Scots for Communicado Theatre Company to perform at the 1992 Edinburgh Festival.

Rostand's play itself is a palimpsest, drawing on historical material from 1640 yet mediating it to *fin-de-siècle* Paris through nineteenth-century versions of the seventeenth century such as Dumas's *Three Musketeers* (1844). Translations of *Cyrano* into English had been published by Christopher Fry in 1975 and Anthony Burgess in 1985, while Rappenau's 1990 film *Cyrano* starring Gerard Depardieu had made the story current and internationally famous. Morgan therefore faced a text which was both familiar and strange, and which had been stamped in English by traditions of poetic drama he found particularly dreary. His views on Fry are clearly stated in his playful verse letter to Ian Dallas on writing for the stage in 1954, 'Extend your range, be flexible, not Fry' and 'Hydroelectric epigrams! Dam Fry!'[9]

Morgan's script was, we know, an extraordinary success, its flexibility and range relished by actors and adored by audiences in Scotland, winning a *Scotsman* Edinburgh Festival Fringe First Award, and a Hamada Foundation prize shared with director Gerry Mulgrew. Critics were quick to note the bravado of its idiom: '[w]here Christopher Fry expected Rostand's hero to warn the foe with whom he is duelling that "the blade begins to flit", Mannion growls "it's kebab time" and means it'.[10] The fizz of the dialogue, while seemingly speaking a language really spoken by men, in fact hugely compounds the artifice of the piece in its juxtaposition with the historicity of the play. Michael Billington drew attention to Morgan's programme note, which identified two features of the play which proved sounding notes for his subsequent drama:

> the real-life Cyrano was, apart from being a poet, Guards officer and sci-fi writer, a gay Gascon. Because it is always presented as a colourful, romantic tear-jerker about heroic self-sacrifice, we have failed to notice that Cyrano is actually a coded, *fin-de-siècle* homosexual play.[11]

These masks – Gascony for Scotland, Roxanne for Christian – align the work with Morgan's political commitment to equality and independence, but Billington regrets that neither was more firmly brought out in performance. It could all too obviously be argued, however, that Morgan's decision to translate the script into the dynamic language of Scottish city streets is hardly a turning away from the nationalist cause, while Cyrano's mesmeric nose placed masculinity centre stage. Mark Fisher, reviewing the revival which opened the Lyceum season in 1996, observed, 'Tom Mannion in the lead role wearing his nose like a naked penis, symbolising at once his embarrassment and his virility', aptly identifies the main source of the multidirectional attention afforded to notions of masculinity by the production.[12]

South of the border the production received more moderate praise; Jeremy Kingston's *Times* review from the Almeida headlined 'Rumbustious Scots let Cyrano slip from their grasp'.[13] This disappointing reception, while neither unusual nor surprising for theatre written in Scots and staged in England, points towards a larger political project of Morgan's linguistic choice for *Cyrano,* confirmed and consolidated later by the critical reception of his Scots translation of *Phaedra.* Morgan's version of Racine's treatment of Euripides was completed in 1997, the year of the successful referendum on Scottish devolution. It was staged at the Royal Lyceum Theatre in Edinburgh in 2000. Often considered together with

Liz Lochhead's Scots *Medea*, written for Theatre Babel and also staged in 2000, it was seen as part of a cumulative cultural move in the construction of a new Scotland.[14] Ian Brown asserts of *Phaedra* and *Medea*,

> They are a high culmination of a long politico-cultural process and not only celebrate political change [...], but are part of a longer creative drive to which earlier writers, including, of course, themselves in their earlier work, had contributed. Creative use and linguistic experimentation in Scots sustained changes in the larger politico-cultural scene that helped it be conceivable that there might be changes of the devolutionary kind.[15]

For Morgan, his engagement with world literature was as much an act of looking-out as it was an act of drawing-in: 'It will be good for outward-looking Scotland,' he announced mysteriously in 2001, 'if I make the name Gilgamesh (don't ask but watch this space) as familiar as William Wallace'.[16] Overarching ambitions are only successfully realised if the theatre itself is commensurately vibrant. Sue Wilson's review of *Phaedra* for the *Independent* captures some of the successes achieved by Kenny Ireland's direction and Morgan's script:

> The stalls have disappeared beneath a raised, near-circular arena, which is surrounded on all sides by the dress circle and additional seating behind the temporarily redundant proscenium arch. Large white sails hang overhead, evoking both the drama's 'seawart' setting and the clouds in the heavens, behind which reside the gods whose cosmic malevolence underpins Phaedra's fate. The edges of the stage area drop precipitously into darkness, with this encompassing void half-lit in rippling green, again suggesting not only the sea but the ominous forces – specifically Neptune – moving within it.
>
> Morgan's text itself is undeniably challenging, both in its conception and in its thoroughgoing nature. Even those with ears well attuned to everyday Scots speech will find many of the words unfamiliar, while Morgan's peppering of the dialogue with earthy colloquialisms can at first seem jarring. This, however, is the point, one element in his project being to reassert the full expressive range of what was once a complete working language; if these jolts make us reconsider the associations particular words or ways of speaking hold for us, then they've succeeded. For at the same time, Morgan is careful to retain the requisite dignity and grandeur in his ordering of the words and his use of rhythm to add rhetorical weight.[17]

Phaedra was an auspicious launch into the last phase of Morgan's theatrical career. *A.D.: A Trilogy of Plays on the Life of Jesus* was commissioned by Robert Carlyle's theatre company, Raindog, for performance at Glasgow's Tramway Theatre to mark the millennial year 2000. Directed by Stuart Davids with Paul Hickey in the title role, and a forty-strong cast, it ran from 20 September to 7 October 2000. It is epic in every sense, and not a drawing room in sight. Each of the three plays tells the story of a phase of the life of Jesus: 'The Early Years'; 'The Ministry'; 'The Execution'. Each play is structured by five acts divided into multiple scenes, and the trilogy as a whole has a preface and an epilogue spoken by the Magi. Brechtian in several respects, attention is focused on how the story is told rather than what happens next, and Morgan deploys a huge range of dramatic expression: swift sequencing of short scenes, song, crowds, soliloquy, public spaces in city and desert, intimate indoor scenes, dream-inducing stichomythia, rhyming verse, blank verse, prose. His dramatic method has range, focus, variety, intensity. It is steeped in changefulness and desire for change, a match for his catalyst hero who broods, 'I see a world / That sits upon the cusp of change, waiting',[18] or later asserts 'O great god of normality! If the normal is wrong, you must change it',[19] after clearing the money lenders from the temple precinct, or, later still, preaching on a hill outside Jerusalem, 'The new is here; I have it! show it! give it!'[20] As with Brecht, the aesthetic exposure of dramatic convention subject to change is designed to show that laws, conventions, and even belief, are in man's gift to change.

Morgan has most narrative freedom in 'The Early Years' since there is 'little about his early years in the Bible. You have to imagine the whole thing.' This was exactly the opportunity Morgan needed, 'I was emphasising Jesus the man as an actual person who existed and grew up in Palestine at that time,' he says. 'I had to make it clear that he was fully a man. Many people believe that he was God at the same time, but he was certainly a man.'[21] While 'The Early Years' serves as an exposition to the trilogy as a whole, like each of the plays it also follows its own internal dramatic structure. Act I begins with Jesus at home with his family in Nazareth and Act V ends after his baptism by John the Baptist, alone in the wilderness with Satan.

The first scene can be read as a dramatic development of John Everett Millais's *Christ in the House of His Parents (The Carpenter's Shop)* (1850) and no doubt would have met with the same public vituperation had Morgan not deferred this opportunity for later in his hero's youthful development. Morgan establishes Jesus within a large family structure, his father a builder keen for his sons to join the family business and shocked that his daughter Ruth is the only volunteer. Beyond this comic domestic world in Nazareth, Morgan paints a vivid picture of Palestine as an occupied region in which Roman rule has factionalised the local population where terrorist cells of Zealots (one of them led by Jesus' brother, Jude) plot their overthrow; as a stonemason in Egypt, Jesus encounters the gods of the Nile; from there, the *Bildungsroman* mode takes Jesus, now aged about twenty, to Sepphoris, '*a sophisticated Greco-Roman city four miles from Nazareth*',[22] where he goes to the theatre to see Sophocles' *Antigone*. The diverse religions and histories of the region, brought into fierce competition by the relentless colonial activity of the Romans, are compellingly presented by Morgan in this exposition, forming the political backdrop for the Act III episodes at Sepphoris in which the hero's *Wanderjahre* are focused on his maturation into manhood. Like Prince Hal or young Hamlet, Jesus must 'by indirections find directions out': he encounters brothels, is tempted by men as well as by his hostess Helen, samples cannabis and alcohol, and fathers an illegitimate daughter, Anna. At the close of this act, Jesus soliloquises self-reflexively on the *Bildungsroman* tradition in which this section of the drama is cast:

> Why do I shake? Why am I so troubled?
> What is there in a play that can do this?
> I am so ignorant. I am shown up.
> In the midst of life I find myself in art.
> In the midst of art I find myself in life.
> I have learned something that does not have clarity.
> A world is pressing in on me – Helen,
> Agathon, Sepphoris, but then it's Antigone.
> The hard bright difficult martyred thing
> With a halter, swinging, darkening,
> Deep in a cavern of the darkening State.
> O she is real! Not more than Helen is real,
> But real too in her own word-given way.
> I must think more about the power of words.[23]

The speech foreshadows his future, but also alerts us to the ultimate artifice of the narrative which contains him. His closing soliloquy of 'The Early Years' begins, 'Not clear, but clearer than it was, my way'.[24] While Morgan insisted that his purpose was to draw out the humanity of Jesus, to show him as a man living amongst men, he deploys conventional *Bildungsroman* methods and motifs in order to achieve this.

'The Ministry' opens with the Salome story and it ends with a meditative night scene between Jesus and John. The tone of this last scene is a modulating, deft conclusion to this section of the story, reflecting with wit and compassion once more on the power of words. 'Think of how people use words. Think / There might be armies using sharp-edged iron, / Wars, massacres, in the name of Jesus,' urges John.[25] He lights a Roman lamp, and the men begin to discuss love:

> JESUS: [...] Let us leave massacres
> And talk about love. My mother, Helen, Anna,
> The kingdom of God, though I cannot define it,
> These I love. And you love – men, am I right?
> JOHN: You are.
> JESUS: I always thought so. To me, it is fine,
> But you must know there are some Pharisees
> Who would vote to stone you tomorrow.
> It must be difficult, being that way?
> JOHN: It is, it was, it always will be, Jesus.
> But we survive. You know, there is in love
> A great strength; by it, indeed, we live.
> And love is love, whatever flesh it inhabits.[26]

Gone is the masked approach to forbidden love of *Cyrano*, gone is the torment which punishes the forbidden love of *Phaedra*; instead we hear a foreshadowing echo of Larkin, 'what survives of us is love'. Morgan did not announce his homosexuality until 1990, the year in which he was seventy and the year when Glasgow was European City of Culture. It was a time to assert solidarity with the widespread protest against the 1988 introduction of Section 28, legislation which stated that local councils 'shall not intentionally promote homosexuality or publish material with the intention of promoting homosexuality' or 'promote the teaching in any maintained school of the acceptability of homosexuality as a pretended family relationship'. One of the first actions of the Scottish Parliament was to repeal this legislation on 21 June 2000. In interview on 3 September 2000, Morgan stated that he was 'disappointed and angry' at the recent furore over the abolition of Section 28. 'It reminds you that there's a dark undercurrent in Scotland which can be tapped into and brought up. It's an ancient feeling of prejudice and something that's not good in the

Scottish bloodstream.'[27] Unsurprisingly, Morgan's representation of John's sexuality and Jesus' acceptance of it, months after the repeal, revivified these channels of prejudice and brought condemnation crashing down on the play.

'The Execution' begins and ends with entrancingly strange stichomythic exchange between Nicodemus and Joseph of Arimathea:

> NICODEMUS: He will have darkness.
> JOSEPH: Darkness and pain.
> NICODEMUS: Not to be measured.
> JOSEPH: But not to be lost, whatever the cost.
> NICODEMUS: Black is the water.
> JOSEPH: The bud is in mud.
> NICODEMUS: The lily makes for light.
> JOSEPH: As if there was no night.[28]

We are taken into a metaphysical realm, where the unfolding drama is larger than life, resonant with the future, richly symbolic of the past, and an oblique picture of the present, Scotland in 2000.

The work was condemned before it had even been written. On 10 January 2000 the *Herald* pronounced 'Holy Outcry Over Jesus Play', and Monsignor Tom Connelly, speaking for the Catholic Church in Scotland, said, 'I suspect the producers are trying to make the play more commercial. But I don't think the people of Glasgow will be fooled. In fact I think people will probably boycott the production.' This was echoed by the 'Convener of the Church of Scotland's Board of Social Responsibility, Ann Allan', who

> criticised the new play for cashing in on the basis of Christianity. Mrs Allan said: 'Works of fiction may produce characters with the same names as those in the Bible but in reality they bear no resemblance to the real figures.'

Morgan's distrust of realism as a dramatic method cannot have anticipated this kind of response, but certainly accommodates it. Stuart Davids, director of the commissioned play, felt compelled to defence in the *Sunday Times* on 16 January 2000: '[i]t saddens me that the Churches in Scotland are so keen to condemn a piece of theatre before they have any information about it. Our intention is to produce a new, epic interpretation of the life of Christ.' Protests flared again once the play opened; several

Catholic schools cancelled their workshops with Raindog, and cancelled their bookings for the show. The press grew exercised over the sex, drugs and gay friends in the representation of Jesus' life. Senior churchmen, however, withheld judgement; Richard Holloway, Bishop of Edinburgh, for example, stated:

> I can sympathise with religious outrage but I rarely feel it myself. The mystery of existence and of Jesus and God is far larger than any human expression of it. I'm not personally shocked by any of this but anything to do with sex and Christianity and people lose their common sense. It's sad. Edwin Morgan is a man of compassion and integrity and a deep honesty; he's not going to go out of his way gratuitously to outrage religious sensibilities. This is Scotland's greatest living poet trying to interpret the challenge of Jesus in a contemporary scene. The Jesus story belongs to humanity; it's not the [...] possession of one religious group. I shall make a point now of going to see it.[29]

While the media furore had little to do with the fabric, technique or even the content of the trilogy itself, overlooking, for example, its fine, poetic treatment of significant instances of violence, torture, beheadings and the crucifixion itself, the legion topics of oppression, prejudice and trust stalked large both on stage and off, demonstrating the timeliness of the trilogy. These heated moral arguments also tended to occlude discussion in the press about the production itself. *The Times* offers a rare glimpse:

> Scenes are punctuated by blaring music, which, again, press all the right emotional buttons but seem at odds with the formal poetry of Morgan's text. The first part is the most interesting and deals with Jesus's unrecorded 'lost' years. Here Paul Thomas Hickey's Jesus is a wide-eyed innocent, [... who ...] meets Kate Dickie's Helen, soon to be mother of his daughter. Watching the pair get it on to a Moby soundtrack as angel dust falls, though, is unintentionally crass. As too is Part Two's introduction of the Disciples, who bound on to the refrains of David Bowie's Heroes, striking a cargo-pant clad pose that looks like something out of a Gap ad. And let's not dwell on Salome's amyl nitrate-induced dance. More interesting is Part Two's revelation that John, Jesus's most beloved follower, is gay, and the quietude of their discourse on the nature of love is one of the most effective moments, not least because high-tech tricksiness is absent.[30]

Juxtaposition of style, apparent breach between content, form and delivery, are not alien features of Morgan's work and indeed are familiar aspects of his previous extensive treatment of Christian themes in his verse, much of which was published in *The Second Life* (1968). 'Message Clear', for example, is a typographical puzzle which resolves into the final line 'I am the resurrection and the life'. It begins stuttering and uncertain, conveying a wounded heroism which looks forward to the way his later hero Jesus would grope towards his path, 'am i / i if / i am he / hero / hurt ...';[31] 'Good Friday', a monologue spoken on the bus by a Glaswegian drunk in search of Easter eggs, raises the fundamental question of Christian faith:

> take today, I don't know what today's in aid of,
> whether Christ was – crucified or was he –
> rose fae the dead like, see what I mean?[32]

The effect is a startling shift in perspective which challenges received understanding, not unlike the theatrical collapse of the drawing room in favour of cave or desert. Together, the technique of such poems anticipates the production style adopted by Raindog for this show and may offer microcosmic glimpses into it.

Morgan's last work for the theatre, *The Play of Gilgamesh*, commissioned by Communicado, but unstaged as result of changes in the company, is a remarkable companion piece for *A.D.* It is a pagan old testament to match the new testament of the Trilogy, originating from the kingdom of Sumer (now southern Iraq) around 2700 BC. Miraculously preserved in cuneiform script on clay tablets, it contains primal versions of the story of the Flood, and the poetry of Ecclesiastes, but also wildly exotic creatures and gods, such as Humbaba, guardian of the cedar forest, or Scorpion-Woman, guardian of a mountain pass, encountered on Gilgamesh's doomed quest for immortality. Morgan's treatment, like that of *A.D.*, places a heroic agent of change at the heart of the epic drama: Enkidu the wild green man of the forest who is brought inside the city walls of Uruk to curb the tyranny of its ruler Gilgamesh. 'I have come to change the nature of things'.[33] He challenges Gilgamesh:

> I am no lout, but a free man whom you know,
> Enkidu, come from the wilderness to show
> How soon I mean to change the order of things.

> GILGAMESH (*laughs*): First then you have to take the measure of kings.[34]

The wrestling match which follows, a naked, homoerotic, mythic contest between these figures of legend, marks the beginning of a thoroughgoing transformation. The fight ends in truce, and a close partnership which encompasses sex as well as brotherhood shapes the destiny of Gilgamesh, Endiku and Uruk. Notions of kingship, masculinity, the relationship between ruler and people, and, eventually, the relationship between mortality and immortality, are all reconfigured. 'This friendship between the two men is the backbone of the poem, and the author, whoever he was, pulls out all the stops to make us understand the depth and intensity of the relationship,' writes Morgan in his introduction. 'The word "love" is used; even the word "bride" is used. Does this mean that it is not only the oldest poem in the world but the oldest gay poem in the world?'[35]

Like *A.D.*, *The Play of Gilgamesh* develops existing, if fractured, narrative, but its currency is largely unknown, giving Morgan greater freedom to place his own emphases. Again he deploys a mixed epic style, structured in five acts, ranging through rhyming couplets, and romping through songs of Brechtian commentary such as the wedding song of 'The Transvestites', or 'The Song of the Lesbian Blacksmith', or, sombrely, 'Song of the Death of Young Men'.[36] He also introduces a Glaswegian Jester as Chorus, his tone familiar from the scene changes in pantomime season and welcomed like an old friend in the welter of the script's strangeness:

> See weddins? Waste a money. A thoosan widny cover this yin. Luk at the lassie – Egyptian cotton, Indian silk, drippin wi gold an lapis-lazuli – aye, an it is gold tae, nane a yer tin an a dip [...] Ah canny get merrit masel, it widny dae for the king's jester. State secrets [...] are safe wi me when Ah've gote nae Delilah nor Mata Hari sharing ma pillow.[37]

Apparently merely comic interlude, yet this too, in its keeping of secrets and its stepping out of the reproductive cycle, supports the central theme of the story which is to question 'What lasts, what changes, what survives?'[38] in a world where, as Ziusura the immortal Flood survivor states, 'Midnight comes; kings are clay; men are earth'.[39]

The final scene of the play completes the healing transformations of the quest and is contained entirely by stage directions:

> *The* PRISONERS, *mostly young, of both sexes, stumble out, or preferably up, from the state dungeons. Their chains are struck off. Bewildered at first, they soon realise they are free, and begin to mingle with the crowd. There are recognition scenes* [...]. *It is now night in the city. Gradually the whole movement of the crowd becomes a solemn dance. Music replaces the voices.* [...] *In the flickering light of the torches, the dance slowly comes to a stop, and the now almost motionless people are transformed into a thick, rustling mass of trees. Perhaps there is some birdsong, as long as it is not overdone. Within this forest, light falls on the statue of* ENKIDU, *its dead but living guardian.*[40]

This boldly lyrical dramatic statement demonstrates in the language of the stage the theme of the entire play, summarised succinctly by Ali Smith: '[i]t begins with a very modern-looking tyranny – a random "disappearing" of Uruk's citizens off the streets to state prisons at Gilgamesh's whim. It goes on to examine what it might mean, mortally, to "disappear".'[41]

All of Edwin Morgan's works for the stage shape existing narratives, and of all he states the same ambition, to make them accessible or credible for 'this generation'.[42] One consistent way in which he achieves this is to be uninhibited about anachronism whether in vocabulary or register: 'it's a logo for the Body Shop';[43] 'Nae mair pussyfootin. Ah'm aff, Theramenes' (*Phaedra*); The Seven Deadly Things in his version of *Doctor Faustus* (1999), Thalidomide, Anthrax, Lobotomy, Defoliation, Napalm, Meltdown and Neutron bomb;[44] '"You must change your life," as the poet said';[45] 'the body-bags lie in rows'.[46] This is more than his translator's art, and it comes most fully into focus in his treatment of the life of Jesus in *A.D.* There we find a radical altering of temporal perspective which is achieved through the language of the story, in the way it is told, and its kaleidoscopic vision of culture across time. The Magi who speak the Prologue remember observing an unusually bright star long ago which they were uncertain how to interpret ('I wonder what happened to the boy').[47] The story is only understood in retrospect, and it has to be brought up to the present to achieve retrospection; the perspective of every present will adjust its backward look according to its own light. In *A.D.* this gives the audience a dizzying sense of all time being continuously present; it is the perspective of Milton's God or T. S. Eliot's voice in *Burnt Norton*, 'Time present and time past / Are both perhaps present in time future'. Morgan's favourite poetry saying, stated on his Poetry Archive page, is Shelley's 'Poets are the mirrors of the gigantic shadows which futurity casts upon the present', an epigram which suggests the poet's command over the plasticity of time.[48] T. S. Eliot, writing in 'Tradition and the Individual Talent', argued that

> historical sense compels a man to write not merely with his own generation in his bones, but with a feeling that the whole of the literature of Europe from Homer and within it the whole of the literature of his own country has a simultaneous existence and composes a simultaneous order. This historical sense, which is a sense of the timeless as well as of the temporal and of the timeless and of the temporal together, is what makes a writer traditional. And it is at the same time what makes a writer most acutely conscious of his place in time, of his contemporaneity.[49]

This captures Edwin Morgan's approach to his stage material, and it is a perspective which he conveys to his audiences. His acute awareness of his contemporaneity fashions his epic subjects, and in so doing adjusts the tradition to which his work belongs, reshaping it for the future. All this is done with a generous humility of spirit, captured in the last speech of his last hero:

> I cannot say I am an ordinary king.
> I am not! But I have learned an ordinary thing:
> Whatever good can be done must be done here.[50]

CHAPTER TEN

Into the Twenty-First Century: From Demon to Dream

Hamish Whyte

Works of Edwin Morgan's last decade – *Demon*, *Cathures*, *Love and a Life*, *Tales from Baron Munchausen* and *Dreams and Other Nightmares* (published or co-published by his Scottish publisher Mariscat Press, some collected in Carcanet Press editions) – can be considered among his most original, surprising and challenging accomplishments. Ranging as they do from prehistory to intimate autobiography to outer space, they explore his concerns at this time for 'first and last things: origins, reward and punishment, willpower, strife and striving, and what remains of us'.[1]

In January 1998 Morgan began work on a sequence of twenty poems featuring a 'demon' and finished it a year later. In opposition to the traditional idea of a demon, Morgan's is more life-force than demonic presence, although he does have some destructive, or at least mischievous, qualities. In effect he is yet another of Morgan's ventriloquising time travellers, flitting in and out of light and darkness, good and evil, myth and history, literature and life. Morgan, of course, was known for seeing Satan as the hero of *Paradise Lost*, or at least having the best lines – and there is a passing reference to Milton's poem in 'The Demon Admires the Stars'.[2] Given his long and deep love of Russian literature and art, James McGonigal very plausibly locates the sources for Morgan's demon in the work of the Russian artist Mikhail Vrubel (1856–1910), who used the image of a demon more in the sense of the Greek *daimon*, a divine force for good or evil, one's guiding spirit. Vrubel also illustrated Lermontov's poem 'The Demon'.[3]

Demon was published by Mariscat Press on 1 August 1999, with a striking black and red cover – 'come to the flames', Morgan commented at the time – incorporating the lettering he had used on the title page of his manuscript and depicting a strange rabbit-headed figure over the legend: 'Lege, intellege, iudica': read, understand, judge. 'What is a demon? Study my life.'[4]

Morgan's demon probes, interrogates, antagonises – 'My job is to rattle the bars'.[5] He encounters Frankenstein's monster on the ice floes and a bunch of neds in Argyle Street, flies to Japan, Poland (Auschwitz) and outer space (specifically the star Algol, whose name comes from the Arabic *Ras al Ghul* – 'Demon's Head' – and which is sometimes called the Demon Star). Blake's 'Energy is Eternal Delight' could be the demon's motto – he pushes on, exploring, constantly curious, eager to kill death, to climb the walls of time: 'go / is all I know'.[6]

However, in the middle of the writing of this sequence another kind of demon struck. Morgan had been experiencing some pain and discomfort for a while and in June 1999 he was diagnosed with terminal prostate cancer. The story is now well known of Morgan asking the consultant how long he had and eventually being told it could be six months – or six years. 'Can I have six years, please?' he replied. In fact he outlived the prognosis by five years, thanks to the slow progress of the disease in one of his age (seventy-nine on diagnosis), a strong heart, and an iron will – the demon drove him forward. Having thought about his situation, Morgan said, he knew what he had to do and he was going to do it. 'It', of course, as always, was work. His mind seemed to become even more concentrated, awareness of his surroundings heightened. '[The] diagnosis of cancer hit me with all the shock of the unexpected. I found myself prowling about the house and the surrounding streets, trying to come to terms with it, and finding a release in the writing of poems which were not directly about the cancer but about how my immediate environment and my state of mind interlocked'.[7]

This small group of poems he called his 'intimations of mortality' poems: about clouds, the Anniesland gasometer, rhododendrons, and, most powerful of all, a seagull which perched on his city balcony and fixed him with its 'cold inspection', as an omen, perhaps

> a visitation
> which only used that tight firm forward body
> to bring the waste and dread of open waters,
> foundered voyages, matchless predators,
> into a dry room.[8]

Another way of coping with illness is to read and find out everything there is on the disease, to approach it more directly, but it is quite another thing to turn that research into a work of art, which is what

Morgan did in *Gorgo and Beau*, a dialogue for radio, broadcast in 2003, between a cancer cell and a normal cell. Gorgo, the cancer cell, typically, gets the best lines: 'I stimulate brain matter, / Your mates are virtual clones'.[9]

In that same momentous year of 1999 Morgan was appointed Glasgow's Poet Laureate, a post he held until 2005. The collection he published in 2002, *Cathures* (Carcanet/Mariscat), as well as including *Demon* and the poems just mentioned, contained the first fruits of his laureateship. There is the 'Changing Glasgow' series: fourteen poems ranging over sperm banks, banks as restaurants, magic mushrooms, Cardinal Winning, a recycled hearse, and a tattooed Celtic fan on a bus – Morgan's gimlet eye still alert to the oddities and ordinarinesses of local life.[10] Also included are nine pen portraits of historical and semi-historical characters with connections to Cathures (an old name for Glasgow), the first being the theologian and heretic Pelagius, an appropriate inclusion as his name is apparently a Latinised form of Morgan. This decade is characterised by more self-reflective and self-referential poems than before – understandably. The poem on the balloonist Vincent Lunardi concludes movingly:

> I wonder who will remember Lunardi
> That soared among the clouds and saw below him
> Trongate and Tontine, and the Saracen's Head
> Where he lodged and talked the night into pleasure?
> It is like a dream of the gay times
> That are possible and to be so cherished
> We have a little comfort to be taken
> As the shadows close in. They do, they do.
> It is cold too. Who is that standing in the door?[11]

But this was just the beginning of a mighty decade. When Morgan meant 'work' he really meant it, a prodigious amount of all kinds: plays (*A.D.: A Trilogy on the Life of Jesus*, 2000; *The Play of Gilgamesh*, 2005); translations (*Christopher Marlowe's Doctor Faustus*, 1999; *Jean Racine's Phaedra: A Tragedy*, 2000; *Attila József: Sixty Poems*, 2001; *The Battle of Bannockburn* by Robert Baston, 2004); and of course poems (*New and Selected Poems*, 2002; *Cathures: New Poems 1997–2001*, 2002; *Love and a Life*, 2003; *Tales from Baron Munchausen*, 2005; *A Book of Lives*, 2007; and his last book, *Dreams and Other Nightmares: New and Uncollected Poems 1954–2009*, 2010).

Morgan tried to carry out his usual round of readings, school visits, talks, reviews and interviews, but his decreasing mobility, increasing pain and fear of falling led eventually to the difficult decision to leave his beloved Anniesland flat and move into a care home. Before this, his last major public appearance was to launch the collection *Love and a Life* (published by Mariscat Press) on 27 May 2003 at Borders bookshop in Glasgow, where he held a large (mainly young, and all clutching their copies of the book, bought before the reading) audience rapt with this amazingly frank and revelatory sequence.

These poems had been written very fast, between September and November 2002, Morgan writing nearly every day, as he said, 'with considerable excitement'. He commented later, 'I honestly don't know how I started writing this, but I got very excited about the ideas. There's something about autumn that made me think back and take stock of my life.'[12] The fifty poems (reprinted in *A Book of Lives*, 2007) not only look back on his life, celebrating love in its many guises (and often in intimate physical detail), but unflinchingly face present illness and the future. They are written in 'Cathurian stanzas', the verse form invented by Morgan himself for his series of 'Cathurian Lyrics', short poems on Glasgow, published in *Cathures*. The stanza consists of six lines of variable length (though usually long) with the same rhyming sound, the last line preceded by a couplet of short lines with a different rhyme, i.e. aaaaabba. The mixture of rigour and freedom seems to suit the sequence, allowing a high degree of flexibility, although there is a danger of the long rhyming lines suffering from Ogden-Nashery; indeed a few of them do clunk a little. But that does not detract from the power of the poems. They burst into intimate detail right from the first poem, with its naming of names. Morgan had come out as gay in 1990, which brought with it a new freedom, no need to 'code' love poems as in earlier decades.

Not everyone, however, was bowled over by the new explicitness. The poet and critic Christopher Whyte expressed reservations. He felt that the 'fascinating doubleness' of Morgan's earlier love poems was lost in the more openly confessional ones. 'They are less transgressive. Gay men of Morgan's generation experienced an intensity of repression which gave even the simplest of gestures a stolen quality, as if the impossible had been realised.'[13] But Colin Nicholson finds 'a greater emotional clarity' in the later work.[14] Morgan, as late as 1988, in an interview with Christopher Whyte expressed an apprehension about publishing overtly gay poems[15] and commented, 'Very often your power [as a writer] comes from things that are not in fact declared and open.'[16]

By 2003, having come out and 'the last dragon' at his heels, Morgan threw caution to the winds.

Love and a Life evokes and explores both the living force of remembered love and lovers and a calmer meditation on time and loss and survival. Morgan considers not only love in his own life but love and desire through the ages, from dinosaurs mating to the spiritual love of Teresa of Avila. All of his armoury of poetical tricks and treats are deployed in the sequence: the lists, the apostrophes, the questions, the fizzing alliterations – and the occasional brilliant rhyme, such as anchor/rancour/tanker/lanker/chancre/flanker in 'War Voyage'.[17] The cover illustration of the Mariscat edition of *Love and a Life* is a photograph, taken by Morgan himself, of the view from his window showing the scaffolding and plastic sheeting put up by the workmen who were refurbishing the building during the time he was writing the sequence. The last poem celebrates the end of the work and the taking down of the scaffolding and sums up, with an echo of the first poem, Morgan's position:

> So now that we are so scoured and open and clean, what shall
> we do?
> There is so much to say
> And who can delay
> When some are lost and some are seen, our dearest heads, and to
> those and to these we must still answer and be true.[18]

On 16 February 2004 Morgan was appointed 'Scots Makar' (a term he himself felt was backward-looking, preferring 'National Poet'). The honour was conferred on him by the First Minister, Jack McConnell, in a ceremony at his care home, Lynedoch House in Bearsden. Morgan declared he was going to be no yes-man (although he would have been in the 2014 referendum campaign), but he took the position seriously and wrote a stirring poem for the opening of the new Scottish Parliament. It was read on the day, 9 October 2004, by Liz Lochhead, Morgan being unable to attend. As well as its forward-looking faith in the future, it was full of humour: 'What do the people want of the place? [...] A nest of fearties is what they do not want.'[19]

Morgan's other main commission that year was from Benno Plassmann, an enthusiastic young German director, who had dramatised some of his work previously. This time he wanted to devise a performance piece based on the eighteenth-century soldier Baron Munchausen and his notorious tall tales. He asked Morgan to retell the stories in a way suitable for theatrical performance. The dramatic monologue had long been a favourite mode and he took to the task with relish. He produced twelve 'poetic reconstructions' as he called them and they were published as a pamphlet (by Mariscat Press) to be sold at performances, the first of which – with poetry, music and dancing – was on 11 March 2005 at the Britannia Panopticon Music Hall in Glasgow – an appropriate venue: Stan Laurel first appeared there and it had also been a zoo at one time. Morgan loved this chance to merge the poet and the story-teller to 'make us think about what is real and what is not real, what is possible and what is not possible'.[20] EM became BM. 'It became such a thorough dramatic projection that I felt confident enough to include one tale he *didn't* tell.'[21] A reading of the original tales will reveal the odd one out. The final tale in the series has a typical Morgan ending. The Baron is flying through the air sitting on a cannonball and encounters an eagle

> Shrieking at the usurper of that space
> Between ground and sky, between friend and foe,
> Between the possible and the impossible.
> I shrieked back to the wild bird in my gladness.
> What an unearthly duet – but life, life![22]

Edwin Morgan may have been confined to a room, but there seemed so far to be no constraints on his imagination and poetic power. Things were changing, though. The care home was put up for sale and the residents had to look for other accommodation. This turned out to be no bad thing for him, as a care home was found for him at Broomhill Cross in Glasgow, just along the road from his old flat and with a view of tenements and a busy street – much more Morgan. His flat was sold, his papers went to Glasgow University Library, his books to the Mitchell Library and his paintings to the Hunterian Gallery, as gifts, by previous arrangement.

Also, the progress of the cancer and the strong medication required were affecting Morgan both physically and psychologically, so that after about October 2005 he found himself unable to write any poems. His famous Blue Bird typewriter had finally broken down and his handwriting was almost illegible. However, work of a kind continued – there was a new collection to be put together – the collection that became the award-winning *A Book of Lives*, his last major collection of new poems.

A Book of Lives, published in 2007 (by Carcanet Press), included the above-mentioned poem for the Scottish Parliament, *Gorgo and Beau* and *Love and a Life* as well as the whole of Morgan's short history of the world, *Planet Wave* (the first half of which had been set to music by Tommy Smith and performed at the Cheltenham Jazz Festival, 1997). In between the reprinting of the sequences were some very interesting poems, two at least based on the care home experience: 'An Old Woman's Birthday' (ninety-four and going strong, in the war she had driven 'an ambulance / through shells, ruins, mines, cries, blood, / frightful, days of frightfulness who could forget?')[23] and 'The Old Man and E.A.P.' – the old man, who dreams of Poe, is asked, 'Had a good nap?' and he answers, 'Better than that: / I sprang a tale of mystery and imagination'.[24] The 'sprang' is very Morganesque – the unexpected word that gives you a slight jolt. So much has sprung from the head of Morgan.

Morgan had been asked by a magazine to contribute something on the theme of humiliation (for reasons he could never fathom). He produced a short series of poems (included in *A Book of Lives*) on the Emperor Charles V, Oscar Wilde and Emperor Hirohito, all men brought low – but each surviving in his own way: Wilde asks, 'Decently dressed in the broad arrows / of humiliation, you cannot go wrong, / can you?' Still the questions. It could be thought humiliating for one so previously in control of life and work to be enclosed, having to be looked after – but there are ways to cope, to accept, to transform if not transcend: '[...] we are alive / With whatever equanimity we can muster / As time burns and bites along our veins'.[25] There is another poignancy in his poem 'Boethius', about the man who wrote *The Consolation of Philosophy* while in prison under sentence of death: life reduced to essentials: 'Take a cell, a shirt, a pen. Amen'. But 'Not quite amen. / [...] working through / to a "Yes" at last [...]'.

> There is no such thing as philosophy.
> There is no such thing as consolation.
> Tyrants have lapis lazuli and porphyry.
> Prisoners, the iron and gold of indignation.[26]

The book teems with life and lives – Morgan is as usual everybody and very much himself – another addition to a life of books. The book was a Poetry Book Society Recommendation, was shortlisted for the T. S. Eliot Prize and won the SMIT Scottish Arts Council Book of the Year Award.

But Morgan's own naps were not springing dreams but nightmares of mystery and imagination. At the end of his term as Glasgow's Poet Laureate he had written, in a note to be read out at an event in the Mitchell Theatre on 21 February 2005, marking the handing over of the Laureateship to Liz Lochhead, 'I was asked [...] whether I had got stocked up with new poetic fuel yet? ... All I can say is I have a sense of poems to come, a dim flotilla of forms, a banging of distant doors, a wheeeeistle, a bandolier of pungencies that I must put on and not refuse or be afraid of ... Gather your forces, man! What lies in wait?' He was never going to say 'enough'.

Unfortunately, as his physical frailty increased and his powers of concentration ebbed, the forms, the banging, the pungencies began to visit him, not so much in imagination as in nightmares. Towards the end of 2007 he experienced a series of dreams that were very intense and frightening. He recounted them to his friend and biographer James McGonigal, who took notes, typed up versions for correcting, and between them they transformed the dreams into poems.[27] Typically, as McGonigal recalled, as soon as the dreams had been realised in 'poetic' form, Morgan wanted to get them published. There was a flotilla after all, albeit a small one, and the sequence formed the first part of his final collection, published by Mariscat Press on his ninetieth birthday, 27 April 2010, as *Dreams and Other Nightmares: New and Uncollected Poems 1954–2009*. (Also published that day, jointly by the Scottish Poetry Library and Mariscat Press, and presented to him at a birthday celebration in the Mitchell Library, was a collection of tributes from friends, colleagues and other writers, *Eddie@90*.)

There were seven dreams, though only four made it into print, dealing with, it seemed, key issues in Morgan's life and work: poetry, translation, isolation, sexuality, journeys – all with that recognisable nightmarish undercurrent of fear: fear of forgetting, of getting things wrong, of not understanding. The first, and possibly strangest, dream begins with his familiar trope of the poet looking out of the window of his flat in Anniesland. It is dark but under a lamp he sees a crowd of men and horses and hears the men whispering (the Horseman's Word – which was the title of his 1970 concrete poetry collection) and the clatter of horses' hooves. Then all the lights go out and Morgan is left with the sound of the hooves 'beating, retreating'.[28]

To intrude a personal note, in 1983 Morgan sent me an old postcard of Brodick Fair (he knew I collected Arran ephemera) on which he mentioned that he had been '(re)reading an old favourite, Jocelyn Brooke, now in King Penguin'. Twenty-four years later this seems to resurface in the dream titled 'Arran', in which he meets a man on the island and goes for a walk with him: 'This was like a Jocelyn Brooke novel.'[29] His parents lurk in the background.

The last dream in the sequence, 'Norwegian', imagines him giving a lecture on a Norwegian poet, 'Norway's answer to Robert Burns', whose name he cannot remember and he is annoyed by this, but happily the dream ends on a positive note, offering some kind of resolution:

> What was astonishing in the dream was
> I could recite whole stanzas of his poetry off by heart.
> Lines, images flew from my tongue. I remembered it all,
> astonishing even myself as I slept.[30]

The rest of the collection was made up from uncollected recent poems (i.e. 2000–2005) and uncollected poems covering his writing career from 1954 on, including some unpublished poems from his papers held by the Special Collections Department, Glasgow University Library. They illustrate most aspects of his work: concrete poems, love poems, dramatic monologues, snapshot poems, translations, science fiction poems – a reminder of the amazing multifariousness of the poet. The academic and critic Patrick Crotty has summed up Morgan in one word: 'fertile' – which seems absolutely apt.

The last poem in the collection was summoned up with an effort of will – and help again from the indefatigable James McGonigal – in the last year of his life. It was a commission to contribute to a book of translations by contemporary poets from Anglo-Saxon. Morgan always responded well to commissions. He commented that 'the thing you've been asked to write can creep in at the back door and become your next poem. Like the man who said to Milton, "You've written about Paradise lost, how about Paradise found?"'[31] Morgan chose one of the Exeter Riddles as his contribution:

> Up beyond the universe and back
> Down to the tiniest chigger in the finger –
> I outstrip the moon in brightness,
> I outrun midsummer suns.

I embrace the seas and other waters.
I am fresh and green as the fields I form.
I walk under hell, I fly over the heavens.
I am the land, I am the ocean.
I claim this honour, I claim its worth.
I am what I claim. So, what is my name?[32]

The answer is 'Creation'. Or maybe Morgan.

Endnotes

Introduction: Presence, Process, Prize

1. Edwin Morgan, 'At Eighty', in Robyn Marsack and Hamish Whyte (eds), *Unknown Is Best: A Celebration of Edwin Morgan at Eighty* (Glasgow and Edinburgh: Mariscat Press and Scottish Poetry Library, 27 April 2000), n.p. (p. 5).
2. Morgan, 'At Eighty'.
3. Edwin Morgan, 'On John MacLean', in *Collected Poems* [hereafter, *CP*] (Manchester: Carcanet Press, 1996), pp. 350–51 (p. 351).
4. Walt Whitman, from section 45 of 'Song of Myself', in *Complete Poetry & Selected Prose and Letters*, edited by Emory Holloway (London: The Nonesuch Press, 1938), pp. 77–78.
5. Charles Olson, *Call me Ishmael* (London: Jonathan Cape, 1967), p. 109.
6. Ibid., p. 110.
7. See T. S. Eliot, *The Waste Land: a facsimile & transcript of the original drafts including the annotations of Ezra Pound*, edited by Valerie Eliot (London: Faber and Faber, 2011); Ezra Pound, *The Cantos* (London: Faber and Faber, 1975); Hugh MacDiarmid, *To Circumjack Cencrastus* (first published October 1930), in *The Complete Poems*, Volume I, edited by Michael Grieve and W. R. Aitken (Manchester: Carcanet Press, 1993); the lines from Dante quoted by Olson are also quoted by MacDiarmid here (p. 205), and there are apposite lines that reflect T. S. Eliot's 'Ash Wednesday' (first published April 1930), section VI, where Eliot has: 'And the lost heart stiffens and rejoices / In the lost lilac and the lost sea voices', and MacDiarmid has: 'My hert'll stiffen and rejoice nae mair / In the lost lilac and the lost sea voices' (p. 259); Derek Walcott, 'The Schooner *Flight*', in *The Star-Apple Kingdom* (London: Jonathan Cape, 1980), pp. 3–20, and *Omeros* (New York: Farrar, Straus and Giroux, 1990).

8. Olson, *Call me Ishmael*, p. 110.
9. Morgan, 'The World', in *CP*, pp. 346–48 (p. 346).
10. Edwin Morgan, from 'Mediterranean', in *Collected Translations* [hereafter, *CT*] (Manchester: Carcanet Press, 1996), p. 9.
11. Alan Spence, in *Eddie@90* (Edinburgh: Scottish Poetry Library and Mariscat Press, 2010), p. 80.
12. Morgan, 'Dies Irae', in *CP*, pp. 21–24.
13. Morgan, *Beowulf* (Manchester: Carcanet Press, 2002), lines 130–34, p. 4.
14. Ibid., p. ix.
15. These poems are from *The Second Life* (1968), in *CP*: 'Glasgow Green', pp. 168–69; 'In the Snack-bar', pp. 170–72; 'Linoleum Chocolate', pp. 163–64; 'Trio', pp. 172–73; 'To Joan Eardley', p. 163; 'At Central Station' is in the 'Uncollected Poems (1978–1981)' section of *CP*, pp. 405–06. For 'To Joan Eardley', see also Alan Riach, 'Poetry and Painting: Sketches for an Essay', in Edwin Morgan, *Beyond the Sun: Scotland's Favourite Paintings* (Edinburgh: Luath, 2007), pp. 14–23, where Eardley's painting is reproduced and Morgan's poem is discussed in detail.
16. The author in a personal conversation with Norman MacCaig, *c.*1984.
17. Jean-Pierre Jeunet (director), *Alien: Resurrection* (1997).
18. Morgan, 'The Solway Canal', in *CP*, p. 455.
19. Morgan, 'The Fifth Gospel', in *CP*, pp. 259–60 (p. 259).
20. Edwin Morgan, *A.D.: A Trilogy of Plays on the Life of Jesus* (Manchester: Carcanet Press, 2000), pp. 163–65.
21. Morgan, 'Preface', in *Essays* (Cheadle: Carcanet Press, 1974), [n.p.]: 'CHANGE RULES is the supreme graffito. Gathering up the shards – "performances, assortments, résumés" – can hope perhaps to scatter values through a reticulation that surprises thought rather than traps it.'
22. These poems are from *From Glasgow to Saturn* (1973), in *CP*: 'The Loch Ness Monster's Song', p. 248; 'The Apple's Song', pp. 237–38; 'Hyena', pp. 246–47.
23. Michael Schmidt, *Lives of the Poets* (London: Phoenix, 1999), pp. 911–12.
24. Edwin Morgan, 'Poetry', in *Grafts / Takes* (Glasgow: Mariscat Press, 1983), [*Grafts*], p. 17; reprinted in *Dreams and Other Nightmares: New and Uncollected Poems 1954–2009* (Edinburgh: Mariscat Press, 2010), p. 28.
25. Morgan, 'The Wanderer', in *CT*, pp. 249–51 (p. 249).

26. Morgan, 'Poetry', in op. cit.
27. Morgan, 'Riddle', in *Dreams and Other Nightmares: New and Uncollected Poems 1954–2009* (Edinburgh: Mariscat, 2010), p. 61; Morgan, 'Pelagius', in *Cathures: New Poems 1997–2001* (Manchester: Carcanet Press, 2002), pp. 9–11.

1: The Once and Future Pilot

1. All such references are to Edwin Morgan, *Collected Poems* (Manchester: Carcanet Press, 1996).
2. Letter dated 16 July 1992, in the Edwin Morgan Papers, Department of Special Collections, Glasgow University Library (MS Morgan DP/4).
3. Reprinted in *Nothing Not Giving Messages: Edwin Morgan, reflections on work and life*, ed. Hamish Whyte (Edinburgh: Polygon, 1990), pp. 264–72.
4. For further analysis of the Scrapbooks, see James McGonigal, *Beyond the Last Dragon: A Life of Edwin Morgan* (Dingwall: Sandstone Press, 2012), pp. 40–45; and also James McGonigal and Sarah Hepworth, 'Ana, Morgana, Morganiana: A Poet's Scrapbooks as Emblems of Identity', *Scottish Literary Review* 4.2 (Autumn/Winter 2012), pp. 1–23.
5. Edwin Morgan, *Hugh MacDiarmid* (Harlow: Longman Group for The British Council, 1976), p. 32. The quotation is from Shelley's *A Defence of Poetry*.
6. 'The Translation of Poetry', *Nothing Not Giving Messages*, pp. 232–35. Originally in *Scottish Review* 2.5 (Winter 1976).
7. Edwin Morgan Papers, Department of Special Collections, Glasgow University Library (MS Morgan V/3/1).
8. Preface to the paperback reissue of his *Beowulf* (Manchester: Carcanet Press, 2002).
9. See Chris Jones, *Strange Likeness: The Use of Old English in Twentieth-Century Poetry* (Oxford: Oxford University Press, 2006); and also Chris Jones, 'While Crowding Memories Came: Edwin Morgan, Old English and Nostalgia', *Scottish Literary Review* 4.2 (Autumn/Winter 2012), pp. 123–44.
10. Holograph poem is dated 30 December 1963–1 January 1963 in the Edwin Morgan Papers, Department of Special Collections, Glasgow University Library (MS Morgan, P/1/260).
11. This paragraph is itself pieced partly from sentences in my introductory study *The Poetry of Edwin Morgan* Scotnote, second edition (Glasgow: Association for Scottish Literary Studies, 2013), p. 59.

12. The notebooks with other memorabilia are now in the Department of Special Collections, Glasgow University Library, and descriptions of these trips in *Beyond the Last Dragon: A Life of Edwin Morgan* are based partly on them: Russia pp. 105–08; Hungary pp. 175–81; Turkey pp. 259–60; United States pp. 226–28.
13. Hungarian notebook. No pagination, but pp. 8–9.
14. The key text here is 'The Beatnik in the Kailyard' (1962), reprinted in Edwin Morgan, *Essays* (Cheadle: Carcanet Press, 1974), pp. 166–76. It is referred to by several contributors to Eleanor Bell and Linda Gunn, eds, *The Scottish Sixties: Reading, Rebellion, Revolution?* (Amsterdam/New York: Rodopi, 2013): Corey Gibson, Margery Palmer McCulloch, James McGonigal and Roderick Watson.
15. Turkish notebook. No pagination, but p. 10.
16. See *Beyond the Last Dragon: A Life of Edwin Morgan*, pp. 259–60.

2. Edwin Morgan's Scrapbooks

1. There are sixteen Scrapbooks. The first two, begun in 1931, were rearranged from earlier jotters in 1937; the last, described by Morgan as unfinished, goes up to 1966. Morgan deposited the Scrapbooks in Glasgow University Library's Special Collections: MS Morgan C/1–16.
2. For STV's *Off the Page* in 1989; the first part of the interview is available online at www.youtube.com/watch?v=cgeGIRzQD40 and the second at news.stv.tv/scotland/76519-off-the-page-edwin-morgan-part-2/
3. www.gla.ac.uk/services/specialcollections/virtualexhibitions/edwinmorganscrapbooks/
4. Morgan mentions these briefly as tiny figures from physique and cinema magazines that 'seemed worth putting in' in the interview with Donny O'Rourke.
5. James McGonigal and Sarah Hepworth, 'Ana, Morgana, Morganiana: A Poet's Scrapbooks as Emblems of Identity', *Scottish Literary Review* 4.2 (Autumn/Winter 2012), pp. 1–23.
6. The phrase 'kilted in Kiev' which McGonigal invokes took on a new resonance in 2014. Like all art the Scrapbooks infinitely renew themselves.
7. James McGonigal, *Beyond the Last Dragon: A Life of Edwin Morgan* (Dingwall: Sandstone Press, 2010), p. 83. 'Women and Poetry', *Cambridge Journal* 3.2 (August 1950), pp. 643–73.
8. 'Strong Lines and Strong Minds: Reflections on the Prose of Browne and Johnson', *Cambridge Journal* 4.8 (May 1957), pp. 481–91.

9. Letter to W. S. Graham, 30 April 1950, Glasgow University Library, MS Morgan D/G10.
10. 'A Hantle of Howlers', *Twentieth Century* (December 1956–January 1957); reprinted in Edwin Morgan, *Essays* (Cheadle: Carcanet Press, 1974), pp. 255–76.
11. 'A Glimpse of Petavius', *Gambit: Edinburgh University Review* (Summer 1963); reprinted in Edwin Morgan, *Essays* (Cheadle: Carcanet Press, 1974), pp. 3–15.
12. 'Three Views of Brooklyn Bridge', *Akros* 3.9 (January 1969); reprinted in Edwin Morgan, *Essays* (Cheadle: Carcanet Press, 1974).
13. X. J. Kennedy, 'The Devalued Estate', *Poetry* 114.4 (July 1969).
14. www.bbc.co.uk/education/guides/zvyqtfr/revision/1
15. Veronica Forrest-Thomson, *Poetic Artifice: a Theory of Twentieth-Century Poetry* (Manchester: Manchester University Press, 1978), p. 162.
16. 'A Trio', *The Second Life*, 1968.
17. 'Stobhill', *From Glasgow to Saturn*, 1973.
18. Of course, he accepted the honours of the United Kingdom – an OBE and the Queen's Gold Medal for Poetry – but that was a long way in the future.
19. The term is used by Barbara Everett to describe the effects of Cleopatra's dying speech, Introduction, *Antony and Cleopatra* (Signet Classics).
20. *Unfinished Poems* in *The New Divan* is a sequence (the quoted lines are from the ninth poem) dedicated to Veronica Forrest-Thomson, who died in tragic circumstances in 1975 at the age of twenty-seven.

3. Full Flourish: Major Collections of the 1960s and 1970s

1. Edwin Morgan, *Collected Poems* (Manchester: Carcanet Press, 1990), pp. 349–50. Hereafter all references to this edition are incorporated into the text in the form *CP*.
2. John Ashbery, *Some Trees* (New Haven: Yale University Press, 1956), p. 6.
3. Reginald Shepherd, 'Only in the Light of Lost Words Can We Imagine Our Rewards: *Some Trees*', *Conjunctions* 49 (Fall 2007). www.conjunctions.com accessed 21 February, 2014. Shepherd refers to Baudelaire's famous sonnet 'Correspondances', which I quote from here in my translation.
4. Gilles Deleuze and Felix Guattari, *A Thousand Plateaus*, trans. Brian Massumi (London: Bloomsbury, 2013 [1980]), p. 15. Further references are given in the text.

5. *Nothing Not Giving Messages*, edited by Hamish Whyte (Edinburgh: Polygon, 1990), p. 22. Hereafter references are incorporated in the text in the form *NNGM*.
6. James McGonigal and John Coyle (eds), *The Midnight Letterbox: Edwin Morgan, Selected Correspondence 1950–2010* (Manchester: Carcanet Press, 2015), p. 143
7. MS Morgan.
8. John Emil Vincent, *Queer Lyrics: Difficulty and Closure in American Poetry* (New York: Palgrave, 2002), p. 61.
9. www.britannica.com/hafiz
10. David Kinloch, 'The Case of the Missing War: Edwin Morgan's "The New Divan"', *Scottish Literary Review* 4.2 (Autumn/Winter 2012), pp. 85–104.
11. D. Smith and J. Protevi, 'Gilles Deleuze' in *The Stanford Encyclopaedia of Philosophy* (Autumn 2008 edn), ed. Edward N. Zalta plato.stanford.edu/archives/fall2008/entries/deleuze/.
12. Jon Clay, *Sensation, Contemporary Poetry and Deleuze* (London: Continuum, 2010), p. 19.
13. Kinloch, pp. 85–104, passim.
14. Rosemary Waldrop, *Against Language?* (Mouton: The Hague, 1971).
15. Edwin Morgan, 'Language, poetry and language poetry', *The Kenneth Allott Lectures* (Liverpool Classical Monthly, Department of Classics and Archaeology, 1990), p. 10.
16. Colin Nicholson, *Edwin Morgan: Inventions of Modernity* (Manchester: Manchester University Press, 2002), p. 69.
17. Edwin Morgan, *Collected Translations* (Manchester: Carcanet Press, 1996), p. 74.
18. Kinloch, p. 97ff.
19. Sarah Ahmed, *Queer Phenomenology* (Durham: Duke University Press, 2006), p. 67.
20. Michael Warner, *The Trouble with Normal: Sex, Politics and the Ethics of Queer Life* (Cambridge, MA: Harvard University Press, 1999), p. 179.
21. Eleanor Bell, 'Experimenting with the Verbivocovisual: Edwin Morgan's Early Concrete Poetry', *Scottish Literary Review* 4.2 (Autumn/Winter 2012), p. 115.
22. Waldrop, p. 25.
23. See this chapter, p. 43.
24. Edwin Morgan, 'MacDiarmid at 75' in *Crossing the Border: Essays on Scottish Literature* (Manchester: Carcanet, 1990), pp. 205–12 (p. 211).

4. Edwin Morgan's Poetry from Scotland

1. *Cencrastus* 38 (Winter 1990–91), 'Editorial', Raymond Ross.
2. Quoted in James McGonigal, *Beyond the Last Dragon: A Life of Edwin Morgan* (Dingwall: Sandstone Press, 2010), p. 456.
3. McGonigal, pp. 431–32.
4. McGonigal, pp. 409–10.
5. *Raster* (Amsterdam) (Autumn 1970), 'Open Letter to All Hyperboreans', p. 268.
6. Kenneth White, *Open World: The Collected Poems 1960–2000* (Edinburgh: Polygon, 2003), p. 21.
7. *Scottish International* 2 (April 1968), p. 2.
8. *The Voice of Scotland* 2.2, p. 29.
9. Ibid., 6.3, p. 3; 6.4, p. 3.
10. *Scottish International* (October 1971), p. 17.
11. Ibid.
12. Ibid., 6.4 (April 1973), p. 3.
13. Ibid., 6.5 (May–June–July 1973), p. 15.
14. Ibid., 'What Kind of Scotland?', p. 11.
15. Ibid., 6.4 (April 1973), p. 7.
16. Ibid., p. 8.
17. Michael Grieve and W. R. Aitken (eds), *Complete Poems of Hugh MacDiarmid* (London: Martin Brien and O'Keefe, 1978), Vol. II, p. 1040.
18. *Scottish International* 1 (January 1968), p. 21.
19. Ibid., pp. 24–25.
20. Ibid., p. 25.
21. This is the burden, for instance, of David Craig's *Scottish Literature and the Scottish People, 1680–1830*, of which Morgan writes in 1971: 'a mixture of Leavis and Marx that might seem to be unholy has worked in fact surprisingly well to produce a serious study of an important period in Scottish life and writing'; despite being 'refreshingly non-parochial, well-documented', it is 'yet at times rather wilfully unsympathetic' (*CB*, 11). 'Unholy' may not have been intended as a pun but Morgan is effectively turning back on Craig the accusation that Scotland was 'un-whole'.
22. *Scottish International*, 1 (January 1968), p. 3.
23. Colin Nicholson, *Poem, Purpose and Place: Shaping Identity in Contemporary Scottish Verse* (Edinburgh: Polygon, 1992), p. 76.

24. Colin Nicholson, p. 76.
25. Edgar Allan Poe, *Prose Tales* (Boston: Dana Estes and Co., n.d.), p. 14.

5. Cold War Morgan

1. See Brian Jamison (ed.), *Scotland and the Cold War* (Dunfermline: Cualann Press, 2003).
2. Alan Dobson, 'Operation Lamachus: The Holy Loch US Nuclear Base and the Dangers of Local Radiation Pollution', in *Military Bases: Historical Perspectives, Contemporary Challenges*, ed. L. Rodrigues and S. Glebov (Amsterdam: IOS Press, 2009), pp. 29–39 (p. 29). The MP for Greenock, Dickson Mabon, raised concerns about radiation pollution in December 1961, from liquid spillage, gamma rays from the hull, iodine gas clouds, and the *Glasgow Herald* buzzed with controversy and counterclaim (Dobson, 34).
3. Robbie Dinwoodie, 'When Polaris arrived, the key question was still unanswered', *Herald* (2 January 1992).
4. 'SSP: FB101 – UK SSP: The British Strategic Systems Programs', Strategic Systems Programme website of the American Navy: www.ssp.navy.mil/fb101/ukssp.shtml (Accessed 3 Feb. 2014): '[*Resolution*] visited Cape Canaveral in February and early March 1968, where both Port and Starboard crews successfully launched a Polaris A3 missile into a downrange target area. HMS *Resolution* made her first deterrent patrol in June 1968. HMS *Renown* was launched in February 1967, HMS *Repulse* in November 1967, and HMS *Revenge* in March 1968.'
5. 'Boats and Places', in *Collected Poems* (Manchester: Carcanet Press, 1990), p. 175.
6. Herbert Kritzer, 'The Military as a Target of Protest', reprint from Gandhi Marg, 1973, Gandhi Peace Foundation: users.polisci.wisc.edu/kritzer/research/protest/GandhiMarg73.pdf (Accessed 15 Feb. 2014).
7. Edwin Morgan, *The Whittrick: A Poem in Eight Dialogues*, in *Collected Poems*, pp. 77–116 (p. 112).
8. 'The Nuclear Tanker', *Time*, Monday, 17 March 1958.
9. Grey's two technicians in the poem, Roddy and Eck, discuss this: '*Roddy* How's the atomic, eh? *Eck* The ba'ery? Fine, fine' (113).
10. H. J.Dunster, quotation from abstract of 'The Disposal of Radioactive Liquid Wastes into Coastal Waters', 31 October 1959. www.osti.gov/scitech/servlets/purl/4264290.

11. W. Grey Walter, *The Curve of the Snowflake* (New York: Norton, 1956), p. 86.
12. In 2056, they have machines called Panphans, which tests out ideas stochastically, aiming at 'a flock of possible verbal meanings and chases the one it brings down as far as it can – it sort of thinks aloud for you' (*Curve of the Snowflake*, p. 159). This matches the Whittrick robot's programming 'with great faith in the logic of choice, to find / The end in every beginning' (*The Whittrick: A Poem in Eight Dialogues*, p. 114). The letter from the future is written in a simple code too, which may have motivated Morgan's line about poets speaking in code.
13. Colin Nicholson, *Edwin Morgan: Inventions of Modernity* (Manchester: Manchester University Press, 2002), p. 92.
14. Edwin Morgan, 'Dunbar and the Language of Poetry', *Essays in Criticism* 2.2 (1952), pp. 138–58 (p. 138).
15. In *Beyond Scotland: New Contexts for Twentieth-century Scottish Literature*, ed. Gerald Carruthers, David Goldie and Alastair Renfrew (Amsterdam: Rodopi, 2004), pp. 95–109.
16. 'From Cathkin Braes: a View of Korea', in *Collected Poems*, pp. 570–71.
17. Printed in *New Selected Poems* (Manchester: Carcanet Press, 2000), p. 165.

6. Morgan and the City

1. Henri Lefebvre, *Qu'est-que penser?* (1985), quoted in Mary O'Connor and Katherine Tweedie, *Seduced by Modernity: The Photography of Margaret Watkins* (Montreal: McGill-Queen's University Press, 2007), p. 229. Watkins was living in Glasgow and photographing the city in the 1930s and 1940s, and also worked in Russia in the early 1930s; Morgan would have been fascinated by her photographs, but she had become a recluse by the 1950s. She died in 1969 and her work was not rediscovered for many years.
2. Interview with Marshall Walker, reprinted in Hamish Whyte (ed.), *Nothing Not Giving Messages* (Edinburgh: Polygon, 1990), p. 81.
3. Irene Maver, *Glasgow* (Edinburgh: Edinburgh University Press, 2000), p. 204.
4. Ibid., p. 253.
5. Ibid., p. 204.
6. Interview with Robert Crawford, reprinted in Hamish Whyte (ed.), *Nothing Not Giving Messages*, p. 120.
7. 'Glasgow', in Edwin Morgan, *Dreams and Other Nightmares: New and Uncollected Poems 1954–2009* (Edinburgh: Mariscat Press, 2010), p. 33.

8. James McGonigal, *Beyond the Last Dragon: A Life of Edwin Morgan* (Dingwall: Sandstone Press, 2010), p. 54.
9. Edwin Morgan, 'Flying with Tatlin, Clouds in Trousers: a Look at Russian Avant-Gardes', in Gerard Carruthers, David Goldie and Alastair Renfrew (eds), *Beyond Scotland, New Contexts for Twentieth-century Scottish Literature* (Amsterdam/New York: Rodopi, 2004), p. 96. He had come across 'the multilingual Russian propagandist magazine *USSR in Construction*' when he was twelve, in 1932.
10. Interview with Robert Crawford, reprinted in Hamish Whyte (ed.), *Nothing Not Giving Messages*, pp. 124–25. In the interview with W. N. Herbert, Morgan mentions Attila József as another influence in the early 1950s, 'a poetry of such deep urban pathos and concern ... Budapest and Glasgow!' Ibid., p. 115.
11. Morgan, 'Flying with Tatlin ...', pp. 96–97.
12. He regretted the disappearance of the word 'railplane' ('once familiar, but now only to be found in the best dictionaries') as well as the machine.
13. 'Tram-Ride, 1939 (F.M.)', in *Hold Hands Among the Atoms*, reprinted in *Sweeping Out the Dark* (Manchester: Carcanet Press, 1994), p. 76.
14. Hamish Whyte (ed.), *Nothing Not Giving Messages*, p. 253.
15. Interview with Marshall Walker, in Hamish Whyte (ed.), *Nothing Not Giving Messages*, p. 68.
16. 'Night Pillion' was first published in *Saltire Review* in 1957, picked by Hamish Whyte for his anthology *Noise and Smoky Breath ... Glasgow Poems 1900–1983* (Glasgow: Third Eye Centre/Glasgow District Libraries Publications Board, 1983), and then collected in *Selected Poems* (1985) and finally *Collected Poems* (Manchester: Carcanet Press, 1990), p. 461.
17. Irene Maver, *Glasgow*, pp. 262–63.
18. James McGonigal, *Beyond the Last Dragon*, p. 41.
19. Malcolm Bradbury, 'The Cities of Modernism', in Malcolm Bradbury and James McFarlane (eds), *Modernism* (Harmondsworth: Penguin Books, 1976), pp. 99–100.
20. Greg Thomas, 'Concrete Poetry in England and Scotland 1962–75: Ian Hamilton Finlay, Edwin Morgan, Dom Sylvester Houédard and Bob Cobbing' (thesis submitted for the degree of Doctor of Philosophy, University of Edinburgh, September 2013), Chapter 4, p. 184. See also Thomas, 'The Tower of Babel: concrete poetry in England and Scotland', in Nicole Sierra and Terri Mullholland (eds), *Spatial Perspectives: Essays on Literature and Architecture* (Oxford: Peter Lang, forthcoming).

21. This block is interestingly located opposite Kelvin Court (1937–38), a block of luxury flats which architectural historians have described as 'almost unique in Glasgow, would be quite at home on one of London's arterial roads', and along from 'Glasgow's last super-suburban cinema, the Ascot (now County Bingo), with its monumental tiled semicircular towers (1938–39)' (Elizabeth Williamson, Anne Riches and Malcolm Higgs, *Glasgow* (London: Penguin Books/NTS, 1990), p. 395). The cinema opened in 1939 with Gracie Fields in *Shipyard Sally*, and was closed in 1975. The auditorium was demolished in 2001, but the art deco façade was retained and apartments built behind it, completed in October 2003, just as Morgan left Whittinghame Court for a care home.
22. Interview with W. N. Herbert, reprinted in Hamish Whyte (ed.), *Nothing Not Giving Messages*, p. 114.
23. In *Noise and Smoky Breath*, Whyte remarks of this group that they are the poems '(by which he is still unfortunately best known – at least in schools)', describing 'In the Snack-bar' as 'over-anthologised' (p. 161). Scottish school pupils are still studying these in 2014.
24. Indeed the architectural historian Charles McKean says that 'by 1914 Glasgow had possibly the most American-like city centre in Europe: grid-iron streets surged up and down hills faced by ever taller red stone-faced commercial buildings. Between the wars that resemblance was intensified in large commercial buildings or banks, principally either at the western edge of the city centre or in the Merchant City.' www.theglasgowstory.com/story.php?id=TGSEF06, accessed 2 April 2014.
25. 'Three Views of Brooklyn Bridge', reprinted in Edwin Morgan, *Essays* (Cheadle Hulme: Carcanet New Press, 1974), p. 43.
26. For Morgan's comparison of Glasgow, Edinburgh and the US, see the interview with Christopher Whyte in Hamish Whyte (ed.), *Nothing Not Giving Messages*, pp. 182–83.
27. He was never a fan of Edinburgh. See also Kasia Boddy, 'Edwin Morgan's Adventures in Calamerica', *Yale Journal of Criticism*, 13.1 (Spring 2000), pp. 177–94.
28. Morgan is referring to the presence of the nuclear submarine base at Faslane, twenty-five miles west of Glasgow; the British government had negotiated throughout the 1960s with the US government to obtain its Polaris system for the submarines.
29. Hamish Whyte (ed.), *Nothing Not Giving Messages*, p. 262.
30. Morgan, *Glasgow Sonnets x*, in *Collected Poems*, p. 292.

31. Morgan, 'Flying Clouds ...', p. 96. 'We are not even having a sit-in strike. Nobody and nothing will come in and nothing will go out without our permission. And there will be no hooliganism, there will be no vandalism, there will be no bevvying because the world is watching us, and it is our responsibility to conduct ourselves with responsibility, and with dignity, and with maturity.' en.wikipedia.org/wiki/Jimmy_Reid, accessed 2 April 2014.
32. Hamish Whyte (ed.), *Nothing Not Giving Messages*, p. 192.
33. Quoted in James McGonigal, *Beyond the Last Dragon*, p. 215.
34. Ian Jack, 'The Repackaging of Glasgow', *Before the Oil Ran Out: Britain 1977–87* (London: Flamingo, 1988), p. 201.
35. Hamish Whyte (ed.), *Noise and Smoky Breath*, p. 11.
36. Michael Pacione, *Glasgow: The Socio-Spatial Development of the City* (Chichester: John Wiley, 1995), p. 250.
37. Ibid., p. 237.
38. Tom Leonard, *Two Members' Monologues and A Handy Form for Artists for use in connection with the City of Culture* (Glasgow: The Edward Polin Press, 1989), p. 10.
39. Edwin Morgan, 'Glasgow Speech in Recent Scottish Literature', reprinted in *Crossing the Border: Essays on Scottish Literature* (Manchester: Carcanet Press, 1990), p. 324.
40. Interview with Christopher Whyte, in Hamish Whyte (ed.), *Nothing Not Giving Messages*, pp. 162–63.
41. Quoted by James McGonigal, *Beyond the Last Dragon*, p. 275.
42. Quoted in Robert Crawford and Hamish Whyte (eds), *About Edwin Morgan* (Edinburgh: Edinburgh University Press, 1990), A46, p. 158.
43. Interview with Christopher Whyte, in Hamish Whyte (ed.), *Nothing Not Giving Messages*, p. 161.
44. Robyn Marsack and Hamish Whyte (eds), *From Saturn to Glasgow: 50 Favourite Poems by Edwin Morgan* (Edinburgh/Manchester: Scottish Poetry Library/Carcanet Press, 2008), p. 7.
45. London was the subject of several poems, and his riff on Soho – 'no mean city of night prophylactic burgess anomalies / Johnson & Johnson john o'hara john calder judo spillane karate ...' – suggests that there is no end to the actual and verbal possibilities the city dangles before the observer ('London', in *Collected Poems*, p. 251). A late sequence, *Planet Wave* (collected in *A Book of Lives*, 2007), includes poems on 'The Siege of Leningrad' and 'The Twin Towers'.
46. Letter to Nicholas Zurbrugg, 25 September 1967: 'Again there is a great range of effects in concrete poetry from "warm" to "cold" [...]

I myself incline to the "warm" rather than the "cold" end, but I recognise that there are other points of view.' (University of Glasgow Library, Special Collections, MS Moragn DZ/1). I am indebted to James McGonigal for this reference.

7. Edwin Morgan and European Modernism

1. Edwin Morgan, 'Gavin Douglas and William Drummond as Translators', in A. J. Aitken, M. P. McDiarmid and D. S. Thomson (eds), *Bards and Makars* (Glasgow: University of Glasgow Press, 1977), p. 198.
2. Peter McCarey, 'Edwin Morgan the Translator', in Robert Crawford and Hamish Whyte (eds), *About Edwin Morgan* (Edinburgh: Edinburgh University Press, 1990), p. 94.
3. Edwin Morgan, 'Afterword', in Sándor Weöres, *Eternal Moment: Selected Poems*, ed. by Miklós Vajda, trans. by Edwin Morgan, William Jay Smith *et al.* (London: Anvil, 1988), p. 147.
4. Edwin Morgan, 'Afterword' (1988), p. 147.
5. Marco Fazzini, 'Edwin Morgan: Two Interviews', in G. Ross Roy (ed.), *Studies in Scottish Literature* 29 (Columbia: University of South Carolina, 1996), pp. 53–54.
6. Edwin Morgan, 'The Translation of Poetry', *Scottish Review* 2.5 (1976), pp. 18–23 (p. 23).
7. Ibid.
8. Ibid.
9. Edwin Morgan, 'Translations from the French', *Studies in Scottish Literature* 35–36, ed. by G. Ross Roy (2007), pp. 464–67.
10. Stephanie Schwerter, *Northern Irish Poetry and the Russian Turn: Intertextuality in the Work of Seamus Heaney, Tom Paulin and Medbh McGuckian* (New York and Basingstoke: Palgrave Macmillan, 2013).
11. Seamus Heaney, *The Government of the Tongue* (London: Faber, 1988), p. 41; also cited in Stephanie Schwerter, *Northern Irish Poetry*, p. 10.
12. Edwin Morgan and Alasdair Clayre, *East European Poets – Poets in Public* (Milton Keynes: Open University Press, 1977), p. 8.
13. Cited in Morgan and Clayre, *East European Poets*, p. 8.
14. Heaney, *The Government of the Tongue*, p. xix; also cited in Stephanie Schwerter, *Northern Irish Poetry*, p. 12.
15. Morgan and Clayre, *East European Poets*, pp. 8–9.
16. Colin Nicholson, *Edwin Morgan: Inventions of Modernity* (Manchester: Manchester University Press, 2002), p. 6.
17. Eugenio Montale, *Collected Poems 1920–1954*, trans. and annotated by Jonathan Galassi (New York: Farrar, Straus and Giroux, 1998), p. 418.

18. Ibid., p. 461.
19. Ibid., p. 540.
20. Morgan, 'The Translation of Poetry', p. 21, also in James McGonigal, *Beyond the Last Dragon: A Life of Edwin Morgan* (Dingwall: Sandstone Press, 2010) p. 114 (referred to in the chapter as *BTLD*) and (worded slightly differently) in *CT* 3.
21. Éanna Ó Ceallacháin, *Eugenio Montale: The Poetry of the Later Years* (Oxford: Legenda, 2001), p. 174.
22. William Jay Smith, 'A Candle in the Window: The Poetry of Sándor Weöres', *American Poetry Review* 17.2 (1988), p. 33.
23. Shona M. Allan, 'Responding, Rewording and/or Resisting', in Adrian Graefe and Jessica Stephens (eds), *Lines of Resistance: Essays on British Poetry from Thomas Hardy to Linton Kwesi Johnson* (Jefferson, NC: McFarland, 2012), pp. 179–93 (p. 186).
24. Edwin Morgan, Scrapbook Three (1936–1953), MS Morgan C/3, p. 54.
25. 'Hungarian poet Sándor Weöres talking about the post-historic human being', www.youtube.com/watch?v=01gkjyo8nVM [accessed 20 May 2014].
26. Nicholson, *Edwin Morgan: Inventions of Modernity*, p. 66.
27. For an analysis of Mayakovsky's agitprop work, see George Bournoutian, 'The Arts in Post-Revolutionary Russia: The Posters of Vladimir Mayakovsky', in David Castriota (ed.), *Artistic Strategy and the Rhetoric of Power: Political Uses of Art from Antiquity to the Present* (Carbondale: Southern Illinois University Press, 1986), pp. 115–20.
28. On Morgan's decision to translate Mayakovsky into Scots, see Nicholson, *Edwin Morgan: Inventions of Modernity*, pp. 66–75.
29. George Reavey translates the title as 'An extraordinary adventure which befell Vladimir Mayakovsky in a summer cottage'; see Vladimir Mayakovsky, *The Bedbug and Selected Poetry*, trans. by Max Hayward and George Reavey (Bloomington: Indiana University Press, 1960), p. 137.
30. W. D. Williams, 'August von Platen', in Alex Natan (ed.), *German Men of Letters*, vol. 5 (London: Wolff, 1969), p. 138.
31. S. S. Prawer, *German Lyric Poetry* (London: Routledge & Kegan Paul, 1965), p. 159.
32. Compare Hugh MacDiarmid's 'Third Hymn to Lenin': 'Unlike the pseudos I am *of* – not *for* – the working class'. Michael Grieve and W. R. Aitken (eds), *The Complete Poems of Hugh MacDiarmid*, vol. 2 (Harmondsworth: Penguin, 1985), p. 900.

33. Attila József, *Sixty Poems*, trans. by Edwin Morgan (Glasgow: Mariscat, 2001), p. 42.
34. József, *Sixty Poems*, p. 50.
35. Peter Sherwood, Review of *Attila József. Leben und Werk*, in *Modern Language Review* 77.3 (1982), p. 768.
36. Tom Hubbard, 'Doing Something Uncustomary: Edwin Morgan and Attila József', *International Journal of Scottish Literature* 1 (2006), p. 6 [online PDF version].
37. Ibid., p. 3.
38. Ibid., p. 6.
39. József, *Sixty Poems*, p. 38.

8. Concrete Realities

1. I am indebted to James McGonigal, David Kinloch, Virna Teixiera and Silke Strohe for their valuable advice in the writing of this chapter (though all infelicities remain my own) and to the Director and staff of the Centro de Referência Haroldo de Campos in São Paulo, Brazil, for help in searching the archives there. I am also grateful to the University of Macau for allowing me research leave to visit the archive.
2. The Scottish contribution to this tradition is anthologised in K. Cockburn and A. Finlay (eds), *The Order of Things: An Anthology of Scottish Sound, Pattern and Concrete Poems* (Edinburgh: Polygon, 2001).
3. W. Bohn, *Reading Visual Poetry* (Lanham: Fairleigh Dickinson University Press, 2010).
4. See A. de Campos, 'poesia concreta' (1955), reprinted in A. de Campos, D. Pignatari and H. de Campos, *Teoria da Poesia Concreta: textos, críticos e manifestos 1950–1960*, 4th edn (Cotia, SP: Ateliê Editorial, 2006), pp. 55–57; also M. E. Solt, (ed.), *Concrete Poetry: A World View* (Bloomington: Indiana University Press, 1970). An online version of the latter is available at www.ubu.com/papers/solt/
5. Reprinted in A. de Campos, D. Pignatari and H. de Campos, *Teoria*, pp. 215–18.
6. See www.ubu.com/papers/
7. See E. Bell, 'Experimenting with the verbivocovisual: Edwin Morgan's early concrete poetry', *Scottish Literary Review* 4.2 (2012), pp. 105–21.
8. M. McLuhan and Q. Fiore, 'The medium is the message', *New York* 123 (1967), pp. 126–28.
9. Much of the biographical detail is taken from J. McGonigal, *Beyond*

the Last Dragon: A Life of Edwin Morgan (Dingwall: Sandstone Press, 2010) [reprinted with additional material, 2012].

10. See H. de Campos, 'Ideograma, anagrama, diagrama: una lectura de Fenollosa', in H. De Campos (ed.), *Ideograma: lógica, poesia, linguagem*, 4th edn (Sao Paulo: EdUSP, 1994 [1977]), pp. 23–108, and J. McGonigal, 'Keeping it Concrete: Edwin Morgan in the Sixties', *PN Review* 214, 40.2 (Nov.–Dec. 2013), pp. 43–48.
11. Cited in T. Neat, *Hamish Henderson, Vol. 2: Poetry Becomes People (1952–2002)* (Edinburgh: Birlinn, 2009), p. 174.
12. See R. Watson, 'Scottish Poetry: the Scene and the Sixties', and J. McGonigal, 'Edwin Morgan, Hugh MacDiarmid and the Direction of the MacAvantgarde', in E. Bell and L. Gunn (eds), *The Scottish Sixties: Reading, Rebellion, Revolution?* (Amsterdam: Rodopi, 2013), pp. 69–92; 115–34.
13. Watson, pp. 75–75, 90n.
14. A. Bartie and E. Bell (eds), *The International Writers Conference Revisited: Edinburgh, 1962* (Glasgow: Cargo Publishing, 2012).
15. Ibid., p. 68.
16. See McGonigal, 'MacAvantgarde', pp. 130–31.
17. Reprinted in Bartie and Bell, p. 167.
18. See A. Bold (ed.), *The Letters of Hugh MacDiarmid* (London: Hamish Hamilton, 1984), pp. 627–28.
19. Watson, p. 75.
20. Morgan Papers, Department of Special Collections, Glasgow University Library, 4848/69. See also J. McGonigal and J. Coyle (eds), *The Midnight Letterbox: Edwin Morgan, Selected Correspondence 1950–2010* (Manchester: Carcanet Press, 2015).
21. Quoted in McGonigal, *Beyond the Last Dragon*, p. 156.
22. De Campos, Pignatari and de Campos, *Teoria da Poesia Concreta*, pp. 276–77.
23. McGonigal, *Beyond the Last Dragon*, p. 159.
24. See M. E. Solt, pp. 101–02; for a commentary on this poem, see also M. Perloff and H. de Campos, '"Concrete Prose" in the Nineties: Haroldo de Campos's *Galáxias* and After', *Contemporary Literature* (2001), pp. 270–93.
25. C. Whyte, *Modern Scottish Poetry* (Edinburgh: Edinburgh University Press, 2004), p. 141.
26. Kinloch, in his response to an earlier version of this paper, presented at a panel organised by Silke Strohe and Alan Riach at the ESSE conference in Košice, Slovakia, in September 2014.

27. Whyte, *Modern Scottish Poetry*, p. 141.
28. Bohn, *Reading Visual Poetry*, pp. 122–23.
29. See D. Kinloch, 'The Case of the Missing War: Edwin Morgan's *The New Divan*', *Scottish Literary Review* 4.2 (2012), pp. 85–103.
30. E. Morgan and A. Scott, *A Double Scotch* (Dublin: Claddagh Records Ltd, 1971).
31. Letter cited in McGonigal, *Beyond the Last Dragon*, p. 156.
32. Bold, p. 673.
33. McGonigal, *Beyond the Last Dragon*, p. 155.

9. Edwin Morgan's Theatre

1. Robyn Marsack, 'From Glasgow to Nineveh', *PN Review* 32.6 (2006), pp. 18–24.
2. Edwin Morgan, 'Another point of departure', *Times*, 7 October 1968, p. 6.
3. Edwin Morgan, Letter to Ian Dallas, 14 September 1956, quoted in full by James McGonigal, 'Exit, in Pursuit of a Bugbear: Edwin Morgan and Poetic Drama', *PN Review* 40.3 (2014), pp. 51–55.
4. Ibid.
5. 'Bitter Play on Abortion', *Times*, 13 September 1967, p. 6.
6. I am grateful to Ian Brown, Arts Council of Great Britain drama director from 1986 to 1994, for this information about the approach of these company members to Morgan.
7. McGonigal, op. cit.
8. Ibid.
9. Ibid.
10. Benedict Nightingale, *Times*, 26 August 1992.
11. *Guardian*, 17 August 1992, p. 33.
12. *Glasgow Herald*, 12 October 1996, p. 20.
13. 15 November 1996.
14. See John Corbett, '"Nae Mair Pussyfoottin. Ah'm Aff, Theramenes": Demotic Neoclassical Drama in Contemporary Scotland', in James McGonigal and Kirsten Stirling (eds), *Ethically Speaking: Voices and Values in Modern Scottish Writing* (Amsterdam: Rodopi, 2006), pp. 1–20.
15. Ian Brown, 'Motivation and Politico-cultural Context in the Creation of Scots Language Versions of Greek Tragedies', in John M. Kirk and Iseabail Macleod (eds), *Scots: Studies in its Literature and Language* (Amsterdam: Rodopi, 2013), pp. 259–76.
16. 'Resolutions for the Year Ahead', *TES*, 5 January 2001.

17. 20 April 2000.
18. Edwin Morgan, 'The Early Years', II.4, *A.D.: A Trilogy of Plays on the Life of Jesus* (Manchester: Carcanet Press, 2000), p. 37.
19. 'The Ministry', IV.1, ibid., p. 124.
20. 'The Execution', I.4, ibid., p. 163.
21. Interview with Peter Ross, 'The Domini Effect', *Sunday Herald*, 3 September 2000, p. 7.
22. 'The Early Years', op. cit., p. 38.
23. Ibid., III.6, p. 54.
24. Ibid., V.3, p. 76.
25. 'The Ministry', ibid., V.4, p. 147.
26. Ibid., V.4, p. 148.
27. Peter Ross, 'The Domini Effect', op. cit.
28. 'The Execution', op. cit., I.1, p. 155.
29. *Scotsman*, 20 September 2000.
30. Neil Cooper, 5 October 2000.
31. *Collected Poems* (Manchester: Carcanet Press, 1990), p. 159.
32. Ibid., p. 164.
33. Edwin Morgan, *The Play of Gilgamesh* (Manchester: Carcanet Press, 2005), p. 16.
34. Ibid., p. 17.
35. Ibid., p. vii.
36. Ibid., p. 14; p. 34; p. 75.
37. Ibid., pp. 13–14.
38. Morgan, 'Introduction', ibid., p. vi.
39. Ibid., p. 92.
40. Ibid., p. 97.
41. Ali Smith, *Guardian* Review, 14 January 2006, p. 18.
42. 9 January 2000, *Sunday Times.*
43. *Cyrano*, Billington, *Guardian* Features, 17 August 1992, p. 33.
44. Edwin Morgan, *Christopher Marlowe's Doctor Faustus* (Edinburgh: Canongate, 1999), pp. 69–72.
45. 'The Ministry', op. cit., p. 124. Jesus is citing Rilke's 'Archaic Torso of Apollo'.
46. *Gilgamesh*, op. cit., p. 75.
47. Op. cit., p. 11.
48. www.poetryarchive.org/poet/edwin-morgan
49. T. S. Eliot, 'Tradition and the Individual Talent', *Selected Essays* (London: Faber and Faber, 1980 [1932]), p. 14.
50. *Gilgamesh*, op. cit., p. 97.

10. Into the Twenty-First Century: From Demon to Dream

1. James McGonigal, *Beyond the Last Dragon: A Life of Edwin Morgan*, 2nd edn (Dingwall: Sandstone Press, 2012), p. 338. For a detailed review of this volume see Patrick Crotty, 'Pride of Scotland', *Times Literary Supplement*, 18 March 2011, pp. 12–13.
2. Edwin Morgan, *Cathures: New Poems 1997–2001* (Manchester and Glasgow: Carcanet and Mariscat Press, 2002), p. 112.
3. McGonigal, p. 343.
4. Edwin Morgan, 'A Little Catechism from the Demon', in *Cathures*, p. 113.
5. Edwin Morgan, 'A Demon', in *Cathures*, p. 93.
6. Edwin Morgan, 'The Demon at the Walls of Time', in *Cathures*, p. 115.
7. Edwin Morgan, Introduction to his poems on the Poetry Archive website: www.poetryarchive.org
8. Edwin Morgan, 'A Gull', in *Cathures*, p. 45. See also 'And not with a whimper', interview with Phil Miller, *Herald*, 24 June 2002, p. 4: 'I always have questions, questions about survival and big changes in life [...] That gull at the window, for instance, that doesn't happen every day. Unless you live in Aberdeen, perhaps [...] What you do ask is: are you ready? Is your life in order? ... It makes you think about your lack of days [...] If you've done things that people like and enjoy, you hope that will survive and that's a good feeling [...] Sputnik did not last very long, but its achievement was something to be celebrated and admired'. Miller concludes: 'he shows me to the stairwell, where the sun burned through the windows, casting shadows on the frail poet, holding his sides, standing alone in his suddenly darkened doorway.' Was this a conscious echo of the ending of Morgan's poem 'Lunardi' in *Cathures*? ('[...] the shadows close in. They do, they do. / It is cold too. Who is that standing in the door?')
9. Edwin Morgan, *Gorgo and Beau*, in *A Book of Lives* (Manchester: Carcanet Press, 2007), p. 56. In an interview with David Stenhouse, 'Still working like a demon', *Sunday Times*, 9 April 2000, Morgan remarks, 'It's interesting to see how it [the cancer] will progress [...] I don't write much about growing old. I like the idea of surviving and keeping going, and not slumping in front of the TV set.' For a review of *A Book of Lives* see Kathleen Jamie, 'The lifeline of love', *Guardian*, 3 March 2007, Review, p. 18.
10. *Cathures*, pp. 31–44.

11. Edwin Morgan, 'Vincent Lunardi', in *Cathures*, p. 21.
12. Interview with Phil Miller, *Herald*, 19 May 2003, p. 7. Morgan had always held out against a conventional autobiography, but he wrote a series of autobiographical snapshots, 'Pieces of Me', for Colin Nicholson's study, *Edwin Morgan: Inventions of Modernity* (Manchester: Manchester University Press, 2002), pp. 195–201. A selection of these is reprinted in *Dreams and Other Nightmares* (Edinburgh: Mariscat Press, 2010), pp. 33–38.
13. Quoted in James Campbell, Profile of Edwin Morgan, *Guardian* Review, 28 February 2004, pp. 20–23.
14. Ibid.
15. Edwin Morgan, *Nothing Not Giving Messages: reflections on work and life*, ed. Hamish Whyte (Edinburgh: Polygon, 1990), pp. 145, 187.
16. Ibid., p. 160. In a review of the BBC Radio 3 programme *Edwin at Eighty*, Ann Donald records Morgan as saying that 'liberating as coming out was, every writer should hold on to a secret room or guard that enemy ticking away within, to add that frisson of the undisclosed to their work. "Don't open the doors straight away," he counselled.' (*Herald*, 15 April 2000)
17. *A Book of Lives*, p. 88.
18. Edwin Morgan, 'The Release', in *A Book of Lives*, p. 103. For a more detailed exposition of *Love and a Life*, see Matt McGuire and Colin Nicholson, 'Edwin Morgan', in *The Edinburgh Companion to Contemporary Scottish Poetry*, ed. M. McGuire and C. Nicholson (Edinburgh: Edinburgh University Press, 2009), pp. 106–10; and David Kinloch, 'It will not be denied' [review of *Love and a Life*], *Poetry Review* 93.3 (Autumn 2003), pp. 81–86.
19. Edwin Morgan, 'Poem for the Opening of the Scottish Parliament 9 October 2004', in *A Book of Lives*, p. 9. For an extended discussion of this poem and Morgan's nationalism, see Robert Crawford, 'Edwin Morgan', in his *Bannockburns: Scottish Independence and Literary Imagination, 1314–2014* (Edinburgh: Edinburgh University Press, 2014), pp. 187–99. Mention is made of Morgan's bequest of nearly a million pounds to the Scottish National Party. He also left an equal amount for the founding of a prize (to be awarded every two years) for a collection of poems by a Scottish poet under thirty. His legacy continues into the twenty-first century in more ways than just through his writing.
20. Edwin Morgan, 'Letter to Baron Munchausen', [introduction to] *Tales from Baron Munchausen* (Edinburgh: Mariscat Press, 2005), p. 8. See

also 'Raising the baron', a review of this book by Rosemary Goring, *Herald*, 26 March 2005, Arts, Books and Cinema supplement, p. 6.

21. Letter to Hamish Whyte, 20 May 2004.
22. Edwin Morgan, 'My Day Among the Cannonballs', in *Tales from Baron Munchausen*, p. 30.
23. Edwin Morgan, 'An Old Woman's Birthday', in *A Book of Lives*, p. 73.
24. Edwin Morgan, 'The Old Man and E.A.P.', ibid., p. 72.
25. Edwin Morgan, 'From a Nursing Home', in *Penniless Press* 22 (Winter 2005); reprinted in Edwin Morgan, *Dreams and Other Nightmares* (Edinburgh: Mariscat Press, 2010), p. 15.
26. Edwin Morgan, 'Boethius', in *A Book of Lives*, pp. 50–51.
27. McGonigal, pp. 4–10.
28. Edwin Morgan, 'Horsemen', in *Dreams and Other Nightmares*, p. 10.
29. Edwin Morgan, 'Arran', in *Dreams and Other Nighmares*, p. 12.
30. Edwin Morgan, 'Norwegian', in *Dreams and Other Nighmares*, p. 13.
31. Poetry Book Society Bulletin, Spring 2007, p. 12.
32. Edwin Morgan, 'Riddle', in *Dreams and Other Nighmares*, p. 61. Written in 2009 for *The Word Exchange: Contemporary Poets Translate Old English Poetry*, ed. G. Delanty and M. Matto (New York: Norton, 2010).

Further Reading

Primary Materials

The Vision of Cathkin Braes and Other Poems (Glasgow: William MacLellan, 1952).
Beowulf: A Verse Translation into Modern English (translator) (Berkeley: University of California Press, 1952).
The Cape of Good Hope (Tunbridge Wells: The Pound Press, 1955).
Poems from Eugenio Montale (translator) (Reading: School of Art, University of Reading, 1959).
Sovpoems: Brecht, Neruda, Pasternak, Tsvetayeva, Mayakovsky, Martynov, Yevtushenko (translator) (Worcester: Migrant Press, 1961).
Starryveldt (Frauenfeld, Switzerland: Eugen Gomringer Press, 1965).
emergent poems (Stuttgart: Hansjörg Mayer, 1967).
gnomes (Preston: Akros Publications, 1968).
The Second Life (Edinburgh: Edinburgh University Press, 1968).
Penguin Modern Poets 15: Alan Bold, Edward Brathwaite, Edwin Morgan (Harmondsworth: Penguin Books, 1969).
Proverbfolder (Corsham, Wiltshire: Openings Press, 1969).
The Horseman's Word: A Sequence of Concrete Poems (Preston: Akros Publications, 1970).
Twelve Songs (West Linton: The Castlelaw Press, 1970).
Selected Poems of Sándor Weöres and Ferenc Juhász (translator and introduction for Sándor Weöres) (Harmondsworth: Penguin, 1970).
Glasgow Sonnets (West Linton: Castlelaw Press, 1972).
Instamatic Poems (London: Ian McKelvie, 1972).
Wi the Haill Voice: 25 Poems by Vladimir Mayakovsky (translator) (Cheadle: Carcanet Press, 1972).
From Glasgow to Saturn (Cheadle: Carcanet Press, 1973).
nuspeak 8. being a visual poem (Glasgow: Scottish Arts Council, 1973).

The Whittrick: A Poem in Eight Dialogues (Preston: Akros, 1973).
Essays (Cheadle: Carcanet Press, 1974).
Words: Seven Modern Poets (ed. Geoffrey Summerfield) (Harmondsworth: Penguin Books, 1974).
Fifty Renascence Love-Poems (translator) (Reading: Whiteknights Press, 1975).
Hugh MacDiarmid (London: Longman, 1976).
Rites of Passage: Selected Translations (Manchester: Carcanet Press, 1976).
The New Divan (Manchester: Carcanet Press, 1977).
Edwin Morgan: An Interview by Marshall Walker (Preston: Akros, 1977).
Platen: Selected Poems by August Graf von Platen-Hallermünde (translator) (West Linton: Castlelaw Press, 1978).
Provenance and Problematics of 'Sublime and Alarming Images in Poetry' (London: The British Academy, 1979).
Star Gate: Science Fiction Poems (Glasgow: Third Eye Centre, 1979).
Seven Poets (ed. Christopher Carrell) (Glasgow: Third Eye Centre, 1981).
'James Joyce and Hugh MacDiarmid', in *James Joyce and Modern Literature* (ed. W. J. MacCormack and Alistair Stead) (London: Routledge and Kegan Paul, 1982).
Poems of Thirty Years (Manchester: Carcanet Press, 1982).
The Apple-Tree: A Medieval Dutch Play (translator) (Glasgow: Third Eye Centre, 1982).
Grafts/Takes (Glasgow: Mariscat Press, 1983).
Master Peter Pathelin (translator) (Glasgow: Third Eye Centre, 1983).
Glasgow Poster Poems (Glasgow: National Book League (Scotland), 1983).
Sonnets from Scotland (Glasgow: Mariscat Press, 1984).
Selected Poems (Manchester: Carcanet Press, 1985).
From the Video Box (Glasgow: Mariscat, 1986).
Newspoems (London: wacy!, 1987).
Twentieth Century Scottish Classics (Glasgow: Book Trust Scotland, 1987).
Themes on a Variation (Manchester: Carcanet Press, 1988).
Tales from Limerick Zoo (Glasgow: Mariscat Press, 1988).
Eternal Moment: Selected Poems of Sándor Weöres (translator) (London: Anvil Press, 1988).
Collected Poems (Manchester: Carcanet Press, 1990).
Crossing the Border: Essays on Scottish Literature (Manchester: Carcanet Press, 1990).
Nothing Not Giving Messages (ed. Hamish Whyte) (Edinburgh: Polygon, 1990).

Hold Hands Among the Atoms: 70 Poems (Glasgow: Mariscat Press, 1991).
Edmond Rostand's Cyrano de Bergerac: A New Verse Translation by Edwin Morgan (Manchester: Carcanet Press, 1992).
Fragments by Attila József (translator) (Edinburgh: Morning Star Publications, 1992).
MacCaig, Morgan, Lochhead: Three Scottish Poets (ed. Roderick Watson) (Edinburgh: Canongate, 1992).
PALABRARmas / WURDWAPPINschaw by Cecilia Vicuña (translator) (Edinburgh: Morning Star Publications, 1994).
Sweeping Out the Dark (Manchester: Carcanet Press, 1994).
'The Poet's Voice and Craft', in *The Poet's Voice and Craft*, ed. C. B. McCully (Manchester: Carcanet Press, 1994), pp. 54–67.
Long Poems – But How Long? W. D. Thomas Memorial Lecture (Swansea: University of Wales Swansea, 1995).
Collected Translations (Manchester: Carcanet Press, 1996).
St Columba: The Maker on High (translator) (Glasgow: Mariscat Press, 1997).
Virtual and Other Realities (Manchester: Carcanet Press, 1997).
Christopher Marlowe's Doctor Faustus. In a New Version (Edinburgh: Canongate Books, 1999).
Demon (Glasgow: Mariscat Press, 1999).
'Scotland and the World', in *Chapman*, 95 (2000), pp. 2–15.
New Selected Poems (Manchester: Carcanet Press, 2000).
A.D.: A Trilogy of Plays on the Life of Jesus (Manchester: Carcanet Press, 2000).
Jean Racine's Phaedra: A Tragedy (translator) (Manchester: Carcanet Press, 2000).
Attila József: Sixty Poems (translator) (Glasgow: Mariscat Press, 2001).
Beowulf: A Verse Translation into Modern English (Manchester: Carcanet Press, 2002 [first publ. 1952]).
Cathures: New Poems 1997–2001 (Manchester: Carcanet Press, in association with Mariscat Press, 2002).
Love and a Life: 50 Poems by Edwin Morgan (Glasgow: Mariscat Press, 2003).
Metrum de Praelio apud Bannockburn by Robert Baston / The Battle of Bannockburn (translator) (Edinburgh: Scottish Poetry Library in association with Akros Publications and Mariscat Press, 2004).
Tales From Baron Munchausen: 12 Poems by Edwin Morgan (Edinburgh: Mariscat Press, 2004).

The Play of Gilgamesh (Manchester: Carcanet Press, 2005).
Thirteen Ways of Looking at Rillie (London: Enitharmon Press, 2006).
Beyond the Sun: Scotland's Favourite Paintings (Edinburgh: Luath Press, 2007).
A Book of Lives (Manchester: Carcanet Press, 2007).
From Saturn to Glasgow: 50 Favourite Poems by Edwin Morgan, eds Robyn Marsack and Hamish Whyte (Edinburgh: Scottish Poetry Library, in association with Carcanet Press, 2008).
Dreams and Other Nightmares: New and Uncollected Poems 1954–2009 (Edinburgh: Mariscat Press, 2010).

Books edited by Edwin Morgan

Collins Albatross Book of Longer Poems (editor) (London: Collins, 1963).
Poems by Alan Hayton, Stephen Mulrine, Colin Kirkwood, Robert Tait: Four Glasgow University Poets (editor) (Preston: Akros, 1967).
Scottish Satirical Verse (editor) (Manchester: Carcanet Press, 1980).

Books co-edited by Edwin Morgan

Scottish Poetry Number One (Edinburgh: Edinburgh University Press, 1966).
Scottish Poetry Number Two (Edinburgh: Edinburgh University Press, 1967).
Scottish Poetry Number Three (Edinburgh: Edinburgh University Press, 1968).
Scottish Poetry Number Four (Edinburgh: Edinburgh University Press, 1969).
Scottish Poetry 5 (Edinburgh: Edinburgh University Press, 1970).
Scottish Poetry 6 (Edinburgh: Edinburgh University Press, 1972).
Scottish Poetry 7 (Glasgow: University of Glasgow Press, 1974).
New Writing Scotland 5 (Aberdeen: Association for Scottish Literary Studies, 1987).
New Writing Scotland 6 (Aberdeen: Association for Scottish Literary Studies, 1988).
New Writing Scotland 7 (Aberdeen: Association for Scottish Literary Studies, 1989).

Periodicals co-edited by Edwin Morgan

Scottish International, from Number 1 (January 1968) to Number 9 (February 1970), then as editorial adviser until the final issue, Volume 7, number 2 (March 1974).

Criticism

Bell, Eleanor, 'Old Country, New Dreams: Scottish Poetry since the 1970s', in *The Edinburgh History of Scottish Literature*, ed. Ian Brown (Edinburgh: Edinburgh University Press, 2007), pp. 185–97.

Brown, Ian and Colin Nicholson, 'The Border Crossers and Reconfiguration of the Possible: Poet-Playwright-Novelists from the Mid-Twentieth Century on', in *The Edinburgh History of Scottish Literature*, ed. Ian Brown (Edinburgh: Edinburgh University Press, 2007), pp. 262–72.

Calder, Angus, 'Morganmania', *Chapman* 64 (Edinburgh: Chapman Publications, 1991), pp. 41–45.

Crawford, Robert and Hamish Whyte (eds), *About Edwin Morgan* (Edinburgh: Edinburgh University Press, 1990).

Dósa, Attila, 'Edwin Morgan: Our Man in Glasgow', in *Beyond Identity: New Horizons in Modern Scottish Poetry* (Amsterdam/ New York: Rodopi, 2009).

Dunnigan, Sarah M. and Margery Palmer McCulloch (eds), *Scottish Literary Review [Edwin Morgan Memorial Number]* 4.2 (Glasgow: Association for Scottish Literary Studies, Autumn/Winter 2012).

Edgecombe, Rodney Stenning, *Aspects of Form and Genre in the Poetry of Edwin Morgan* (London: Cambridge Scholars Press, 2003).

Fulton, Robin, 'Edwin Morgan', in *Contemporary Scottish Poetry: Individuals and Contexts* (Loanhead: Macdonald Publishers, 1974).

Houston, Amy, 'New Lang Syne: *Sonnets from Scotland* and Restructured Time', *Scottish Literary Journal* 22.1 (Aberdeen: Association for Scottish Literary Studies, 1995), pp. 66–73.

Marsack, Robyn and Hamish Whyte (eds), *Unknown Is Best: A Celebration of Edwin Morgan at Eighty* (Edinburgh and Glasgow: Scottish Poetry Library and Mariscat Press, 2000).

Marsack, Robyn and Hamish Whyte (eds), *Eddie@90* (Edinburgh: Scottish Poetry Library and Mariscat Press, 2010).

McCarra, Kevin, 'Edwin Morgan's "Cinquevalli"', *Scottish Literary Journal* 12.2 (Aberdeen: Association for Scottish Literary Studies, 1985), pp. 69–75.

McGonigal, James, *The Poetry of Edwin Morgan* (Glasgow: Association for Scottish Literary Studies, 2013); the first edition of this book was Thomson, Geddes, *The Poetry of Edwin Morgan* (Aberdeen: Association for Scottish Literary Studies, 1986).

McGuire, Matt and Colin Nicholson, 'Edwin Morgan', in Matt McGuire and Colin Nicholson (eds), *The Edinburgh Companion to Contemporary Scottish Poetry* (Edinburgh: Edinburgh University Press, 2009).

Nicholson, Colin, 'Living in the utterance: Edwin Morgan', in *Poem, Purpose and Place: Shaping Identity in Contemporary Scottish Verse* (Edinburgh: Polygon, 1992).

Nicholson, Colin, *Edwin Morgan: Inventions of Modernity* (Manchester: Manchester University Press, 2002).

Nicholson, Colin, 'Edwin Morgan's Sonnets from Scotland: towards a republican politics', in Marco Fazzini (ed.), *Alba Literaria: A History of Scottish Literature* (Venezia Mestre: Amos Edizioni, 2005).

Piette, Adam and Alex Houen (eds), *Blackbox Manifold* [Edwin Morgan Tribute number, contributions from Dorothy Alexander, Tom Leonard, Jim McGonigal, nick-e melville, Alan Riach, Dilys Rose], number 6 (2011): www.manifold.group.shef.ac.uk/issue6/index6.html

Schmidt, Michael, 'Edwin Morgan', in *An Introduction to Fifty Modern British Poets* (London: Pan Books, 1979), pp. 314–20.

Schmidt, Michael, 'The Other War', in *Lives of the Poets* (London: Phoenix, 1998), pp. 895–913.

Walker, Marshall, 'Poems and spaceships: Edwin Morgan', in *Scottish Literature Since 1707* (London and New York: Longman, 1996).

Watson, Roderick, 'New visions of old Scotland: Edwin Morgan', in *The Literature of Scotland: The Twentieth Century*, 2nd edn. (Basingstoke: Palgrave Macmillan, 2007).

Whyte, Christopher, 'Now You See It, Now You Don't: The Love Poetry of Edwin Morgan', *The Glasgow Review* 2 (Glasgow: University of Glasgow, 1993), pp. 82–93.

Whyte, Christopher, 'The 1960s', in *Modern Scottish Poetry* (Edinburgh: Edinburgh University Press, 2004).

Whyte, Hamish (ed.), *Nothing Not Giving Messages: Reflections on Work and Life* (Edinburgh: Polygon, 1990).

Wood, Barry, 'Scots, Poets and the City', in *The History of Scottish Literature Vol. IV: Twentieth Century*, ed. Cairns Craig (Aberdeen: Aberdeen University Press, 1987), pp. 337–48.

Young, Alan, 'Three "Neo-Moderns": Ian Hamilton Finlay, Edwin Morgan, Christopher Middleton', in *British Poetry Since 1970: A Critical Survey*, eds Peter Jones and Michael Schmidt (NY: Persea, 1980), pp. 112–24.

Young, Alan, 'Edwin Morgan', in *Poets of Great Britain and Ireland 1945–1960*, ed. Vincent B. Sherry, Jr. [*Dictionary of Literary Biography*, vol. 27], (Detroit: Gale Research Company, 1984), pp. 247–53.

Biography

McGonigal, James, *Beyond the Last Dragon: A Life of Edwin Morgan* (Dingwall: Sandstone Press, 2010; revised edition, 2012).

Archives

Edwin Morgan Papers, Special Collections, University of Glasgow Library, Glasgow.

Edwin Morgan Collection, Special Collections, Mitchell Library, Glasgow.

Edwin Morgan Archive, Scottish Poetry Library, Edinburgh.

Notes on Contributors

John Corbett is a Full Professor and the Head of the English Department at the University of Macau. He has published widely on Scottish language, Scots language and translation, as well as on linguistics and language education.

Cairns Craig is Glucksman Professor of Irish and Scottish Studies and Director of the Centre for Irish and Scottish Studies at the University of Aberdeen. He was general editor of the four-volume *History of Scottish Literature* (1987–89) and his books include *The Modern Scottish Novel* (1999) and *Intending Scotland: Explorations in Scottish Culture since the Enlightenment* (2009).

David Kinloch is from Glasgow and is currently Professor of Poetry and Creative Writing at the University of Strathclyde. He is the author of five collections of poetry, including *Finger of a Frenchman* (Carcanet Press, 2011), and of many studies in the fields of French, Translation and Scottish Studies.

James McGonigal is Emeritus Professor of English in Education at Glasgow University. He has published on modernism, Scots-Irish writing and children's literacy and language learning. His *Beyond the Last Dragon: A Life of Edwin Morgan* (Sandstone Press, 2010, 2012) was a Saltire Scottish Research Book of the Year.

Dorothy McMillan is Honorary Research Fellow in English Literature at Glasgow University where she taught for nearly forty years. She has worked and published mainly in the field of women's writing. She is a former, and until 2015 the only female, president of the Association for Scottish Literary Studies.

Robyn Marsack has been Director of the Scottish Poetry Library since 2000. She is an editor, critic and translator. With Hamish Whyte she co-edited the anthologies *Unknown is Best* (2000), *From Saturn to Glasgow: 50 Favourite Poems by Edwin Morgan* (2009) and *Eddie@90* (2010).

Adam Piette is Professor at the University of Sheffield, author of *Remembering and the Sound of Words, Imagination at War* and *The Literary Cold War, 1945 to Vietnam*. He co-edited *The Edinburgh Companion to Twentieth-Century British and American War Literature* and co-edits the poetry journal *Blackbox Manifold*.

Alan Riach is Professor of Scottish Literature at Glasgow University, author of five books of poems, including *Homecoming* (2009), and co-author with Alexander Moffat of *Arts of Independence* (2014) and *Arts of Resistance* (2008), described by the *Times Literary Supplement* as 'a landmark book'.

Ernest Schonfield is Lecturer in German in the School of Modern Languages and Cultures, Glasgow University. He writes on modern German and comparative literature: *Art and its Uses in Thomas Mann's Felix Krull* (2008); essays on Brecht, Hubert Fichte and Emine Sevgi Özdamar. He is the editor of a website on German literature: www.germanlit.org

Anne Varty is Professor of English Literature at Royal Holloway, University of London. She has a long-standing interest in British drama since the Victorian period, and has published on modern Scottish theatre, Liz Lochhead, and Victorian Theatre. She is currently working on contemporary women's poetry.

Hamish Whyte was Edwin Morgan's friend, bibliographer and, through Mariscat Press, his Scottish publisher. He edited Morgan's *Nothing Not Giving Messages* (Polygon) and co-edited, with Robert Crawford, *About Edwin Morgan* (Edinburgh University Press). He is an Honorary Research Fellow in Scottish Literature at Glasgow University. His poetry collections include *Hannah, Are You Listening?* (Happen*Stance*, 2014).

Index

Lightning Source UK Ltd.
Milton Keynes UK
UKOW06f0755041115

262057UK00001B/19/P

9 781908 980144